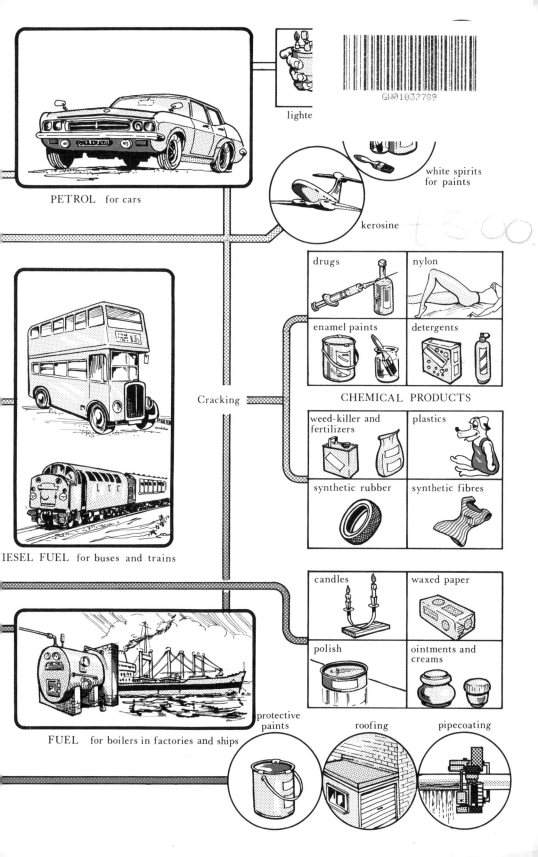

PETROL for cars

lighte

white spirits
for paints

kerosine

GW01032789

drugs

nylon

enamel paints

detergents

CHEMICAL PRODUCTS

Cracking

weed-killer and
fertilizers

plastics

synthetic rubber

synthetic fibres

IESEL FUEL for buses and trains

candles

waxed paper

polish

ointments and
creams

FUEL for boilers in factories and ships

protective
paints

roofing

pipecoating

Chemistry by experiment and understanding

Secondary Science Series

Chemistry: Consulting Editor
R C Whitfield, BSc, PhD, MA, MEd, ARIC
Department and Faculty of Education,
University of Cambridge

Chemistry by experiment and understanding

John R Gerrish BSc, ARIC
Director of Studies,
Bassaleg School, Monmouthshire
(formerly Senior Chemistry Master,
The Perse School for Boys, Cambridge)

David H Mansfield BSc
Head of Chemistry Department,
Harvey Grammar School,
Folkestone
(formerly Senior Chemistry Master,
Braintree County High School)

London · New York · St Louis · San Francisco · Düsseldorf ·
Johannesburg · Kuala Lumpur · Mexico · Montreal · New Delhi ·
Panama · Rio de Janeiro · Singapore · Sydney · Toronto

Published by

McGRAW-HILL Book Company (UK) Limited

MAIDENHEAD · BERKSHIRE · ENGLAND

Pupil's edition: 07 094381 8
Teacher's edition: 07 094382 6

PRINTED AND BOUND IN GREAT BRITAIN

Contents

Preface

This book is intended to provide suitable material for the two or three years of a chemistry course immediately prior to O-level, a time-table allocation of eight to ten period-years having been assumed. Some topics, such as electronic structure, periodicity, complex ions, free energy, and activation energy have been included which are unusual at this stage, but the teacher may be reassured that they have all been successfully taught by the authors to average pupils. However, if these topics are thought to be too difficult, or if any of the material is covered in too great a depth, the teacher can make a selection suitable for his classes and their particular examination requirements. The fullest possible integration of practical and theoretical work has been attempted and applications of the chemistry outside the laboratory have been continually stressed.

It is assumed that the pupils will have previously undertaken some chemical studies either as a single subject or as part of a course in combined science. In particular, it is assumed that they will have encountered:

(*a*) Simple exercises in separation involving dissolution, filtration, centrifuging, evaporation, and chromatography.

(*b*) The pH scale as an empirical method of comparing relative acidity and alkalinity.

(*c*) The elementary chemistry of the air and the simple properties of nitrogen and oxygen.

(*d*) The concept of 'elements'; metals and non-metals; simple competition experiments leading to the development of an activity series for the metals; the properties of hydrogen.

(*e*) Tests for oxygen, nitrogen, carbon dioxide, chlorine, and hydrogen gases; other simple tests possibly introduced through open-ended investigations on substances such as malachite.

SI units are used exclusively (except when considering gas pressures), as is IUPAC nomenclature; however, trivial names that are in common use will be mentioned in brackets when a new compound is first encountered.

The teacher's edition of the book contains notes on the apparatus and chemicals required for each experiment, together with sample results and comments, where appropriate. This edition should be of assistance to both teachers and laboratory stewards.

The book contains sufficient material to cover the syllabuses of all GCE examination boards and, in the introduction to the teacher's notes, ways of using the text to suit several of these are suggested.

For the sake of clarity, all experimental details are printed in a different colour from the main body of the text, and questions are marked by a coloured bar on the left-hand side of the page.

Acknowledgements

The main inspiration for the writing of this book lies in the work of the Nuffield O-level Chemistry Project, to which we freely acknowledge an enormous debt, as we do also to our pupils and to our laboratory assistants, all of whom have contributed to the development of new ideas and techniques.

We should like to thank Dr R. C. Whitfield of the University of Cambridge Department of Education and Mr M. Mander of the Royal Grammar School, High Wycombe, for their careful reading of the manuscript and for the many helpful suggestions made to improve the text.

Various items in the book are reproduced by kind permission of the following:

Inner front cover   The Shell Petroleum Company

Photographs   Department of Metallurgy, University of Cambridge
                Morris Laboratory Instruments Limited
                Oxfam
                The Shell Petroleum Company
                The United Kingdom Atomic Energy Authority

Examination Questions   The source of these is shown in the text by the letters in brackets.

   The Joint Matriculation Board (JMB)
   The Oxford and Cambridge Schools Examination Board (O & C)
   The University of Cambridge Local Examinations Syndicate (CT)
   The University of London School Examinations Department (L) and
      (NL)*

John R Gerrish
David H Mansfield

* The 'Nuffield' examination set by the University of London.

Editorial introduction

Dr Richard Whitfield, University Lecturer in Education and the
Teaching of Chemistry, University of Cambridge

The formalization of curriculum development under the auspices of organi-
zations such as the Nuffield Foundation and Schools Council within the last
few years has provided individual textbook authors with new and higher
standards of scholarship and pedagogic insight, for the new curricula have
been able to pool the expertise of large sections of the teaching profession.
The authors of this text have wide experience of teaching both traditional and
Nuffield courses in chemistry and have sought to distil this experience for
sharing with a wider audience; they have in my opinion met the stringent
requirements for a class text in a post-Nuffield era. Perusal of the text indicates the following strengths in the authors' treatment:

(*a*) Practical work is thoroughly integrated with theory and a wealth of
experiments with an investigatory flavour are provided for pupils, or as
teacher demonstrations.

(*b*) Questions are provided alongside the practical experiments and
throughout the text to test and stretch the pupils' understanding as the course
proceeds.

(*c*) The conceptual structure of the text is clear and is reinforced by useful
end of chapter summaries.

(*d*) Applications of chemistry outside the laboratory are frequently
mentioned.

(*e*) The descriptive chemistry is up-to-date, extensive, and cogently
presented; this will compensate for some of the omissions in this area in the
Nuffield O-level Sample Scheme; again, the heuristic flavour of the experiments should help to maintain pupils' interest during these parts of the course.

(*f*) The teacher's notes will be most useful during lesson preparation by
both the teacher and the laboratory technician; the text itself is clearly
designed to be *used* during almost every lesson—it will not be, like so many,
a mere adjunct to the course.

This is a most important and original book, combining the best of past and present practice in school chemistry teaching. It deserves to be widely used.

Cambridge
  March 1971.

Introduction

To the pupil

As we all know, Earth is a tiny planet and yet the complexity and variety of different chemical substances found in and on it are enormous. Thus it seems obvious that an understanding of chemistry, even at an elementary level, and its relevance to everyday life is important to everybody.

The contents of this book are so arranged that you may work through them in sequence or alternatively your teacher may choose just some of the various topics, depending on the requirements of the examination that you will eventually take. Whichever approach is used, you will find detailed instructions for a large number of experiments that you may carry out; the teacher will only perform those experiments that are too dangerous for you to do.

Throughout the text you will be asked numerous questions which should test and help to improve your understanding of what you have done. If, after serious thought, you cannot answer a particular question you should then refer to the summary of that chapter for the answer. You could, of course, read the summary first, but 'cheating' in this way will not help you to understand much chemistry!

Apart from learning how to make careful observations of experimental work and using these to come to sensible conclusions, you should also make a habit of using the chemistry section of the library in order to look up additional material for the topic that you are studying.

You should read through the next section and then refer back to it when necessary, as you proceed with the course.

Numbers and units

In science we sometimes encounter numbers that are either very large or very small. For example, the number of hydrogen atoms in one gramme of the element is about six hundred, thousand, million, million, million. In figures this is:

$$600\ 000\ 000\ 000\ 000\ 000\ 000\ 000\ 000$$

Carrying out calculations with such numbers would obviously be cumbersome and it is much more convenient to express the number in the form:

$$6 \times 10^{23}$$

The mass, in grammes, of each hydrogen atom is then the reciprocal of this number:

$$\frac{1}{6 \times 10^{23}} = \frac{1}{6} \times 10^{-23} = 1{\cdot}7 \times 10^{-24}\,\text{g}$$

These two examples, respectively involving numbers multiplied by ten raised to the appropriate positive and negative powers, illustrate a method of expressing numbers known as **standard form**.

SI units

The United Kingdom, in common with most countries throughout the world, has agreed to adopt the 'Système International d'Unités', abbreviated to SI, for expressing scientific measurements. The basic units that concern us in our chemical work at this level are shown in the following table:

Physical quantity	Unit	Symbol
Length	metre	m
Mass	kilogramme	kg
Time	second	s
Electrical current	ampere	A
Quantity of substance	mole	mol
Temperature	kelvin	K

Prefixes for SI units

In general, prefixes involving powers that are multiples or submultiples of three are preferred, e.g., 10^3, 10^{-9}, but some others will continue in use, as shown in the following table. This is not a complete list but will cover our requirements.

Multiple or submultiple	Prefix	Symbol
10^3	kilo	k
10^{-1}	deci	d
10^{-2}	centi	c
10^{-3}	milli	m
10^{-6}	micro	μ
10^{-9}	nano	n

Derived units

A number of units in common use are derived from the basic SI units, as shown below:

Physical quantity	Unit	Symbol
Volume	cubic metre	m^3
Volume	cubic decimetre	dm^3
Volume	cubic centimetre	cm^3
Density	gramme per cubic centimetre	$g\ cm^{-3}$
Energy	joule	J
Electrical charge	coulomb	C
Electromotive force	volt	V
Power	watt	W
Temperature	degree Celsius	°C

Units other than SI still in common use

(*a*) The litre (l) and millilitre (ml) are not SI units and will not be used in this book. For practical purposes, the litre is identical with the cubic decimetre and the millilitre with the cubic centimetre.

(*b*) The calorie and kilocalorie are sometimes used for measuring heat energy. The calorie is related to the SI unit, the joule, by the equation:

$$1 \text{ calorie} = 4 \cdot 2 \text{ joules}$$

(*c*) Pressure is most conveniently expressed in millimetres of mercury or atmospheres for work at this level, and we shall use these throughout the book:

$$1 \text{ atmosphere} = 760 \text{ mm of mercury}$$

Energy changes

A convenient method of measuring an energy change is to determine the temperature rise or fall in a measured quantity of water or aqueous solution. The specific heat capacity of water, and also (without appreciable error) of many aqueous solutions, is $4 \cdot 2$ kJ kg^{-1} K^{-1}, which means that 4·2 kilojoules of energy are required to raise the temperature of one kilogramme of water (or solution) by one kelvin.

An alternative method of determining energy changes involves electrical measurements and the use of the following relationships.

The product of electromotive force (in volts) and current (in amperes) gives the power supplied (in watts), so that:

$$V \times A = W$$

Power can also be expressed as the energy supplied (in joules) in a given time (in seconds), so that:

$$\frac{J}{s} = W$$

Thus:

$$\frac{J}{s} = V \times A$$

and

$$J = V \times A \times s$$

Electrical charge (in coulombs) is the product of current (in amperes) and time (in seconds), so that:

$$C = A \times s$$

Hence:

$$J = V \times C$$

i.e.,

Energy in joules = electromotive force in volts
× electrical charge in coulombs

1

Atoms

The word **atom** is nowadays familiar to most people, who are only too aware of the devastating power of atomic explosions produced by the atomic bomb (Fig. 1.1) and its more modern development, the hydrogen bomb. These devices are obviously used for destructive purposes and although it is possible that small versions may be suitable for excavation, the most important peaceful use of the tremendous energy available from the atom is in the generation of **atomic power** (see Fig. 1.2). An increasing proportion of electricity is being produced in this way and smaller units are already in use for driving the engines of ships.

There is much evidence to show that atoms are, in fact, minute particles of matter. The idea of atoms was first suggested by the Hindus (1200 BC) and later by the Greeks, but John Dalton (1803) developed the theory. He thought that each atom was indivisible and that the atoms of any one element were identical, compounds being formed by the joining together of these atoms in simple, whole number proportions. These 'compound atoms' were later called **molecules** (see chapter 2). Dalton's ideas are still largely correct although they have had to be modified in certain important respects due to more recent discoveries.

Experiment 1.1   *The effect of certain chemicals on photographic film*

Take an envelope of X-ray film and put it where it need not be disturbed for some time. Place a coin or key on top of the film which should be 'tube side' up, and then cover it with the sealed Polythene bag containing a thorium or a uranium compound. Take care to distribute the chemical within the bag, if necessary. (See Fig. 1.3.)

After several days, remove the bag of chemical and, under safelight conditions, take the sheet of film out of the envelope and develop and fix it according to the manufacturer's instructions. After thorough washing in

Figure 1.1   An atomic explosion

running water or by soaking in several changes of water, the film should be hung up to dry and then examined.

Figure 1.2   Trawsfynydd Nuclear Power Station at dusk

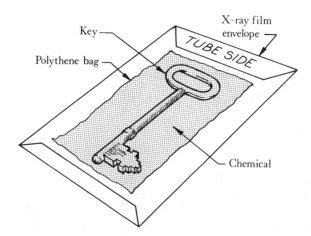

Figure 1.3   The 'Becquerel Experiment'

Describe what you can see on the film when it is dry and try to explain what has happened.

7

Natural radioactivity

The effect you have just seen in Experiment 1.1 was first observed by Henri Becquerel in 1896. He realized that the chemicals concerned must be giving off some form of radiation which was capable of much greater penetration than visible light. X-rays had been discovered by Wilhelm Röntgen a year earlier but Becquerel was satisfied that the new radiation was different from X-rays. Shortly after, Ernest Rutherford showed that the Becquerel radiation consisted of at least two different types of particles, which he called alpha (α) and beta (β). Pierre Curie later discovered a third component gamma (γ) which was proved to be an electromagnetic radiation and not particulate. These three components can be distinguished by their interaction with an electrostatic field (see Fig. 1.4), when α-particles are found to be positively charged, β-particles negatively charged and γ-rays to have no charge.

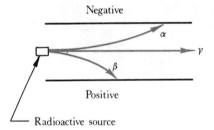

Figure 1.4   The effect of an electrostatic field on radioactive emissions

Substances that emitted this invisible penetrating radiation were described by Marie Curie as being **radioactive** and the phenomenon as **radioactivity**.

What effect does the discovery of radioactivity have on the Dalton idea of an atom?

The structure of the atom

Hans Geiger and Ernest Marsden in 1909 carried out a series of experiments in which they caused a stream of α-particles to fall onto very thin metal foils. The foil appeared to be unaffected and most of the α-particles passed straight through, while some suffered slight deflections as shown by the flashes of light called scintillations on a zinc sulphide screen (see p. 15). However, approximately 1 in 20 000 of the particles suffered a very large deflection of more than $90°$. This was a very surprising result, as described by Rutherford '. . . it was as if you had fired a 15-inch shell at a piece of tissue-paper and it came back and hit you . . .'. (See Fig. 1.5.)

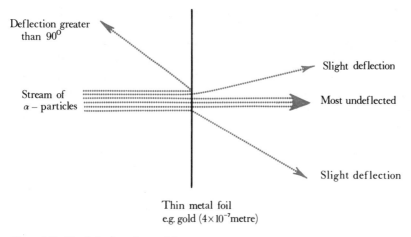

Figure 1.5   The deflection of α-particles

Rutherford in 1911 explained these results by assuming that the atom was not uniform in structure but had most of its mass concentrated in a small, positively charged core or **nucleus**. Only when a positively charged α-particle passed very close to this positive nucleus would repulsion between the two like charges occur (Fig. 1.6). Rutherford was able to calculate from the number and size of the deflections just how small the nucleus is and found that the diameter of the atom is approximately 10 000 times that of the nucleus!

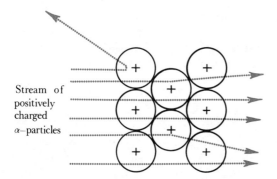

Figure 1.6   The interaction of α-particles and nuclei

J. J. Thomson in 1897 discovered the first sub-atomic particle, which he called the **electron**, evidence for its existence being obtained from a wide range of experiments. Although electrons occur in all matter, they always have the same negative charge and the same mass.

The number of electrons in a particular atom must be such that their total negative charge is equal to the positive charge of the nucleus, so that the atom overall is electrically neutral. In certain circumstances, it is possible to remove one or more electrons from the atom and the resultant particle will then have a net positive charge equal to the number of electrons removed. Conversely, it is also possible to add one or more electrons to certain atoms to produce new particles which have a resultant negative charge. These charged particles are called **ions**.

As most of the mass of the atom is concentrated in the nucleus, the mass of the electron is very small (approximately 1/2000 that of the lightest atom, hydrogen). The diameter of the electron is similar to that of the nucleus and thus most of the atom is empty space!

We now have a simple picture of the atom (Fig. 1.7) as consisting of the nucleus surrounded by a region containing the appropriate number of electrons and making up the total volume of the atom.

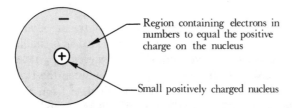

Figure 1.7   A simple picture of the atom (very much out of scale)

It has been found to be impossible to predict the exact positions of any of the electrons, but it is known that they are arranged in definite regions called **orbitals** and that these orbitals are grouped together in **shells**. Each type of orbital can contain electrons up to a maximum number as shown in Table 1.1.

Table 1.1—Types of orbitals

Type of orbital	Maximum number of electrons
s	2
p	6
d	10
f	14

It does not follow that all types of orbitals must occur in each shell and the actual distributions are shown in Table 1.2.

The arrangement of electrons within a particular atom can be worked out by reference to Table 1.2. Thus the element with eleven electrons has the electronic structure $1s^2\, 2s^2\, 2p^6\, 3s^1$, which indicates that there are two electrons

Table 1.2—Orbital electron distributions

Shell		Orbitals	Maximum number of electrons in shell
Name	Number		
K	1	s	2
L	2	s, p	(2+6) = 8
M	3	s, p, d	(2+6+10) = 18
N	4	s, p, d, f	(2+6+10+14) = 32
O	5	s, p, d, f	(2+6+10+14) = 32
P	6	s, p, d	(9)
Q	7	s	(2)

NB: The P and Q shells are incomplete, the numbers given in the last column being those for lawrencium, element number 103.

in the $1s$ orbital, two in the $2s$ orbital, six in the $2p$ orbital and one in the $3s$ orbital.

The structures of individual atoms are discussed in more detail in chapter 9.

Write down the electronic structures of the elements that contain: (a) three electrons, (b) eight electrons, (c) fourteen electrons, (d) seventeen electrons.

The mass of the atom

The masses of atoms can be compared with great accuracy (up to 1 part in 100 000) using an instrument called a **mass spectrometer** (see Fig. 1.8).

The material, M, under test is admitted to the instrument through a heated inlet, where it immediately vaporizes (if not already a gas) because of the heat and the very low pressure maintained within. It is then bombarded with a stream of high speed electrons passing from X to Y which causes ionization:

$$M(g) + e^- \xrightarrow{\text{(fast)}} M^+(g) + 2e^- \text{(slower)}$$

The beam of positive ions produced is accelerated by an electrostatic field between two plates, the second of which (Q) is more negative than the first (P), so that when the beam emerges through the slit at Z, all the particles are travelling at the same speed.

Application of a strong magnetic field causes the beam to be deflected and if there are ions of different mass present, the lightest will be deflected the most. The strength of the magnetic field is adjusted to cause all the ions of a particular mass to fall onto a detecting instrument called an electrometer. This produces a small current which, when amplified, is recorded in the form of a graph. Further adjustment of the magnetic field causes ions of a different mass to be recorded and in this way the masses of all the particles present can

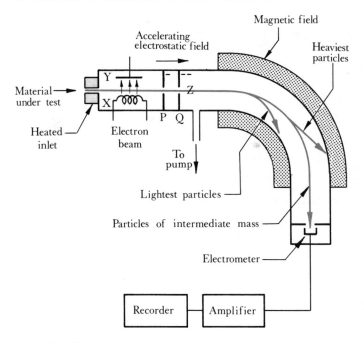

Figure 1.8   The mass spectrometer

be measured. An example of the graph obtained when using chlorine is shown in Fig. 1.9.

The structure of the nucleus

The lightest particle detectable in the mass spectrometer is obtained when using hydrogen gas. This particle which is, in fact, the nucleus of the hydrogen atom, has a charge that is equal and opposite to that of the electron and is called the **proton**. It has a mass of approximately 1.7×10^{-27} kg which is obviously far too small for convenient use and so this mass is called one **atomic mass unit** (amu).

It is now known that the nuclei of all other elements contain protons. The number of protons in a particular atom is called the **atomic number** of the element and is equal to the number of electrons surrounding the nucleus in the neutral atom. *For a given element, all atoms have the same atomic number.*

Mass spectrometer measurements show that for all atoms other than hydrogen, the mass of the nucleus, represented by the **mass number** which is the number of amu to the nearest whole number, cannot be accounted for by protons alone. Some examples are shown in Table 1.3.

The 'missing' mass units are due to the presence in the nucleus of another

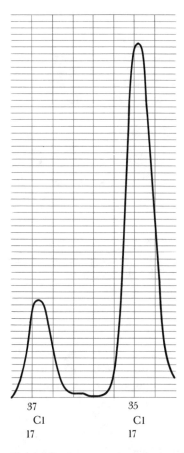

$$\begin{array}{cc} 37 & 35 \\ \text{Cl} & \text{Cl} \\ 17 & 17 \end{array}$$

Figure 1.9   A mass spectrometer trace for chlorine

Table 1.3—Some atomic numbers and mass numbers

Element	Symbol of element	Atomic number (Z)	Mass number (A)
Helium	He	2	4
Aluminium	Al	13	27
Iron	Fe	26	56
Iodine	I	53	127
Lead	Pb	82	207

type of particle called the **neutron**, which has a mass virtually the same as that of the proton (one amu) but with no electric charge, so that its presence will not affect the atomic number of the atom. This particle was first suggested by

Rutherford in 1920 but was not actually detected until 1932 by James Chadwick. Thus:

Number of neutrons in the nucleus of an atom $= A - Z$

For each of the elements listed in Table 1.3 write down the number of (a) protons, (b) neutrons and (c) electrons in one atom of the element.

The particles present in the nucleus are called **nucleons**. Thus:

Number of nucleons = number of protons + neutrons $= A$

The existence of neutrons suggests that it should be possible to have atoms of the same element (i.e., with the same number of protons) which have differing numbers of neutrons in their nuclei and hence differing masses. The mass spectrometer has shown that this is the case and such atoms are called **isotopes**. If chlorine gas is analysed in the mass spectrometer, two peaks are obtained on the resulting graph corresponding to atoms with mass numbers of respectively 35 and 37 (Fig. 1.9). The relative heights of the peaks show the relative proportions of each isotope.

The stability of the nucleus

A radioactive atom emits particles from its nucleus indicating that the nucleus is unstable. Most naturally occurring elements have stable nuclei and are not radioactive. There are some notable examples of light elements that have naturally occurring radioactive isotopes, such as potassium-40 and carbon-14, but it is much more common for radioactivity to be shown by the very heavy elements from lead (atomic number 82) to uranium (atomic number 92), although it does not follow that all isotopes of these elements are unstable. Such elements all have a high ratio of neutrons to protons, for example uranium with 143 neutrons to 92 protons (in the isotope of mass number 235). Elements with atomic numbers greater than 92 do not occur naturally but may be prepared artificially. They are all highly radioactive. Radioactive isotopes of most other elements can be prepared by suitable treatment and many are of vital importance in a wide variety of uses, as described later in this chapter.

Radioactive emissions

An unstable nucleus will undergo a spontaneous rearrangement of its nucleons in an attempt to achieve stability and in so doing will eject either an α-particle or a β-particle, together with γ-rays. It was once thought that the nucleus actually contained α- and β-particles but this idea has now been discarded.

(a) α-particles

These have little penetration, travelling only a few centimetres in air and being stopped by a thin sheet of paper. They have a positive charge (see p. 8) and Rutherford was able to prove that they are the nuclei of helium atoms with mass number four and atomic number two. They may be represented by the symbol $^4_2$He.

(b) β-particles

These will travel several metres in air and can penetrate thin sheets of metal such as a few centimetres of aluminium. They have a negative charge and are in fast-moving electrons, which may be represented by the symbol $^0_{-1}$e, showing the mass number zero and charge of -1 as compared with the proton charge of $+1$.

(c) γ-rays

These are not particles but electromagnetic waves similar to visible light and X-rays, with very short wavelength (approximately one-tenth that of X-rays). γ-rays are highly energetic and will travel about 100 metres in air and will penetrate thick shields such as several centimetres of lead. They are unaffected by an electrostatic field.

Which type of radiation could not have been discovered by Becquerel in his photographic experiments? Explain your answer.

Detection of radiation

(a) Photographic method

This has already been seen in Experiment 1.1 and the pattern obtained is called an **autoradiograph**.

(b) The Geiger-Müller tube (G-M tube)

When radiation falls on a G-M tube each emission causes an electric current to flow which, after amplification, may be detected by suitable equipment such as audible clicks from a loudspeaker, the movement of the needle of a **ratemeter** or flashing lights in the **scaler**.

(c) The scintillation counter

Certain minerals such as zinc sulphide fluoresce or glow when exposed to radiation. (This is the principle that gives the picture on a television set.) The glow is made up of tiny flashes of light or **scintillations** and these may be seen under a microscope or counted with suitable equipment.

The hazards of radiation

Great care has to be taken when handling radioactive materials and stringent regulations exist to eliminate all risk. Workers exposed to radiation in the course of their work in laboratories, hospitals, etc., are checked regularly to ensure that they do not receive more than the permitted dose.

Mild doses of radiation can cause changes in the cell structure and behaviour in the body which may not become apparent until a number of years later. Cancer, and in particular leukaemia, is common in these cases and also, if the young are exposed, mutations (changes in cell structure, resulting in deformities) in future generations may occur.

Exposure to massive doses of radiation is usually fatal but some people, hideously scarred and crippled, have survived, notably in Japan following the use of the atomic bombs in World War II.

Everybody is exposed to some radiation from minerals in the earth's crust and from cosmic rays from outer space, but the quantity is so small that there are no known harmful effects. This is known as **background radiation**.

Radioactive decay

When a radioactive atom emits radiation, the nucleus changes and a new element is produced.

When an α-particle is emitted, the new nucleus must have a mass number smaller by four units and an atomic number smaller by two units since an α-particle, which is a helium nucleus, consists of two neutrons and two protons. This may be represented by an equation:

$$^{238}_{92}U \longrightarrow {}^{234}_{90}Th + {}^{4}_{2}He$$

This shows that the isotope of mass number 238 of the element uranium (atomic number 92) **decays** to the isotope of mass number 234 of the element thorium (atomic number 90) by the loss of an α-particle.

When a β-particle is emitted it is thought that a neutron in the nucleus splits to form an electron, which is the β-particle, and a proton which remains in the nucleus. Thus, in this case, the new element formed will have a mass number that is unaltered, since an electron has virtually no mass, and an atomic number *greater* by one since there is now an extra proton in the nucleus. This may again be represented by an equation:

$$^{234}_{90}Th \longrightarrow {}^{234}_{91}Pa + {}^{0}_{-1}e$$

Thus the isotope of mass number 234 of the element thorium (atomic number 90) decays to the isotope of mass number 234 of the element protactinium (atomic number 91) by the loss of a β-particle.

The isotope protactinium-234 is also a β-emitter and so:

$$^{234}_{91}\text{Pa} \longrightarrow {}^{234}_{92}\text{U} + {}^{0}_{-1}\text{e}$$

Thus it can be seen that an α-emission followed by two β-emissions will produce a lighter isotope of the original element.

There is unfortunately no way of predicting which type of particle will be emitted from a particular isotope, but by various combinations of α- and β-emissions a series of changes occurs which finally leads to the formation of a non-radioactive isotope, often of lead.

The rate of radioactive decay

Experiment 1.2   *To investigate the rate of a
radioactive decay*

This experiment must be performed by the teacher.

Measure out into a separating funnel 3 cm^3 of a 35 per cent solution of uranyl nitrate, 7 cm^3 of concentrated hydrochloric acid, and 10 cm^3 of 4-methylpentan-2-one (isobutyl methyl ketone). Shake the mixture well for several minutes, run off the lower (aqueous) layer and immediately transfer the remaining (organic) layer to a G-M liquid counter. Start a stop-clock and the scaler simultaneously and as soon as possible. Leave the clock to run continuously and count for 20 second periods with 10 second intervals, reading and re-setting the scaler during each interval. Record your results as in Table 1.4, filling in the blank column with the appropriate figures.

Table 1.4

Counting period (in seconds)	Number of counts (in 20 seconds)
0—20	
30—50	
60—80	
90—110	
120—140	
150—170	
180—200	
210—230	

Plot a graph of the count rate (counts per 20 seconds) against the starting time of each count, i.e., 0, 30, 60, etc. (in seconds).

The uranium in the sample of uranyl nitrate used consists mainly of the isotope uranium-238 but this is decaying slowly and there will also be other radioactive isotopes present. Only one of these, protactinium-234, is soluble in the organic solvent, 4-methylpentan-2-one. The decay product of protactinium-234 itself decays so slowly that its activity will not affect the experiment.

Taking this into account, what do you think the graph represents?
Using the graph, determine the time taken for the count rate to drop by half and repeat this determination between different points on the graph to obtain several values for this result. What deductions can you make?

The rate of radioactive decay is found to depend only on the mass of the radioactive substance present and is usually expressed as a **half-life**.

What do you think is meant by the term 'half-life'?
From your results, what is the half-life of protactinium-234?

The half-lives of radioisotopes vary considerably, as shown in Table 1.5.

Table 1.5—Half-lives of some natural radioisotopes

Isotope	Half-life
Uranium–238	4.5×10^9 years
Thorium–234	24.5 days
Radium–226	1.59×10^3 years
Polonium–214	1.5×10^{-4} second
Lead–210	22 years

The uses of radioisotopes

(a) Medical uses

Intense γ-radiation can be used to destroy cancerous growths but great care must be taken that healthy tissue is not also damaged. The radiation may be focussed onto the growth by special machines (Fig. 1.10), or a tiny capsule of the isotope is implanted in the affected part of the body. Cobalt-60 is commonly used for this treatment.

In 1970, a nuclear battery was first used to provide power for a heart pacemaker (Fig. 1.11) which maintains the heartbeat of patients suffering from heart disease. The pacemaker is implanted in the patient and will last for ten years compared with the two years for one operated by a conventional chemical battery.

(b) Sterilization

Very large doses of γ-radiation will completely destroy bacteria and similar organisms and leave the objects concerned perfectly sterile with no residual radioactivity. This is particularly useful for surgical equipment which can be so treated when already sealed in the appropriate container or packing and thus there is no risk of further contamination.

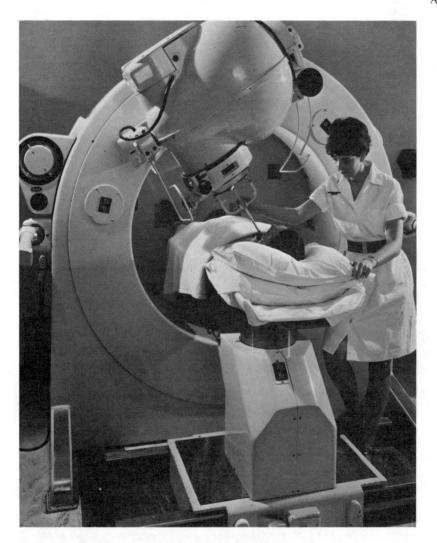

Figure 1.10   The treatment of cancerous growths by radiation

(c) Industrial uses

β- or γ-sources are used for thickness gauges which can automatically monitor and control the thickness of sheet material such as plastic, paper, metal, etc., as it is being processed, by detecting variations in the intensity of the radiation passing through it. Another type of thickness gauge can be used for measuring the wall thickness of pipework to check for internal corrosion (Fig. 1.12).

Figure 1.11   A nuclear heart pacemaker

Similar sources are used to control the mechanical filling of packets, tins, tanks, etc. When the level of the material reaches a pre-determined height the radiation beam is cut and filling is stopped.

Industrial radiography is rather similar to the use of X-rays but by using intense γ-sources greater penetration can be achieved. This technique is particularly useful for checking welds and castings for faults. A welded pipeline, for example, is tested by placing the γ-source inside and wrapping a piece of film around the weld. After suitable exposure, the film is processed and any flaws that show up in the pipe can be corrected.

(d)   Radioactive 'tracers'

The movement or behaviour of a radioactive atom can be traced because of its activity and this fact is utilized in many different ways. Pipelines may be tested for leaks by adding the radioisotope to the flowing liquid and testing for activity along the length of the pipe. The flow of water through a dam (see Fig. 1.13) or the movement of silt in rivers and estuaries can be followed in a similar manner.

Figure 1.12　Checking the wall thickness of pipework using a radiation gauge

In medicine, many metabolic processes can be traced, such as the uptake of iodine by the thyroid gland using iodine-131, and such techniques are frequently of importance in diagnosis.

Tracers are also of vital importance to the chemist in the investigation of many reactions which would otherwise be impossible to follow (see chapter 6).

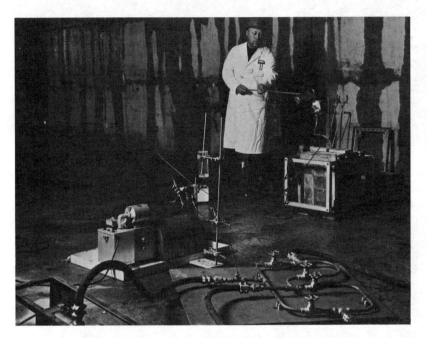

Figure 1.13   Adding a radioactive tracer to check the flow of water through a dam

(e) Dating techniques

The presence of very long-lived radioisotopes in the earth's crust (e.g., uranium-238) makes it possible to estimate the age of the earth by comparing the activity now with that which it was presumed to be when the earth was first formed. A figure of 4000 million years has been suggested by this method.

The radioactive carbon-14 occurs in the atmosphere and is absorbed by plants in the form of carbon dioxide together with the ordinary inactive carbon-12. When the plant dies, uptake of carbon ceases, and from the activity of the plant remains the age of the plant can be estimated. This method is accurate for ages up to about 10 000 years old and can still be used to date material of up to about 40 000 years old.

What type of radioisotope, in terms of half-life, would you think most suitable for use (*a*) in a thickness gauge, (*b*) as a tracer in medical work? Explain your answers.

The natural occurrence of isotopes

Many elements exist naturally as a mixture of isotopes, but the proportions present vary tremendously from one element to another. For example, the ratio of the isotopes of hydrogen, hydrogen-1 to hydrogen-2, is approximately 6900 to 1, while in bromine, bromine-79 and bromine-81 are present in nearly equal quantities. Table 1.6 gives some common elements and their isotopes and Table 1.7 shows some elements that are 'simple' (i.e., only one isotope occurs).

Table 1.6—Some elements and their isotopes

Element	Symbol of element	Atomic number	Mass numbers
Hydrogen	H	1	1, 2
Carbon	C	6	12, 13
Nitrogen	N	7	14, 15
Oxygen	O	8	16, 17, 18
Sulphur	S	16	32, 33, 34, 36
Chlorine	Cl	17	35, 37
Copper	Cu	29	63, 65
Zinc	Zn	30	64, 66, 67, 68, 70
Tin	Sn	50	112, 114, 115, 116, 117, 118, 119, 120, 122, 124
Lead	Pb	82	204, 206, 207, 208
Uranium	U	92	*234, *235, *238

* radioactive.

Table 1.7—Some common 'simple' elements

Element	Symbol of element	Atomic number	Mass number
Fluorine	F	9	19
Sodium	Na	11	23
Aluminium	Al	13	27
Phosphorus	P	15	31
Manganese	Mn	25	55
Iodine	I	79	127

Atomic masses

The mass of an atom relative to those of other atoms is called its **atomic mass** which, being a ratio, has no unit. The early determinations of atomic masses were carried out by measuring the relative masses in which elements combined. These methods were usually extremely tedious but surprisingly good results were often obtained. The first standard used was the lightest element, hydrogen, which was given an atomic mass of one. Later it was found more convenient to use oxygen as the standard, this being assigned an atomic mass of sixteen. The atomic masses of most other elements were then very close to whole numbers.

With the greater accuracy of the mass spectrometer and the discovery of isotopes it has been shown that the isotopic composition of some natural elements, although remarkably constant in most cases, does show slight variations from one sample to another. Thus it has become desirable to use as the standard of atomic mass a specific isotope, which cannot vary in mass, rather than a natural element which can.

By international agreement the carbon-12 isotope is now used as the standard of atomic mass. However, except for very accurate work, the differences between the values obtained for atomic masses on the different scales are so small that they are not really significant.

In order to determine the atomic mass of a natural element using the mass spectrometer, the accurate mass of each isotope present relative to the carbon-12 isotope, this being called the **isotopic mass**, is measured, together with the relative abundances of the isotopes, these being proportional to the heights of the peaks on the graph. In the case of chlorine (see p. 13) the isotopic masses are 35 and 37 and the relative abundances are respectively 75·5 per cent and 24·5 per cent. The results are then calculated as follows:

$$\text{Atomic mass of chlorine} = \frac{75\cdot5}{100} \times 35 + \frac{24\cdot5}{100} \times 37$$
$$= 26\cdot41 + 9\cdot05$$
$$= 35\cdot46$$

As shown in this example, the presence of various isotopes in a natural element explains why the atomic masses of some elements are far from being whole numbers. A full table of atomic masses is given at the back of this book.

The mole

In 12 g of the isotope carbon-12, it can be calculated that there are approximately 6×10^{23} atoms. This number is called the **Avogadro Constant** (L). Two different methods of estimating a value for this constant are given on pages 30 and 50.

The **mole** is the amount of substance that contains a number of particles equal to the Avogadro Constant. It can be shown that one mole of atoms of any element has a mass in grammes equal to the atomic mass of that element.

Thus one mole of carbon-12 atoms has a mass of 12 g, one mole of bromine atoms has a mass of 80 g and so on.

In addition to atoms, the mole may refer to molecules, ions, electrons or a group of such entities.

NB: The mole replaces the terms formerly in use gramme-atom, gramme-molecule, gramme-ion, etc. Thus a gramme-atom is now described as a mole of atoms, a gramme-molecule as a mole of molecules, and so on.

Summary

All matter is made up of tiny particles called **atoms**. The atoms of certain elements are unstable and give off penetrating radiations. The discovery of this effect, which is called **radioactivity**, led to important changes in the theory of the atom. The original Dalton idea of the atom as being indivisible and indestructible had to be modified to account for radioactive atoms that are constantly changing to other atoms and thus must be splitting in some way. At about the same time, a negatively charged particle called the **electron** had been discovered and found to be contained in all atoms. It was thus the first sub-atomic particle known. Later experiments showed that in addition to electrons, each atom contains a small **nucleus** which has a positive charge equal to the negative charge of the electrons, so that overall the atom is electrically neutral. If the atom has more or less electrons than necessary for neutrality, a charged particle called an **ion** results. The volume occupied by the nucleus is very small compared with the volume of the whole atom, which is thus very largely empty space. The electrons are arranged around the nucleus in **orbitals**, which in turn are grouped in **shells**, each of which can contain a certain maximum number of electrons. Further examination of the nucleus led to the discovery of two more sub-atomic particles called respectively the **proton** and the **neutron** and collectively **nucleons** (since they occur in the nucleus). The masses of the proton and the neutron are nearly the same and for convenience this mass is called one **atomic mass unit**. The total mass of protons and neutrons in atomic mass units, to the nearest whole number, is called the **mass number**. The properties of the important sub-atomic particles are summarized in Table 1.9.

Table 1.9—Sub-atomic particles

Particle	Mass (in atomic mass units)	Charge
Proton	1	+1
Neutron	1	0
Electron	0 (approx)	−1

The **atomic number** of an element is the number of protons in the nucleus and the number of neutrons is the difference between the mass number and the atomic number. Measurements with the mass spectrometer show that atoms of the same element can have different masses. This is because the nuclei can contain differing numbers of neutrons without altering the atomic number, as the neutron has no charge. Atoms with the same atomic number but differing mass numbers are called **isotopes**. Mixtures of isotopes occur in many natural elements, but many more can be made artificially and these are often radioactive. If the neutron to proton ratio in the nucleus is high, the atom is likely to be radioactive but, with few exceptions, only those elements of high atomic number are naturally radioactive.

There are three types of radioactive emissions, two of which are particulate, α-particles, which are fast-moving helium nuclei, and β-particles, which are even faster-moving electrons, and the third, γ-radiation, which is an electromagnetic radiation moving with the speed of light and having great penetrative properties. All are produced by changes in the nucleus and all are a serious hazard to health, so that strict precautions are necessary at all times to prevent exposure to them. Some atoms are α-emitters while others are β-emitters, γ-radiation being given out simultaneously with both, but in each case an isotope of a new element will be produced. This will in turn decay into another isotope until finally a non-radioactive isotope, often of lead, is formed. The rate of decay is measured by the **half-life** (the time taken for half of the active atoms of that isotope to decay) and this varies tremendously from millions of years to fractions of a second. Radioactive isotopes have many uses, notably in the fields of medicine, industry, and general scientific research.

The mass spectrometer measures the relative masses of individual isotopes and these values, in conjunction with the relative quantities of each isotope present, can be used to calculate the **atomic mass** of the naturally-occurring element, which is in most cases a mixture of isotopes. This atomic mass is the mass of that element relative to the mass of a standard, that currently in use being the mass of the carbon-12 isotope, and for most elements is very close to a whole number, any significant differences being due to unusual isotopic mixtures.

The **mole** is an amount of substance which may refer to atoms, molecules, ions, electrons, or groups of these particles. The number of particles in one mole is equal to the **Avogadro Constant** (6×10^{23}).

Questions

1. The table below shows the results obtained in an experiment to investigate the decay of the radioactive isotope iodine-128, using a scaler connected to a liquid counter:

Time (in minutes)	0	10	20	30	40	50	60
Count rate per minute	2900	2200	1700	1300	980	750	570

Plot the decay curve and use it to determine a value for the half-life of the isotope.

2. The element lithium has an *atomic mass* of 6·939, an *atomic number* of 3 and is composed of *isotopes* of *mass numbers* 6 and 7. Explain the meaning of the terms in italics and make a table to show how lithium atoms are made up of protons, neutrons, and electrons.

3. Use the Periodic Table at the back of the book to complete the following decay sequence:

$$^{232}_{90}\text{Th} \xrightarrow{\alpha} \text{X} \xrightarrow{\beta} \text{Y} \xrightarrow{\beta} \text{Z} \xrightarrow{\alpha} {}^{224}_{88}\text{Ra}$$

4. The table below gives some information concerning certain isotopes of sodium:

Mass number	20	21	22	24
Half-life	0·3 s	23 s	2·6 y	15 h

It has been decided to use one of these to test the efficiency of the heart of a patient in hospital in a Scottish city. The isotopes are produced at Harwell in Berkshire. Which of these isotopes do you consider should be chosen? Give reasons for your choice.

Molecules

Most atoms are unable to exist by themselves and have to join up with other atoms, which may be of the same element or of other elements, to form either a **giant structure** (see chapter 4) or a **molecule**, this being the smallest particle of an element or compound, other than an ion, capable of existing by itself. It is also possible for atoms to be converted to ions and exist in this form, but this will be dealt with in later chapters (3 and 4).

Some elements exist as molecules at atmospheric temperature and pressure, the number of atoms in each molecule of the element, which is called the **atomicity**, being small (Table 2.1).

Table 2.1—Some elements that exist as molecules

Element	Symbol of element	Formula of molecule	Atomicity
Helium	He	He	1
Neon	Ne	Ne	1
Hydrogen	H	H_2	2
Nitrogen	N	N_2	2
Oxygen	O	O_2	2
Chlorine	Cl	Cl_2	2
Bromine	Br	Br_2	2
Iodine	I	I_2	2
Phosphorus	P	P_4	4
Sulphur	S	S_8	8

The **monatomic** elements such as helium do in fact exist as single atoms but for the sake of consistency they are referred to as molecules. The **di-atomic** and **polyatomic** elements cannot normally exist as separate atoms, the smallest particle of these being the appropriate molecule.

Many compounds occur as molecules and although some are small, many are very large such as in plastics in which there are thousands of atoms in each molecule.

NB: The term atomicity is not used for compounds.

The size of molecules

We know that atoms and molecules are very small but is it possible to measure their size? The following experiment gives a rough idea of the size of a fairly large molecule.

When a drop of oil is placed on water it will spread out, if free to do so, into a very thin film which will be approximately one molecule thick. Thus if we measure the volume of the oil drop and the area of the film, it will be possible to calculate the thickness of the film which is the approximate size of one molecule.

Experiment 2.1 *To measure the approximate size of a molecule of oil*

Fill a large bowl or tray with water to a depth of approximately 1 cm and sprinkle a very small amount of fine powder (e.g., baby powder) onto the surface.

Using a ruler for measurement, make a loop 1 mm in diameter in the piece of wire provided (as in Fig. 2.1). Cut off the length of excess wire on one side of the loop and bend the loop to an angle of about 45° to the remaining wire.

(*a*) Wire with loop

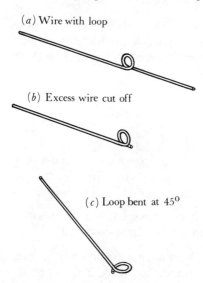

(*b*) Excess wire cut off

(*c*) Loop bent at 45°

Figure 2.1   Making the wire loop

Dip the end of the piece of wire cut off into some olive oil and transfer the drop that clings to the wire to the loop, so that the loop is just filled with oil. The volume of oil is thus approximately 1 mm^3.

Touch the drop of oil onto the dusted surface of water. The oil should spread out immediately into a large film. If it does not do so, it is better to start again. You may have used too much powder or the tray may not have been clean. In the latter case, the tray should be washed with detergent to remove all traces of oil.

Calculate the volume of oil in cubic centimetres. Estimate the area of the oil-patch in square centimetres and hence calculate the thickness of the film in centimetres.

This will be the approximate size of one molecule of the oil. The answer will be very small and an appropriate unit is the nanometre (nm).

$$1 \text{ nm} = 10^{-9} \text{ metre}$$

Express your answer in nanometres. What will be the approximate size of an atom, relative to your result? Explain your answer. If each molecule were assumed to be a cube of side equal to your answer, calculate the number of molecules in 1 cm^3 of olive oil. If one mole of olive oil occupies a volume of 316 cm^3, calculate the number of molecules in one mole of the oil, i.e., the Avogadro Constant, L.

The behaviour of molecules

We know that molecules are very small particles consisting of one or more atoms grouped together in such a way that the particle can lead a stable and independent existence. It would be very useful if we could discover how these particles behave.

Experiment 2.2 *To investigate some properties of molecules*

Carry out each of the following experiments:

(*a*) Place a drop of bromine in a gas-jar with a greased rim and immediately place a similar inverted jar on top, so that a seal is formed between the two rims. Place a piece of white paper behind the jars and observe carefully.

NB: **Bromine, both as liquid and vapour, is dangerous and must be handled with extreme care, dispensing being carried out in a fume-cupboard.**

(*b*) Fill a 50 cm^3 beaker to the brim with an aqueous solution (i.e., solution in water) of potassium permanganate and then place it in an empty 600 cm^3 beaker. Carefully pour water into the large beaker until the potassium permanganate solution in the small beaker is covered completely. If this is done slowly, a minimum of spontaneous mixing will occur. Leave to stand for some time and observe occasionally.

(c) Fit a piece of glass tubing, approximately 1 metre in length and 0·5 cm in internal diameter, with a small piece of cotton wool at each end and seal with a cork, as shown in Fig. 2.2. Clamp the tube so that it is horizontal, preferably against a dark background.

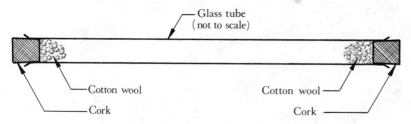

Figure 2.2   The tube for Experiment 2.2(c)

Remove the corks and, with a teat-pipette, add a few drops of concentrated hydrochloric acid to the cotton wool at one end and a few drops of concentrated ammonia solution to that at the other end. Replace the corks and observe the tube from time to time. The fumes given off from hydrochloric acid are of the gas hydrogen chloride and those from ammonia solution are of the gas ammonia.

(d) Drop a large crystal of ammonium dichromate into a beaker of water and leave to stand. Observe occasionally.

(e) Fill two test-tubes with nitrogen dioxide gas. Place one of these underneath an inverted empty test-tube and invert the second over another empty test-tube. Observe what happens.

The effect that you have observed in each of these experiments is called **diffusion**.

In the light of your observations, suggest a meaning for this term.
What must be happening to the molecules in order that diffusion may occur?

If you have come to the correct conclusions in the previous experiments, the following experiment should confirm those conclusions.

Experiment 2.3   *The 'smoke-cell' experiment*

Using the smoke-cell provided (see Fig. 2.3), carry out the instructions and describe what you can see.

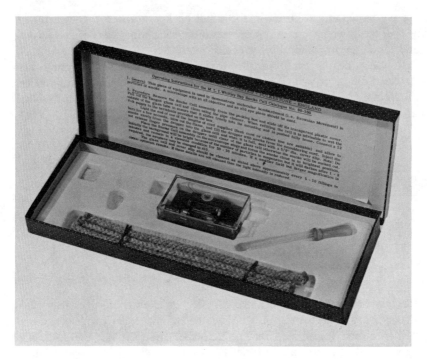

Figure 2.3   A smoke cell

In this experiment are you looking at actual molecules? If not, try to explain what is happening.

What you have observed is called **Brownian Movement**.

The kinetic theory of matter

The previous experiments show that molecules of a gas or a liquid are constantly moving in a completely random manner and undergoing collisions with each other and the walls of the container. In air at room temperature there are over 7000 million collisions by each molecule in every second! In between collisions, it has been found that the molecules travel in straight lines, this being called **translational** movement, but while doing so they are also **rotating** about their own axes and undergoing **vibration** (see Fig. 2.4). The average speed at which the molecules move increases with increase of temperature because their energy of movement (or kinetic energy) is increased. The energy of a particular molecule will be constantly changing due to collisions, so that at any one temperature some molecules will be moving very quickly and some very slowly, but most will have near average speeds.

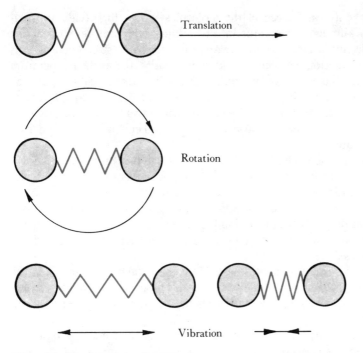

Figure 2.4   The three types of movement

The typical distribution of speeds is shown in Fig. 2.5 and the effect of temperature on this distribution is discussed in chapter 6.

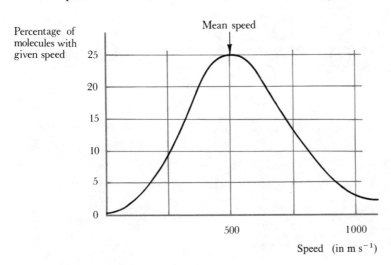

Figure 2.5   The distribution of molecular speeds

In a gas the average speed of the molecules is very high (e.g., approximately 1600 kilometres per hour in air at room temperature) so that the molecules occupy a large volume relative to their own size. There is thus virtually no attraction between individual molecules, but as the temperature is reduced so is the energy of the molecules and hence the distance between them, until eventually they are sufficiently close for the attractive forces to hold them together. At this point the gas condenses to a liquid with a tremendous reduction in volume, e.g., approximately 1600 cm^3 of steam condenses to 1 cm^3 of water.

In a liquid, the molecules are still able to undergo the three types of movement but on a much more limited scale than in a gas, due to their lower energy and greater closeness to one another, resulting in considerable mutual attraction. As the temperature is reduced the energy of the molecules drops still further until finally the attraction between them is so great that they are unable to move from one point to another (i.e., translationally) and the liquid solidifies.

The molecules in the solid still have some energy and this appears in the form of vibration and occasionally rotation. Only at the absolute zero of temperature ($-273°C$) will the molecules have zero energy, when they will not move at all.

On raising the temperature the above changes will be reversed. A representation of these changes is shown in Fig. 2.6.

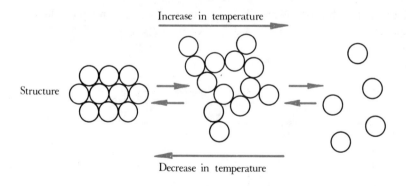

State	Solid	Liquid	Gas
Movement	Vibration	Vibration	Vibration
	Rotation	Rotation	Rotation
	(sometimes)	Translation	Translation

Figure 2.6   Changes of state

This explanation of the three states of matter in terms of the movement of molecules is called the **Kinetic Theory** (kinetic meaning 'motion').

Summary

Most atoms are not capable of existing independently and normally join up in various ways to form larger structures such as **molecules**. Even the largest molecules are very small and thus atoms are even smaller (of the order of 0·1 nm). The molecules of elements usually contain small numbers of atoms, the number of atoms per molecule being called the **atomicity**.

Molecules are in a constant state of movement, the amount and freedom of which depend on the temperature. In the solid state, the degree of movement is very limited because of attraction between the particles, and only vibration and sometimes rotation are normally possible. When the solid melts there is still appreciable attraction between the particles but their greater energy enables them to undergo translation as well as vibration and rotation and thus the amount of movement is very much greater. At higher temperatures, when the particles have sufficient energy, they will break away from all mutual attractive forces and the substance will then be in the gaseous state and the particles will have almost complete freedom of movement. In gases at a particular temperature, the molecules have a wide range of different speeds, but the average is very high, which explains the phenomenon of **diffusion** (the rapid and complete mixing together of different gases when in contact). Diffusion also occurs in liquids but at a much slower rate due to the lower speeds of the particles concerned. The completely random motion of particles in a liquid or gas explains **Brownian Movement** where large particles (such as smoke in the smoke-cell) are bombarded from all directions by smaller particles and move accordingly. The movement of particles is described by the **Kinetic Theory of Matter**.

Questions

1.

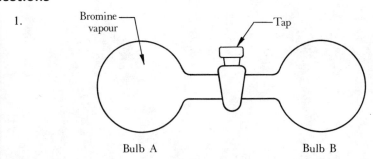

Bulb A   Bulb B

The apparatus shown above was used to investigate the diffusion of bromine. In the first experiment, the bulb B was filled with air and when the tap was opened the bromine slowly diffused to fill both the bulbs. In the second experiment, the air was first pumped out of bulb B and this time when the tap was opened, the bromine diffused at a very rapid speed. In terms of the Kinetic Theory of Matter, explain the difference in these results.

2. The symbol for hydrogen is H but the hydrogen molecule is always represented as H_2. Explain carefully why this is so.

3. A grain of sand can be assumed to be a sphere of diameter 10^{-4} m. It can further be assumed to consist of atoms that are 10^{-10} m in diameter. Use this data to estimate the number of atoms in a grain of sand.

3

Chemistry and electricity

Electricity has many obvious uses both in the home for lighting, heating, and for operating the vast range of household utensils, and in industry for driving machinery, heating furnaces, etc. The chemist uses electricity in many of these ways but of particular interest to him is what effect the current has, if any, on the material through which it is passing.

As a start, he needs to know what types of substances conduct electricity.

Conduction

Experiment 3.1 *Investigating the electrical conduction of various substances*

Set up a circuit as shown in Fig. 3.1 with the substance under test at point X. The electricity is supplied by a battery or a 6 V d.c. source. The lamp is an

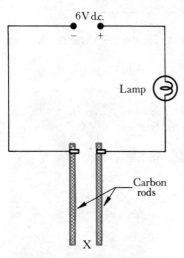

Figure 3.1 The test circuit

ordinary 6 V 'pea-bulb' and the 'probes' at X are two carbon rods that serve as **electrodes**.

Test the solid substances by pressing the two electrodes firmly against each in turn for several minutes.

If a substance does conduct, what would you expect to happen to the lamp?

At the end of the time look carefully at the substance under test to see whether it has changed in any way.

Place each liquid in turn in a small beaker and dip the electrodes into it. As before, observe the lamp and the substance under test for several minutes. When one liquid has been tested, wash the beaker and the electrodes with distilled water before proceeding to the next test.

Test as many of the following substances as time allows.

Solids: carbon, iron, perspex, sulphur, copper, Polythene.
Liquids: distilled water, ethanol, lime-water, dilute sulphuric acid, copper sulphate solution, zinc sulphate solution, sugar solution, mercury.

Record your results as shown in Table 3.1.

Table 3.1

Substance	Conductor	Non-conductor	Changes observed

Do all solids conduct electricity? When solids conduct electricity, do they change in any way?
Do all liquids conduct electricity? When liquids conduct electricity, do they change in any way?

A liquid that conducts an electric current, the conduction being accompanied by chemical changes, is called an **electrolyte**.

Experiment 3.2 *Do metals always conduct electricity?*

Use the same circuit as for Experiment 3.1.

Dip the electrodes into a small beaker or dish of iron filings.

Sprinkle a little fine copper powder onto some water in a small beaker and insert the electrodes.

What conclusions can be drawn from your observations?

Experiment 3.3 *Do crystals conduct electricity?*

Use the same circuit as for Experiment 3.1.

Dip the electrodes into a small beaker or dish of each of the following crystalline substances: lithium chloride, potassium iodide, lead chloride, lead bromide.

What conclusions can be drawn from your observations?

Experiment 3.4 *Investigating the effect of heat on solid non-conductors*

The laboratory must be well-ventilated during this experiment because of the fumes produced.

For this experiment use the same circuit as for Experiment 3.1 but if a 12 V d.c. supply is available this will give a better result. As the material under test is to be heated, the insulated wires must be shielded from the heat. A simple method of doing this is shown in Fig. 3.2. Care must be taken to ensure that the electrodes are not touching.

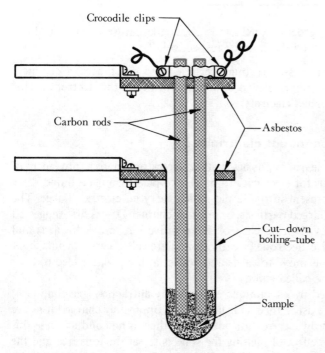

Figure 3.2 The electrode assembly and support

The electrode attached to the positive terminal of the supply is called the **anode** and that attached to the negative terminal is called the **cathode**.

Test in turn those solids that have been found not to conduct by placing them in the boiling-tube and heating until the substance melts. Insert the electrodes and observe the lamp.

A molten substance is said to be in the **fused** condition. If any of the substances do conduct when fused, remove the lamp from the circuit and continue to pass the electric current for several minutes, observing any changes that occur.

Record your results as in Table 3.2.

Table 3.2

Substance	Conduction	Changes at	
		Anode	Cathode

Can you make any general conclusions about the nature of any products formed at the anode and the cathode respectively?

When electricity is passed through certain fused substances, a chemical reaction is seen to occur and new products are formed at the electrodes. This type of reaction is called **electrolysis**.

Why do electrolytes conduct electricity?

You have probably learnt in physics that an electric current is a movement of electric charge. Thus for electricity to be able to pass through a liquid there must be particles present in the liquid which carry an electric charge. The existence of these charged particles, or **ions** (see chapter 1), was first suggested by Michael Faraday. During electrolysis, positive ions move towards and collect at the negative electrode or cathode and are called **cations** while, conversely, negative ions move towards and collect at the positive electrode or anode and hence are called **anions**.

It has been proved by a technique called **X-ray diffraction** (see chapter 4) that these ions can exist in the solid state but, as oppositely charged ions are held rigidly together by electrostatic attraction, there is no conduction in this state. However, the effect of melting the solid is to set the ions free and the material then becomes an electrolyte.

An electrolyte is overall electrically neutral. Thus the positive charges of the cations must exactly balance the negative charges of the anions. For example, in the case of lead bromide each lead ion (Pb^{2+}) must be associated with two bromide ions (Br^-).

What happens at the electrodes?

Let us consider the case of fused lead bromide. Lead ions collect at the cathode during electrolysis and are changed into uncharged particles of lead (i.e., atoms). In this process, called **discharge**, each lead ion must gain two negative charges (i.e., electrons) to neutralize the two positive charges. These electrons can be gained from the cathode because it has a negative charge and thus an excess of electrons. Thus:

$$\underset{\text{ion}}{Pb^{2+}} + \underset{\text{electrons}}{2e^-} \longrightarrow \underset{\text{atom}}{Pb} \tag{1}$$

The atoms gradually become, and can eventually be seen as, globules of lead.

Likewise, at the anode, bromide ions collect and as each one has one electron too many, this electron is lost to the anode, the positive charge of which means that it is short of electrons. Thus:

$$\underset{\text{ion}}{Br^-} - \underset{\text{electron}}{e^-} \longrightarrow \underset{\text{atom}}{Br} \tag{2}$$

Bromine atoms, once formed, are not stable individually and they very rapidly join up in pairs to form molecules. Thus:

$$\underset{\text{atom}}{Br} + \underset{\text{atom}}{Br} \longrightarrow \underset{\text{molecule}}{Br_2}$$

The familiar brown bromine gas consists of bromine molecules.

NB: The equations (1) and (2) are examples of **ionic half-equations**.

Quantity of electricity

The quantity of electricity passed through any conductor depends on the size of the current and the time for which it passes. The size of an electric current is measured in amperes. If one ampere is passed for one second, the quantity of electricity is said to be one **coulomb**. Thus:

$$\text{Quantity of electricity (coulombs)} = \text{current (amperes)} \times \text{time (seconds)}$$

Experiment 3.5 *To determine the quantity of electricity needed to deposit one mole of lead atoms*

This experiment should be performed by the teacher.

Set up the circuit as shown in Fig. 3.3 with a 12 V d.c. supply (6 V d.c. is satisfactory if 12 V is not available) and an ammeter capable of taking up to 4 A. The electrode assembly and support is that used in Experiment 3.4 and the electrolyte is lead bromide to a depth of 1 to 2 cm when molten.

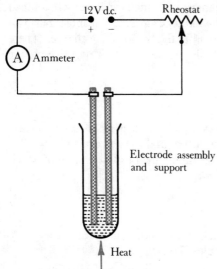

Figure 3.3   The circuit for Experiment 3.5

Heat the electrolyte until completely molten, insert the electrodes and immediately adjust the current to a value in the range of 2 to 4 A. At the same time start a stop-clock. Keep the current steady and allow to run for approximately fifteen minutes. Switch off the current and stop the clock.

Withdraw the electrodes and pour off the molten lead bromide into a *dry* dish or beaker and immediately pour the molten lead into a second *dry* dish. When the bead of lead has solidified, prise it off the glass with a spatula, place it in a small dish or on a tile, chip off any adhering lead bromide and weigh the clean lead.

Calculate the number of coulombs passed.

This has produced the mass of lead that you have recorded.

Calculate the number of coulombs that would be required to deposit one mole of lead atoms (207 g).

The part played by water in electrolysis

Experiment 3.6   *Does the presence of water affect
                   the products of electrolysis?*

Connect the carbon electrodes of the electrolysis cell shown in Fig. 3.4
into the circuit used in Experiment 3.1. Fill the cell to about two-thirds of
its depth with pure (i.e., distilled) water.

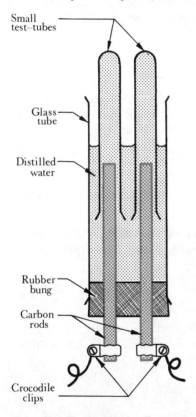

Small
test–tubes

Glass
tube

Distilled
water

Rubber
bung

Carbon
rods

Crocodile
clips

Figure 3.4   The electrolysis cell

❚ Does this water conduct electricity?

With the circuit still connected drop a *small* piece of sodium into the water
and observe the bulb. When this sodium has dissolved, add a second small
piece.

NB: **Stand well back when the sodium is being added to the water.**

43

When all the sodium has dissolved and your observations are complete, remove the bulb and continue to pass the current for several minutes. Collect any gases evolved in the small tubes provided (these must of course be filled with water as shown in Fig. 3.4) and try to identify them.

What happens to the water when sodium is added to it? Can you now explain your observations and, in particular, what is the source of your products? Does the presence of water affect the products of electrolysis?

You have discovered that solutions of some substances in water (i.e., aqueous solutions) conduct electricity and you are now to investigate more closely what happens in these cases.

Experiment 3.7 *The electrolysis of aqueous solutions*

Use the same circuit as for Experiment 3.1 with the solution under test in the electrolysis cell used in Experiment 3.6. Test each of the following solutions: copper chloride, zinc bromide, potassium iodide, dilute hydrochloric acid.

In each case, first test for conduction and, if positive, remove the lamp and electrolyse for approximately five minutes. Observe carefully what happens and attempt to identify any gases evolved.

Record your results in the same form as was used in Table 3.2 for Experiment 3.4.

Compare the products obtained when fused potassium iodide and an aqueous solution of potassium iodide are electrolysed. Attempt an explanation of your answer.

Conduction by aqueous solutions

As we have seen, when a fused electrolyte is electrolysed there are only two species of ions present and the products must be formed from these. In the case of fused lead bromide:

$$\text{at the cathode,} \quad Pb^{2+} + 2e^- \longrightarrow Pb$$
$$\text{at the anode,} \quad Br^- - e^- \longrightarrow Br$$
$$\text{(then} \quad Br + Br \longrightarrow Br_2)$$

However, when water is present there are some ions from ionization of the water:

$$\underset{\substack{\text{water} \\ \text{molecule}}}{H_2O} \longrightarrow \underset{\substack{\text{hydrogen} \\ \text{ion}}}{H^+} + \underset{\substack{\text{hydroxide} \\ \text{ion}}}{OH^-}$$

Water is, in fact, only very slightly ionized but may nevertheless produce sufficient ions for there to be competition for discharge between these ions and the ions of the other compound since, generally, only one species of ion is discharged at a particular electrode at any one time.

To distinguish between ions in aqueous solution and those in the fused state, a convention of subscripts is used, for example:

$Pb^{2+}(s)$ represents a lead ion in a solid,
$Pb^{2+}(l)$ represents a lead ion in a fused state,
$Cu^{2+}(aq)$ represents a copper ion in aqueous solution.

Thus in an aqueous solution of copper chloride there are four species of ions present:

from the water, $H^+(aq)$ and $OH^-(aq)$,
from the copper chloride, $Cu^{2+}(aq)$ and $Cl^-(aq)$.

In Experiment 3.7 which of the four ions mentioned above were in fact discharged? Illustrate your answer by writing ionic equations.
Consider in turn each of the other aqueous solutions that you tested and write ionic equations to explain your observations.
Which ions are apparently unaffected by the presence of water?

Further work on quantity of electricity

Experiment 3.8 *To measure the quantity of electricity required to liberate one mole of hydrogen atoms*

Set up the apparatus as shown in Fig. 3.5 with dilute hydrochloric acid in the U-tube.

With the syringe disconnected, switch on the supply and adjust the current to 1 A (or some other convenient value). Switch off the current and connect the syringe, ensuring that the levels of liquid in the two arms of the U-tube are equal. Simultaneously switch on the current and start a stop-clock. Take volume readings every minute, levelling the acid in the arms before each reading, for fifteen minutes. Throughout this time, check that the current remains constant.

Plot a graph of volume of gas evolved against time and read off from it convenient corresponding values of volume and time. Why is this method likely to give more accurate results than measuring the total volume for a given time? Can you deduce anything from the shape of the graph?
Convert the volume obtained as above to a mass of hydrogen. (The density of hydrogen at room temperature is 0.083 g dm^{-3}.) Calculate the number of coulombs used in the experiment from the values for current (in amperes) and time selected from the graph (in seconds). Hence calculate the number

of coulombs that would be required to liberate one mole of hydrogen atoms (i.e., 1 g). How many moles of hydrogen *molecules* would be liberated by this quantity of electricity?

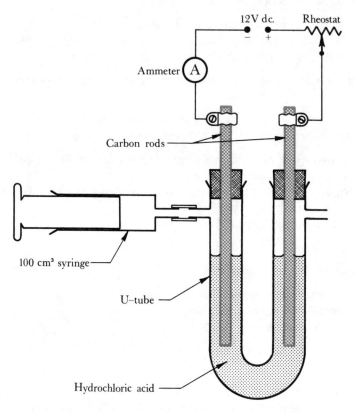

Figure 3.5   The electrolysis of hydrochloric acid

Experiment 3.9   *To measure the quantity of electricity required to deposit one mole of copper atoms*

Set up a circuit as shown in Fig. 3.6. The current is measured by a milli-ammeter reading to 0·2 A. The 50 cm³ beaker contains a solution of copper sulphate in dilute sulphuric acid. The electrodes are two pieces of copper foil.

Clean both electrodes with steel wool, wash them with water, rinse with propanone (acetone) and dry with a paper tissue.

NB: **Propanone is very inflammable and must be handled carefully.**

Mark the electrodes A (anode) and C (cathode), weigh them accurately and connect them into the circuit. Switch on the current and adjust it quickly to a convenient value in the range 0·1 to 0·2 A and simultaneously start a stop-clock. Different groups in the class should arrange to carry out their experiment for various times between twenty-five and forty minutes so that the effect of varying the quantity of electricity can be studied. The current, for any one experiment, must be kept constant throughout.

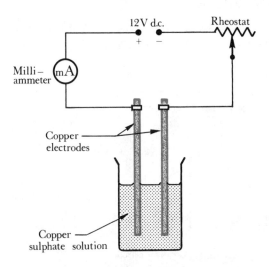

Figure 3.6   The electrolysis of copper sulphate solution

Switch off the current, stop the clock, and remove the electrodes. Wash them with water, rinse in propanone and dry with a paper tissue. Reweigh each in turn and compare the respective masses with the original values.

What has happened to the mass of the cathode?
What has happened to the mass of the anode?
Attempt an explanation of these results using ionic equations. (Remember that the cathode is willing to donate electrons and the anode is willing to accept them.)
Using the values that you have obtained for the time (in seconds) and the current (in amperes), calculate the number of coulombs of electricity that have passed. Then calculate the number of coulombs that would be required to deposit one mole of copper atoms (i.e., 64 g) on the cathode.
With the class results, plot a graph of the mass (in grammes) of copper deposited on the cathode against the quantity of electricity (in coulombs) passed. Comment on the shape of the graph.

The shapes of the graphs that you have obtained in Experiments 3.8 and 3.9 effectively express **Faraday's First Law of Electrolysis.**

| Can you suggest a statement for this law, consistent with your observations?

Experiment 3.10   *To measure the quantity of electricity required to liberate one mole of copper atoms under differing conditions*

Set up a circuit as shown in Fig. 3.7. The current is measured by a milli-ammeter reading to 0·2 A. The two 50 cm³ beakers contain respectively a solution of copper sulphate in dilute sulphuric acid and a mixture of sodium chloride and sodium hydroxide dissolved in water. The latter beaker must be so arranged that it can be heated to and maintained at a temperature of 75 to 85°C. The electrodes are four pieces of copper foil.

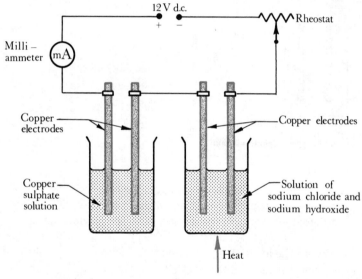

Figure 3.7   The circuit for Experiment 3.10

Clean two copper electrodes with steel wool, wash them with water, rinse with propanone and dry with a paper tissue. Weigh them accurately and connect them into the circuit as the respective *anodes*, taking care that you know which is which. The two unweighed copper electrodes are connected as the cathodes.

Heat the sodium chloride/sodium hydroxide solution to the required temperature and check throughout the experiment that this temperature is maintained.

Switch on the current, adjust it quickly to a convenient value in the range 0·1 to 0·2 A and simultaneously start a stop-clock. Allow the experiment to run for approximately thirty minutes, checking that the current remains constant throughout and moving the anodes about repeatedly to dislodge any deposit that forms on them.

Switch off the current, stop the clock and remove the anodes. Wash them with water, rinse in propanone and dry with a paper tissue. Reweigh each in turn and compare the respective masses with the original values.

What have the changes in mass of the two anodes in common? What has happened to the copper of the anodes to cause these changes?

Calculate the number of coulombs passed. This quantity of electricity has caused the changes in mass. Hence calculate, for each of the two anodes, the number of coulombs that would be required to liberate one mole of copper atoms (i.e., 64 g). By comparing these two results, can you deduce anything about the nature of copper ions?

The faraday

You have seen that the number of coulombs required to liberate one mole of atoms of various elements differs but is always a very large number. For this reason an alternative unit is used, the **faraday** (given the symbol F), which is equal to approximately 96 500 coulombs.

Consider the results that you have obtained in the experiments on electrolysis and complete the following table (Table 3.3).

Table 3.3

Element	Number of coulombs to liberate one mole of atoms	Number of faradays to liberate one mole of atoms
Lead Hydrogen Copper (in copper sulphate) Copper (in sodium chloride/ sodium hydroxide)		

NB: Calculate the number of faradays to the nearest whole number.

The equation for the discharge of the hydrogen ion is:

$$H^+ + e^- \longrightarrow H$$

Hence one mole of hydrogen ions will produce one mole of hydrogen atoms and to do so will need one mole of electrons. From the results of Experiment 3.8 we have seen that the quantity of electricity required to discharge one mole of hydrogen atoms is one faraday. Thus **one faraday is one mole of electrons**.

You may meet an experiment in your physics lessons in which the charge on one electron is determined as $1·6 \times 10^{-19}$ coulomb. This enables us to calculate the value of the Avogadro Constant (L), as L times the charge on one electron is equal to the charge on L electrons. Thus:

$$L = \frac{\text{Charge on L electrons}}{\text{Charge on 1 electron}} = \frac{96\,500}{1·6 \times 10^{-19}} = 6 \times 10^{23}$$

More about ions

If an ion has a single charge, one faraday of electricity is required to discharge one mole of it. If it has a single negative charge one faraday must be lost and if a single positive charge, one faraday must be gained. For example:

$$H^+ + e^- \longrightarrow H \quad \text{(then } H + H \rightarrow H_2\text{)}$$

and

$$Cl^- - e^- \longrightarrow Cl \quad \text{(then } Cl + Cl \rightarrow Cl_2\text{)}$$

If the ion has a double charge, two faradays are required to discharge one mole. For example:

$$Pb^{2+} + 2e^- \longrightarrow Pb$$

Ions with a double negative charge are not normally discharged during electrolysis.

There are relatively few ions with a triple charge but those that do exist require three faradays to discharge each mole. For example:

$$Al^{3+} + 3e^- \longrightarrow Al$$

Some elements are able to form more than one species of ion and these are discussed in more detail in later chapters, e.g., the iron(II) ion and the iron(III) ion. (Note the use of the Roman numerals in brackets to designate the specific variety.)

How many faradays would be required to discharge one mole of the iron(II) and iron(III) ions respectively?
Which other element that you have met can form more than one species of ion? Write the formulae of the ions concerned and state the number of faradays required to discharge one mole of each.

As can be seen from the above examples, the quantity of electricity required to liberate one mole of atoms of any element is a simple multiple of that required to liberate one mole of atoms of the simplest atom (hydrogen). This is a statement of **Faraday's Second Law of Electrolysis**.

'Compound' ions

A number of ions exist that contain more than one element such as the hydroxide ion (OH^-) which contains the elements oxygen and hydrogen. Most of these are anions and the only common cation of this type is the ammonium ion (NH_4^+) which contains the elements nitrogen and hydrogen.

If these ions are present in a solution that is being electrolysed, they are rarely discharged. The hydroxide ion is one of the few of this type that can easily be discharged:

$$OH^- - e^- \longrightarrow OH$$

then $$4OH \longrightarrow 2H_2O + O_2$$

NB: The life of the hydroxide radical (OH) is very short.

The movement of ions

We have assumed that the electrical conduction observed in many liquids is due to the movement of ions under the effect of the electric current. Is it possible to see this movement?

Experiment 3.11 *Observing the movement of ions*

For both of the following experiments the apparatus used is shown in Fig. 3.8. Fold a piece of filter paper several times to form a thick strip, approximately 1 cm in width. Saturate it with tap-water and fasten it to a microscope slide by means of two crocodile clips connected to a 6 (or 12) V d.c. supply.

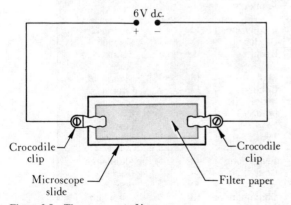

Figure 3.8 The movement of ions

(*a*) Place a small crystal of potassium permanganate in the centre of the filter paper, as marked by a pencil, and leave with the current switched on for about twenty minutes.

(*b*) Place a small crystal of copper(II) sulphate in the centre of the filter paper and leave, with the current switched on, for about twenty minutes. In this case, the blue colour of the copper(II) ion will not be sufficiently strong to be seen clearly and so it must be located by conversion to a more highly coloured form. This may be done by exposing the strip of filter paper briefly, at the end of the experiment, to the gas hydrogen sulphide.

In each case, comment on your results and explain them as far as you are able to.

A catalogue of ions

You have already met a number of ions and the corresponding atoms. These are included in the following catalogue together with some new ones. Copy out Table 3.4 but leave room to add further examples that you may come across in the future. It should be noted that some of the ions listed are not

Table 3.4—A catalogue of ions (*a*) cations

	Formula of ion	Name of ion	Symbol of atom	Name of element
Ions with a charge of one	H^+ Ag^+ Li^+ Na^+ K^+ Cu^+ Hg^+ NH_4^+	Hydrogen Silver Lithium Sodium Potassium Copper(I) Mercury(I) Ammonium	H Ag Li Na K Cu Hg —	Hydrogen Silver Lithium Sodium Potassium Copper Mercury —
Ions with a charge of two	Mg^{2+} Ca^{2+} Ba^{2+} Zn^{2+} Mn^{2+} Cu^{2+} Hg^{2+} Fe^{2+} Pb^{2+} Sn^{2+}	Magnesium Calcium Barium Zinc Manganese Copper(II) Mercury(II) Iron(II) Lead(II) Tin(II)	Mg Ca Ba Zn Mn Cu Hg Fe Pb Sn	Magnesium Calcium Barium Zinc Manganese Copper Mercury Iron Lead Tin
Ions with a charge of three	Al^{3+} Au^{3+} Fe^{3+} Cr^{3+}	Aluminium Gold Iron(III) Chromium	Al Au Fe Cr	Aluminium Gold Iron Chromium

normally discharged during electrolysis, in particular many of the 'compound ions' and anions with a charge greater than one.

Table 3.4—A catalogue of ions (b) anions

	Formula of ion	Name of ion	Symbol of atom	Name of element
Ions with a charge of one	Cl^-	Chloride	Cl	Chlorine
	Br^-	Bromide	Br	Bromine
	I^-	Iodide	I	Iodine
	OH^-	Hydroxide	—	—
	NO_3^-	Nitrate	—	—
	HCO_3^-	Hydrogen carbonate	—	—
	HSO_4^-	Hydrogen sulphate	—	—
Ions with a charge of two	O^{2-}	Oxide	O	Oxygen
	S^{2-}	Sulphide	S	Sulphur
	CO_3^{2-}	Carbonate	—	—
	SO_4^{2-}	Sulphate	—	—
	SO_3^{2-}	Sulphite	—	—
Ions with a charge of three	PO_4^{3-}	Phosphate	—	—

NB: The formulae and symbols listed are conventionally regarded as representing one mole of either ions or atoms respectively. Thus the formula Pb^{2+} represents one mole of lead ions and the symbol Zn represents one mole of zinc atoms, etc.

Electroplating

You have observed that when a solution of copper(II) sulphate is electrolysed, the cathode is plated with copper. This is the principle of electroplating.

The article to be plated is made the cathode in the cell which contains an aqueous solution of ions of the plating metal. Frequently, the anode is made of the plating metal but this is not essential. Careful control of the concentration and purity of the solution is necessary if the plated object is to receive a satisfactory coating.

Experiment 3.12 *Electroplating with various metals*

Set up the circuit as shown in Fig. 3.9. The lamp controls the current flowing to a suitable level. In both cases use a copper cathode cleaned very thoroughly with steel wool, followed by a wash with water, a rinse with propanone and drying with a paper tissue. Place the appropriate solution in the 50 cm^3 beaker with an anode of the metal which is to plate the cathode.

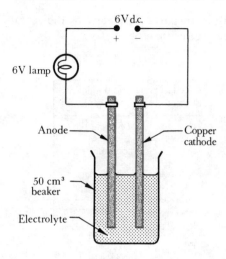

Figure 3.9   Electroplating

(a) Zinc-plating

The anode in this case is a piece of zinc foil and the solution is aqueous zinc sulphate, acidified with dilute sulphuric acid and with a small quantity of boric acid added to improve the quality of the coating. Pass the current for about ten minutes.

(b) Nickel-plating

The anode in this case is a piece of nickel foil and the solution is aqueous nickel ammonium sulphate. Again pass the current for about ten minutes.

In both cases, after switching off the current, remove the cathodes, wash them carefully with water, rinse with propanone and allow to dry. The coating should be quite firm and difficult to remove.

Make a list of as many electroplated objects as you can, together with the metal that has been used for plating.

Anodizing

The surface of aluminium and certain other metals can be specially treated so that they can be coloured with dyes, a process that is superior to painting in that it is quite permanent. This surface treatment, called **anodizing**, involves oxidation of the surface by making the metal the anode in a suitable electrolytic cell. It is, in fact, the oxide film thus produced that is actually dyed.

Experiment 3.13 *Anodizing and dyeing aluminium*

Set up the circuit as shown in Fig. 3.10, with the cylinder of aluminium connected as the cathode. Clean the piece of aluminium to be used as the anode with propanone, followed by water, and then connect it into the circuit, handling with forceps to avoid touching the metal with the fingers. Pour dilute sulphuric acid into the beaker so that the anode is covered as much as possible and then connect the 6 V d.c. supply. Leave for about fifteen minutes, disconnect the supply, remove the anode, wash it with water and examine it.

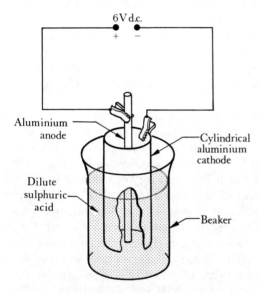

Figure 3.10   Anodizing aluminium

Warm the given dye solution until nearly boiling and then dip the anodized aluminium into it until the required colour is achieved. Finally, immerse the dyed metal in boiling water for a few minutes to seal in the dye.

Summary

All metallic elements conduct electricity when in the liquid (fused) state and also when solid, provided that they are not in a finely-divided condition as powder, filings, etc., when generally they do not. The majority of non-metallic elements, with the notable exception of carbon, do not conduct electricity. When elements do conduct electricity, they do so without undergoing any change.

Crystalline substances, other than crystals of metals or carbon, are non-conductors in the solid state but frequently become conductors when fused or made into aqueous solution. Such liquids and solutions are known as **electrolytes**. Certain other solutions such as dilute sulphuric acid are also electrolytes.

When electricity is passed through an electrolyte a chemical reaction occurs and new products are formed at the **electrodes**. This process is called **electrolysis**. The product at the **cathode** (the negative electrode) is, in almost all cases, either a metal which often plates the electrode thus causing an increase in mass, or hydrogen gas. At the **anode** (the positive electrode) the product is always a non-metal, unless conditions are such that the anode dissolves, thereby causing a decrease in mass.

Conduction in electrolytes is due to the presence of ions. During electrolysis, ions gain or lose one or more electrons to form neutral atoms or radicals. These either deposit as a metal or join together very rapidly to form molecules. If the anode dissolves, it does so by forming ions of the metal of which it is made.

Water is a very poor conductor because it is only very slightly ionized but it plays a very important part in the electrolysis of aqueous solutions and often controls the nature of the products formed. When there is a mixture of ions present in an electrolyte, as for example in an aqueous solution, there is a preferred order of discharge which, however, may be modified by other factors, notably the concentration of the solution and the material of the electrode. Thus in an aqueous solution of potassium iodide containing the cations hydrogen, (H^+), and potassium, (K^+), hydrogen gas is evolved at the cathode, but in an aqueous solution of copper(II) sulphate containing the cations hydrogen and copper(II), (Cu^{2+}), the cathode is plated with copper. Examples of cations in increasing order of difficulty of discharge, under conditions of equal concentration, are copper(II), (Cu^{2+}), hydrogen, (H^+), zinc, (Zn^{2+}), and potassium, (K^+). Examples of anions in increasing order of difficulty of discharge, under conditions of equal concentration, are iodide, (I^-), hydroxide, (OH^-), bromide, (Br^-), and chloride, (Cl^-).

Quantity of electricity is measured in **coulombs** and **faradays** (one faraday = 96 500 coulombs). To liberate one mole of atoms of any element during electrolysis, a simple number of faradays is required.

Faraday's First Law of Electrolysis states that the mass of product liberated at an electrode is directly proportional to the quantity of electricity passed.

Faraday's Second Law of Electrolysis states that the quantity of electricity required to liberate one mole of atoms of an element is a simple multiple of that required to liberate one mole of hydrogen atoms.

Certain elements are able to form more than one species of ion, e.g., copper as copper(I), (Cu^+), and copper(II), (Cu^{2+}), and iron as iron(II), (Fe^{2+}), and iron(III), (Fe^{3+}). Some ions exist that contain more than one element, e.g., the sulphate ion, $(SO_4{}^{2-})$, but these, with the exception of the hydroxide ion, (OH^-), are not usually discharged during electrolysis.

The movement of individual ions cannot be seen as they are much too small but by using coloured compounds it can be proved that cations do in fact move to the cathode and anions to the anode.

Electroplating, which is the covering of one material, usually metal or plastic, with a thin layer of metal is carried out for a number of reasons. Silver, gold, and chromium-plating improve the appearance of the article and the latter is also used for protection from corrosion, as for example on car bumpers. For economy purposes a thin layer of metal such as silver or gold is obviously much cheaper than making the entire article of that metal.

Anodizing is the process by which certain metals, notably aluminium, are given a surface film of oxide by being made the anode in a suitable electrolytic cell. This oxide film can be dyed to give a permanent and brilliant colour.

Questions

1. Make a Venn diagram to show how the sets 'conductor', 'insulator', and 'electrolyte solution' are related. Place the names of five typical substances in their correct positions on the diagram.

2. A current of 0·1 A is passed through a solution of a gold compound for 5 hours. 1·22 g of gold (atomic mass 197) are plated on the cathode. What charge do these results suggest is carried by the gold ions?

3. Suppose you wanted to demonstrate that ions of a metal element X, in aqueous solutions, each carried twice the charge as ions of the metal element Y. Describe an apparatus and procedure which would enable you to do this. State what measurements you would make and how you would use them in calculation. (Let x and y represent the atomic masses of the two metal elements.)   (LN)

4. Suppose that you have to plate a graphite rod with copper. Describe, with the help of a labelled diagram and a brief description, how you would do this. State what changes occur during the operation. Calculate the mass of copper (atomic mass 64) that would be deposited on the graphite during the passage of 500 coulombs.

(O & C)

5. Find out how 'masters' are produced in the record industry, using electrolysis.

4

The structure of substances

A mole of water has a volume of 18 cm^3 at 4°C. If this is made into steam at its boiling point, the volume swells to about 30 dm^3. As the water and steam both contain the same number of molecules, it follows that in the steam the molecules must be much more widely separated. The steam molecules have extra energy (as discussed in chapter 2) which is necessary to overcome the attractive forces between the molecules and to keep them 'airborne'. The energy required to turn a mole of water into vapour is called the **molar latent heat of vaporization**.

As one mole of any liquid contains the same number of molecules, will the molar latent heat of vaporization be the same for other liquids?

Experiment 4.1   *To determine the molar latent heats of vaporization of liquids*

Set up the apparatus as shown in Fig. 4.1 with distilled water in the flask. Switch on the electrical supply and let it operate until liquid is collecting in the receiver at a steady rate. Use the rheostat to control the power at between twenty and thirty watts. When steady conditions are achieved, collect the liquid distilling in a previously weighed beaker for a known time (five minutes is suitable) and reweigh.

Repeat the experiment using cyclohexane (C_6H_{12}).

In each case, calculate the energy supplied in joules (this is the product of power in watts and time in seconds). Calculate the mass of one mole of the liquid under test and then the energy required to convert this quantity of the liquid into vapour.

As the energy expressed in joules is rather large, it is normal to divide each value by 1000 to convert it to kilojoules (kJ).

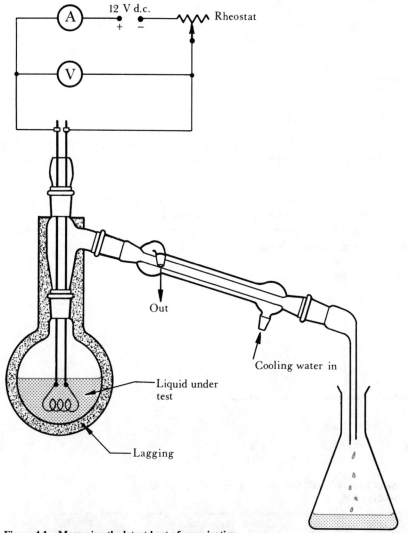

Figure 4.1   Measuring the latent heat of vaporization

What conclusions can you come to from the differences in the values you have obtained for the two liquids?

Experiment 4.2   *Finding out more about the nature of the forces between the molecules in a liquid*

A piece of Polythene rod rubbed vigorously with cat's fur acquires a negative charge. Fill a burette with water and adjust the tap so as to allow the liquid to run out in a slow, steady stream. Charge a Polythene rod in the manner described and hold it about 2 cm from the stream of emergent liquid. Repeat the experiment with cyclohexane in the burette.

What additional evidence does this experiment provide about the forces between the molecules of the liquids?

Boiling point and structure

It might be expected that the boiling point of a liquid would be affected by the same factors as those that affect the magnitude of its latent heat of vaporization.

Using the data provided in Table 4.1, plot a graph of molar latent heat of vaporization against boiling point as shown in Fig. 4.2.
What would be the expected boiling point of a liquid having a molar latent heat of vaporization of zero?

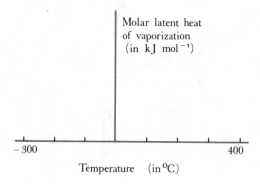

Figure 4.2

Table 4.1—Some values of molar latent heats of vaporization and the corresponding boiling points

Liquid	Molar latent heat of vaporization (in kJ mol^{-1})	Boiling point (in °C)
Benzene	31	80
Carbon disulphide	27	46
Cyclohexane	30	81
Ethanol	38·5	79
Mercury	56·5	356
Methanol	35	65
Sulphuric acid	50	326
Tetrachloromethane	30·5	77
Trichloromethane	29	61
Water	40·5	100

Melting points and latent heats of fusion

Experimental methods are also available for the determination of **molar latent heats of fusion** of solids. These correspond to changes of the type:

$$X(s) \longrightarrow X(l)$$

Some of the results are shown in Table 4.2. Inspection of these figures will show that no simple relationship exists between melting points and molar latent heats of fusion.

Table 4.2—Some values of molar latent heats of fusion and the corresponding melting points

Solid	Molar latent heat of fusion (in kJ mol^{-1})	Melting point (in °C)
Lead	4·8	327
Lithium chloride	13·5	610
Magnesium chloride	43	708
Phosphorus (white)	2·5	44
Potassium chloride	25·5	776
Sodium chloride	28·5	801
Sulphur	1·7	119
Tin	7·1	232

Some of these solids have high melting points and large molar latent heats of fusion. Obviously, particularly strong forces are involved in holding these structures together.

What do those compounds with high values of molar latent heat of fusion have in common?

Compound formation

When warm sodium is placed in chlorine a vigorous reaction takes place (see chapter 9). We believe that a compound is formed by a transfer of electrons from the atoms of the metal to the atoms of the non-metal:

$$Na(s) \longrightarrow Na^+(s) + e^-$$
$$\tfrac{1}{2}Cl_2(g) + e^- \longrightarrow Cl^-(s)$$

The sodium and chloride ions thus formed are held together by the electrostatic attraction between the oppositely charged ions in a rigid, regular, solid structure. Such an arrangement is known as a **crystal lattice**. A method for studying the exact arrangement of the particles in crystalline solids was discovered by Sir Lawrence Bragg in the early part of this century.

Experiment 4.3   *A light analogue of the X-ray diffraction method of investigating the arrangement of the particles in crystalline structures*

The 'Nuffield' diffraction grids consist of a window that contains a piece of film on which is printed an arrangement of transparent dots too small to be distinguished by the naked eye. Cards are available which show three different arrangements of dots (square, diamond, and jumbled) in green squares.

Hold each card before the eyes, one at a time, so that a low voltage bulb is viewed through the film at a distance of about three metres by the right eye. For each of the three arrangements, a distinctive diffraction pattern will be observed. Using these three cards as standards, identify the arrangement of dots in some of the numbered cards.

What we have been able to do in this experiment is to produce an observable **diffraction pattern** from which the arrangement responsible for this pattern can be deduced. With a suitable mathematical approach, it is possible to work out from first principles the arrangement from the observed diffraction pattern without using standards. In this way Sir Lawrence Bragg was able to identify the arrangement of ions in a crystal of sodium chloride. Before diffraction patterns are produced, it is necessary that the wavelength of the radiation is of about the same magnitude as the distance between the particles. X-rays have wavelengths of suitable size to obtain diffraction patterns from crystals.

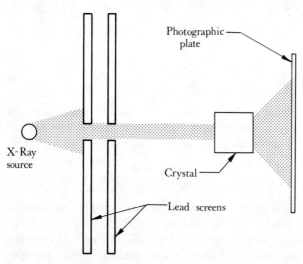

Photographic plate

X-Ray source

Crystal

Lead screens

Figure 4.3   The measurement of X-ray diffraction

The experimental arrangement shown in Fig. 4.3 was originated by the German scientist von Laue and a typical diffraction pattern obtained by him is shown in Fig. 4.4.

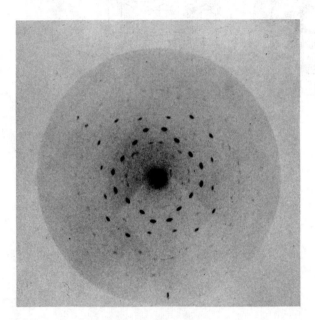

Figure 4.4   A Laue diffraction pattern

Sir Lawrence Bragg discovered that it was an improvement to use diffraction patterns obtained by reflection of X-rays from crystals rather than by their transmittance through crystals and this method is now preferred. The arrangement of the ions in sodium chloride determined by this method is shown in Fig. 4.5. This is known as the **cubic** crystal lattice. Different types of crystalline arrangements may occur in other substances.

The structures of non-ionic substances

We shall now consider the structures of some non-ionic substances. A simple example is furnished by the hydrogen molecule which consists of two hydrogen atoms. If each of these atoms pool their single electron to form a negative **electron cloud**, the positive nuclei can be envisaged as being embedded in this. (See Fig. 4.6.) The distance between the nuclear centres will be such that the repulsion due to their similar charge is just balanced by the attraction exerted on them by the electron cloud. The link formed in this way is known as a **covalent bond**.

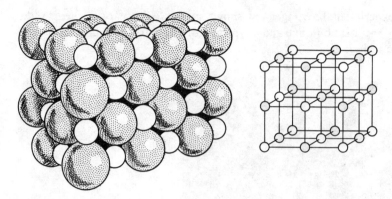

Figure 4.5   The structure of sodium chloride

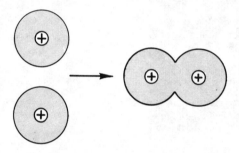

Two hydrogen atoms become one hydrogen molecule

which may be represented
by showing the electron
cloud between the atoms

or more simply as   H—H

Figure 4.6   The hydrogen molecule

Hydrogen chloride gas consists of molecules each containing one hydrogen and one chlorine atom. The hydrogen atom donates its single electron and the chlorine atom donates one of its seven outer electrons to form a covalent bond between the atoms. In this case, however, the electron cloud is not shared between two identical nuclei and the chlorine atom exerts a stronger pull on the electron cloud than the hydrogen atom. Chlorine is said to be more **electronegative** than hydrogen. This unequal sharing of the electron cloud results in the molecule having a positive end (represented by $\delta+$) and a negative end (represented by $\delta-$), as shown in Fig. 4.7. Such a molecule is known as a **dipole** and is said to be **polar**.

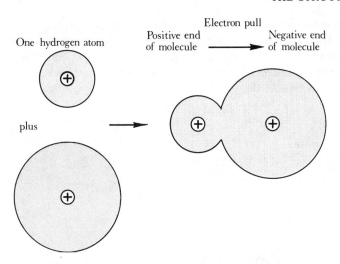

One hydrogen atom

Electron pull

Positive end
of molecule   Negative end
of molecule

plus

one chlorine atom become one hydrogen chloride molecule

The electron cloud picture

and the representation of
the polar molecule

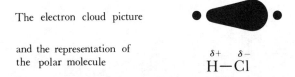

$$\overset{\delta+}{H}-\overset{\delta-}{Cl}$$

Figure 4.7   The hydrogen chloride molecule

Another polar molecule is water in which the two hydrogen atoms are arranged at an angle of 104° 40' to each other (see Fig. 4.8). Owing to the greater electronegativity of the oxygen atom, this end of the molecule is negative and that of the hydrogen atoms is positive.

We can use this idea to better explain the results obtained in Experiment

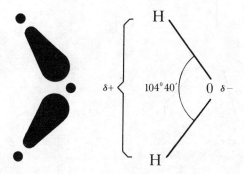

H

$\delta+$ 104° 40'   0 $\delta-$

H

Figure 4.8   The water molecule

4.2. The negative electrostatic field extends radially from the charged Polythene rod and polar molecules placed in this field will orientate themselves in the manner shown in Fig. 4.9. The attraction for the positive end of the molecule will be greater than the repulsion of the negative end and so the molecule will move as indicated.

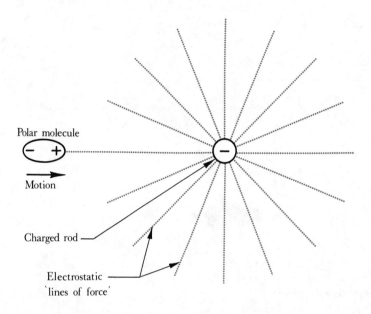

Polar molecule

Motion

Charged rod

Electrostatic
'lines of force'

Figure 4.9   The movement of a polar molecule in an electrostatic field

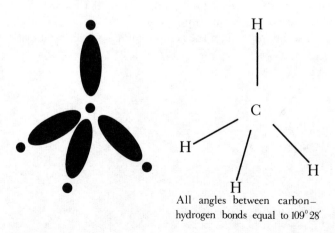

All angles between carbon–
hydrogen bonds equal to $109^{\circ}28'$

Figure 4.10   The methane molecule

Methane has the formula CH_4. The carbon atom has four electrons in its outermost orbital and it can use these to form covalent linkages with four hydrogen atoms in the manner described previously. The four negative clouds so formed will be mutually repellent and the shape of the methane molecule will be dictated by the four clouds taking up positions in which this repulsion is minimized. This shape is one in which the carbon atom is situated at the centre of a regular tetrahedron with the four hydrogen atoms at the corners, as shown in Fig. 4.10.

Is methane a polar molecule? Explain your answer.

It should be clear that the covalent bond differs from the ionic bond in being directional, with the result that the molecule has a definite shape.

Experiment 4.4   *Is there any evidence that metals are crystalline?*

(*a*) Set up the tubes illustrated in Fig. 4.11 and examine the metals displaced in each case for evidence of crystal structure. A low-powered microscope or hand-lens may prove useful in this work.

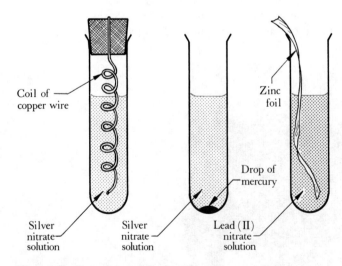

Coil of copper wire

Zinc foil

Drop of mercury

Silver nitrate solution

Silver nitrate solution

Lead (II) nitrate solution

Figure 4.11   Preparing crystals of metals

(*b*) Hang weights on the iron rod suspended in the manner shown in Fig. 4.12 and find the weight required to bend the rod through a convenient angle. Straighten the rod once more and repeat the experiment. Remove the iron rod from the support and bend it rapidly several times at the same point. Place a finger on the bent portion.

(c) Take a piece of tin rod about 10 × 0·5 cm, hold it close to your ear and bend it slowly.

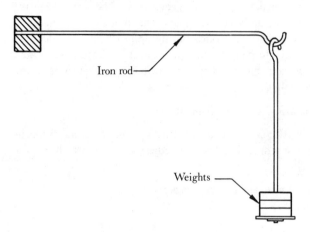

Iron rod

Weights

Figure 4.12   The iron rod experiment

What evidence for the crystalline nature of metals do each of these exercises provide? Examine the photograph of a metal sample in Fig. 4.13. Is the appearance of the metal consistent with your experimental conclusions?

Figure 4.13

Experiment 4.5 *Comparing the hardness of metals*

Tape the ball-bearing to the metal sample being studied and drop the 1 kg weight on it from a height of 25 cm as shown in Fig. 4.14.

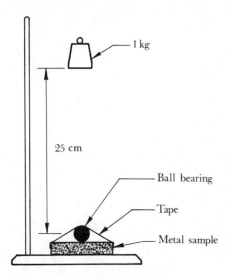

Figure 4.14   The hardness of metals

Measure the diameter of the indentation produced. Test each of the metals shown in Table 4.3.

Table 4.3—Measuring the hardness of metals

Metal	Diameter of indentation (in mm)
Copper Brass (copper, zinc) Bronze (copper, tin) Aluminium Duralumin (aluminium, magnesium, copper, manganese)	

What is the relationship between the diameter of the indentation and the hardness of the metal?

What is the general effect of alloying on the hardness of a metal?

The structure of metals

Experiment 4.6 *Investigating the structure of metals using models*

Use rafts of polystyrene spheres glued together as shown in Fig. 4.15 to see if it is possible to arrange a second and third layer in more than one way.

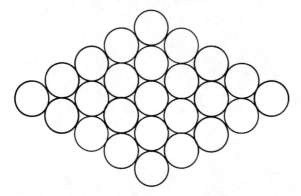

Figure 4.15   The raft of 'atoms'

The arrangement of atoms in metallic copper is shown in Fig. 4.16.

Metals must be held together in the solid state by some forces between the atoms. A simple theory of the structure of metals postulates that each of the atoms in the metal contributes some of its electrons to a general 'electron-plasma' in which the ions resulting are embedded (Fig. 4.17).

Figure 4.16   The structure of copper

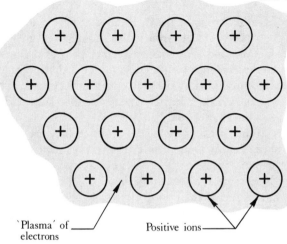

'Plasma' of electrons

Positive ions

Figure 4.17   The 'electron-plasma' theory

This model of metal structure provides a convincing explanation of the good electrical conducting properties that metals exhibit. If a potential difference is applied between two positions on the metal, the 'electron-plasma' is considered to flow from negative to positive. This flow constitutes the electrical current.

Other properties that are said to be characteristic of metals are good thermal conductivity, malleability (the capability of being hammered or pressed into some new shape), and ductility (the capability of being drawn out, for example, into wire). In terms of what you have learnt about metals, try to explain why they have these particular properties. Suggest a reason why alloying affects the hardness of metals.

Summary

Ionic substances have comparatively high values for **molar latent heats of fusion** and melting points because of the strong electrostatic forces of attraction between the ions of which they are composed. Ionic substances are formed by the donation of electrons from the atoms of a metallic element to the atoms of a non-metallic element.

Non-ionic, or **covalent**, substances exist as molecules in which a directional bond is formed between the two atoms concerned by the pooling of one electron from each. These form an **electron cloud** in which the nuclei of the participating atoms are embedded. The shape of a molecule, such as that of methane, in which more than one covalent bond is present is dictated by the mutual repulsion between the electron clouds. When a covalent bond is formed between atoms of two different elements, equal sharing of the electron cloud is not achieved. The more **electronegative** atom has a greater attraction for the electron cloud and thus such molecules possess a **dipole** and are said to be **polar**. Direct evidence for the existence of such dipoles in the molecules of liquids can be obtained by observing their deflections by an electrostatic field. Such liquids also have higher values of **molar latent heat of vaporization** and boiling point than would be expected.

In crystalline solids, the atoms, ions, or molecules of which they are composed are arranged in a regular fashion. The exact arrangement of the particles in such solids can be investigated by observing the **diffraction pattern** that results when X-rays are incident upon them.

Metals are crystalline in nature and their good electrical conductivity can be explained in terms of the 'electron-plasma' theory of the structure of metals. Some of the outer electrons of each metallic atom are considered to be donated to a common 'electron-plasma' in which the ions that remain are embedded. Metals are good conductors of heat for a similar reason, the heat energy being transferred easily through the 'electron-plasma'. The characteristic malleability and ductility of metals are due to the relative ease with which layers of atoms can slide over one another, since there are no rigid directional bonds between neighbouring atoms. If atoms of other elements are added by alloying, this ease of movement is restricted and the metal becomes less malleable and ductile and consequently harder and stronger. The chemistry of some of the more important metals is studied in chapters 10 and 11.

Questions

1. Complete the following table:

Liquid	Formula mass	Volt	Ampere	Mass distilled (in $g\ s^{-1}$)	Latent heat of vaporization (in $kJ\ mol^{-1}$)
A	160	10	2·7	0·15	
B	123	10	3·3	0·10	

If streams of liquids A and B were allowed to run from burettes, which stream would be the more likely to be deflected by a charged rod of Polythene? Which liquid would you expect to have the higher boiling point?

2. Magnesium oxide is an ionic solid forming a cubic crystal lattice similar to that of sodium chloride.

(a) Explain what happens, in terms of electron transfer, when magnesium burns in oxygen.

(*b*) Outline the method by which the arrangement of the ions in such solids has been discovered.

(*c*) Suggest a reason why the latent heat of fusion, in kJ mol^{-1}, for magnesium oxide is considerably greater than that for sodium chloride.

3. Write an account of the structure of metals and explain how the physical properties of metals agree with these ideas about their structure.   (LN)

Formulae, equations, and molecular masses

The composition of water by mass

Dumas, in 1842, used the apparatus shown in a simplified form in Fig. 5.1 to determine the composition of water by mass. Parts A and B were weighed separately. Hydrogen was passed over the heated black copper oxide, taking oxygen from it and forming water, and then both parts of the apparatus were reweighed. The *loss* in mass of A is the mass of oxygen used and the gain in mass of B the mass of water formed. Subtracting the former from the

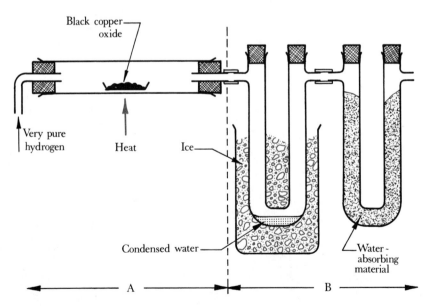

Figure 5.1 A simplified version of Dumas' apparatus

latter gives the mass of hydrogen used. After nineteen such experiments, Dumas stated the ratio of oxygen to hydrogen to be close to 8:1. Little was known at that time about the proportions in which atoms combined to form molecules. Working on the principle that the simplest case is the most acceptable one unless there is evidence to the contrary, the hydrogen and oxygen in water were assumed to combine in the proportion of one atom to one atom and the formula of water was thus considered to be HO. Applying Dumas' results to this formula indicated that each oxygen atom had eight times the mass of a hydrogen atom. The atomic mass was thus taken as 8, assuming that hydrogen had a mass of 1 (the hydrogen scale).

Due principally to the work of Avogadro, it became apparent a little later that water was better represented by the formula H_2O. In order to conform with the mass ratio observed by Dumas, the accepted value for the atomic mass of oxygen had then to be amended to 16. Modern determinations of the atomic mass of oxygen using a mass spectrometer and employing the scale $^{12}C = 12.0000$, give a value of 15·9994 for this constant. (See chapter 1.)

Using atomic masses to find some formulae

On analysis, aluminium oxide is found to contain 53 per cent of the metal. The atomic masses of aluminium and oxygen are 27 and 16 respectively and thus, as 53 g of aluminium are combined with 47 g of oxygen, almost two moles of aluminium atoms are combined with almost three moles of oxygen atoms. The simplest formula for aluminium oxide is therefore Al_2O_3 since atoms combine in whole number ratios (see p. 5). In the next three experiments the formula of a simple compound will be determined. Whenever the formula of a chemical is stated, some such experimental work has gone into its determination.

Experiment 5.1   *To determine the formula of black copper oxide*

As in the Dumas experiment, if hydrogen is passed over heated black copper oxide, the oxygen is removed as water, leaving copper. A convenient source of hydrogen is town gas.

Weigh the tube shown in Fig. 5.2 empty and then with about two spatula measures of black copper oxide. Connect the tube to the gas supply, turn on the gas, and allow it to flow for about ten seconds to displace all the air before igniting it at the small hole. Adjust this flame to a height of about 2 cm. Heat the tube and its contents with a small, non-luminous bunsen flame until the reaction which is seen to occur is complete. Remove the burner but continue to pass gas over the product until it is cool.

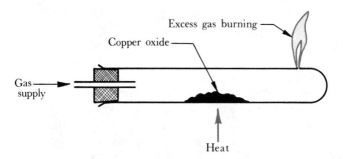

Figure 5.2   The analysis of black copper oxide

What evidence is there that a reaction has taken place? Why is it necessary to continue passing gas until the tube and its contents are cool? From your results calculate the percentage of copper in the black copper oxide. Pool the class results to obtain the most acceptable value.

If the percentage of copper is x, then x g of copper are combined with $(100 - x)$ g of oxygen. The atomic masses of copper and oxygen are respectively 64 and 16. Hence $x/64$ moles of copper atoms are combined with $(100 - x)/16$ moles of oxygen atoms.

Using your value of x, calculate the number of moles of oxygen atoms that are combined with one mole of copper atoms and hence write the formula of black copper oxide.

Experiment 5.2   *To determine the formula of magnesium oxide*

When magnesium is heated in air, it combines with the oxygen to form magnesium oxide.

Weigh a crucible and lid empty and then with 0·24 g of clean magnesium ribbon. Place the crucible with its lid on a pipe-clay triangle on a tripod (Fig. 5.3) and heat gently with a bunsen flame. Gradually increase the heat until the magnesium ignites, lifting the lid occasionally with a pair of tongs to assist burning, but taking care not to allow too much magnesium oxide smoke to escape. Finally, when burning seems to have finished, remove the crucible lid and heat the crucible strongly to ensure complete combustion. Replace the lid and allow the crucible to cool. Reweigh the crucible and lid and then repeat the heating procedure. If on cooling the mass is the same as after the first heating, it may be assumed that all the magnesium has reacted.

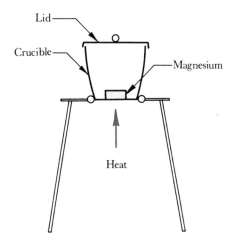

Figure 5.3   The analysis of magnesium oxide

> What fraction of a mole of magnesium atoms is 0·24 g?
> What mass of oxygen combines with 0·24 g of magnesium? Hence calculate what fraction of a mole of oxygen atoms combines with 0·24 g of magnesium and deduce the formula of magnesium oxide.

Experiment 5.3   *To determine the formula of a*
                 chloride of mercury

This experiment should be carried out by the teacher.

Mercury chloride is reduced to the metal by reacting it with hypophosphorous acid.

Weigh a 100 cm³ beaker empty and then containing 5 g of mercury chloride. Add 30 cm³ of distilled water, heat on a water-bath and then add 10 cm³ of hypophosphorous acid solution. Some globules of the metal will form and when the reaction appears to be complete, decant off the liquid and wash the metal with water, following by propanone. Remove the last drops of propanone with filter-paper and after standing for several minutes to allow any remaining propanone to evaporate, reweigh the beaker and its contents.

> What fraction of a mole of mercury atoms has been produced? Calculate the mass of chlorine and hence what fraction of a mole of chlorine atoms is combined with the mass of metal formed. Deduce the formula for mercury chloride.

77

Concentrations of solutions

For many chemical purposes, the concentration of a solution is most conveniently expressed in mol dm^{-3}. A 1 M solution is one that contains one mole of solute in one dm^3 of solution. The formula-mass of hydrated magnesium chloride ($MgCl_2.6H_2O$) is 203. A 1 M solution of magnesium chloride would thus be prepared by dissolving 203 g of the hydrated solid in water and making the volume up to 1 dm^3. Such a solution can also be described as '1 M with respect to Mg^{2+} ions' and as '2 M with respect to Cl^- ions'. A solution of magnesium chloride containing 20·3 g of solid hydrate in each dm^3 is said to be 0·1 M.

NB: This expression of the concentration of the solution has been known as its molarity.

Writing equations for chemical reactions

Like most chemistry books this volume contains a large number of chemical equations. In the section that follows we shall learn how the evidence for writing a particular equation is obtained and interpreted. You should realize that whenever a chemical equation is written, evidence of this type has first had to be obtained.

Experiment 5.4   *Investigating a reaction involving the formation of a precipitate*

When solutions of lead nitrate and potassium iodide are mixed, a yellow precipitate forms which is obviously a product of the chemical reactions between some of the free ions in the solution. To find out more about which ions are involved, we shall carry out the reaction using definite quantities of solutions of particular concentrations.

Using a burette, measure out 5 cm^3 of 1 M potassium iodide solution into a test-tube and add, from a second burette, 1 cm^3 of 1 M lead nitrate solution. Remembering to balance the tube, centrifuge it for fifteen seconds and measure the height of the precipitate. Add a further 0·5 cm^3 of the lead nitrate solution, centrifuge again for fifteen seconds and re-measure the height of precipitate. Continue adding 0·5 cm^3 portions of lead nitrate solution, centrifuging and measuring the height of precipitate after each addition. Enter the precipitate height corresponding to the total volume of lead nitrate solution added, as in Table 5.1.

Table 5.1

Volume of 1 M lead nitrate solution (in cm³)	Height of precipitate (in mm)
1·0 1·5 2·0 ⋮ 6·0	

Plot the results of the experiment on a graph as shown in Fig. 5.4.
Why does the height of precipitate reach a maximum value and then cease to grow as more lead nitrate solution is added? What is the smallest volume of lead nitrate solution that will produce this maximum precipitate height? Try to write an equation for the reaction that is consistent with the experimental results.

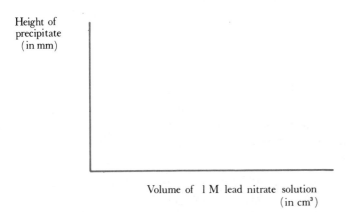

Height of precipitate (in mm)

Volume of 1 M lead nitrate solution (in cm³)

Figure 5.4

Experiment 5.5 *Investigating the reaction between mercury(II) ions and iodide ions*

Place some mercury(II) chloride solution in a test-tube and add a little potassium iodide solution. Then add a further amount of potassium iodide solution, constantly shaking the tube, until the precipitate first formed is redissolved.

The salmon-pink precipitate formed initially is due to a reaction that can be represented by the equation:

$$Hg^{2+}(aq) + 2I^-(aq) \longrightarrow HgI_2(s)$$

79

On adding an excess of potassium iodide solution, the reaction taking place involves the formation of a soluble **complex ion** of mercury:

$$HgI_2(s) + nI^-(aq) \longrightarrow [HgI_{2+n}]^{n-}(aq)$$

We shall now carry out the experiment under more quantitative conditions, in order to find a value for 'n'.

Place 25 cm^3 of 0·2 M mercury(II) chloride solution in a conical flask. Using a burette, find the quantity of 1 M potassium iodide solution that must be added to just redissolve the precipitate that forms initially.

From a comparison of the volumes and concentrations of the two solutions, deduce a value for 'n'.
Write the correct formula for the complex ion of mercury.

NB: The chemistry of complex ions is considered further in chapter 9.

Experiment 5.6   *Investigating the reaction between iron and a solution of copper(II) sulphate*

When iron is added to a solution of copper(II) sulphate it goes into solution by forming ions and causes the precipitation of copper metal. As discussed in chapter 3, iron can form either double or treble positively charged ions and this experiment is designed to see which are produced in this reaction. The equations for the two possible reactions are:

$$Fe(s) + Cu^{2+}(aq) \longrightarrow Fe^{2+}(aq) + Cu(s)$$
or
$$2Fe(s) + 3Cu^{2+}(aq) \longrightarrow 2Fe^{3+}(aq) + 3Cu(s)$$

Weigh a boiling-tube empty and then place in it 0·56 g of finely divided iron filings. Add 20 cm^3 of an almost boiling 1 M solution of copper(II) sulphate, this constituting a reasonable excess. When the reaction has ceased, allow the precipitated copper to settle and decant off the liquid above it. Add about 10 cm^3 of water and rinse the precipitate with this to remove any remaining ions. Decant off the water and repeat the rinsing once more with water and then twice with propanone. Surround the boiling-tube with boiling water to evaporate any propanone that remains. When the copper is thoroughly dry, dry the outside of the tube and reweigh to find the mass of copper deposited.

Calculate the number of moles of iron atoms that react and the number of moles of copper atoms that are precipitated. Which of the above equations best represents the reaction that has taken place?

Molar volume

Before we can investigate some reactions involving gases, we must first study the way in which the volumes of gases are related to the quantity in moles. We shall consider these gases at room temperature and pressure, although these conditions are not constant and changes in them will affect gases much more than they do liquids and solids. This is therefore an approximate treatment of the problem which is, however, adequate for our immediate purposes. Later work in this chapter takes into account such variations more accurately.

A mole of nitrogen gas has a mass of 28 g and a density, at room temperature and pressure, of $1 \cdot 17$ g dm^{-3}. The volume occupied by one mole of nitrogen under these conditions is therefore calculable as shown below:

$1 \cdot 17$ g of nitrogen occupies 1 dm^3 at room temperature and pressure, thus 28 g of nitrogen occupies $(1 \times 28)/1 \cdot 17$ dm^3 at room temperature and pressure,
or 1 mole of nitrogen occupies 24 dm^3 at room temperature and pressure.

The volume occupied by one mole of a gas is called the **molar volume**.

| Carry out similar calculations to complete Table 5.2.

Table 5.2—Molar volumes of some different gases

Gas	Formula	Density (in g dm^{-3})	Mass of 1 mole (in g)	Molar volume (in dm^3 mol^{-1})
Hydrogen	H_2	0·08	2	
Chlorine	Cl_2	2·99	71	
Carbon dioxide	CO_2	1·81	44	
Methane	CH_4	0·72	16	
Ethene	C_2H_4	1·14	28	
Hydrogen chloride	HCl	1·50	36·5	

NB: These figures apply at room temperature and pressure.

It can be seen from the table that the molar volume is almost the same in each case and thus we can summarize what we have learnt as:

One mole of any gas occupies a volume of about 24 dm^3 *at room temperature and pressure.*

As one mole of any gas contains the same number of molecules, it follows that:

Equal volumes of all gases, under the same conditions of temperature and pressure, contain the same number of molecules.

This statement is known as **Avogadro's Law**.

Experiment 5.7 *A reaction in which a gas is evolved*

Place a piece of magnesium ribbon of mass 0·024 g in the inner tube of the apparatus shown in Fig. 5.5, and about 10 cm³ of dilute hydrochloric acid in the outer tube, and then complete the assembly. By carefully shaking the tube the two can be mixed. When all the magnesium has reacted and the apparatus has cooled back to room temperature, measure the volume of hydrogen that has been produced.

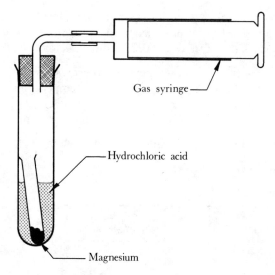

Gas syringe

Hydrochloric acid

Magnesium

Figure 5.5 The magnesium/hydrochloric acid reaction

What fraction of a mole of magnesium atoms was taken? What fraction of a mole of hydrogen molecules was evolved? Balance the equation outlined below in a manner consistent with these results, supplying a suitable value for 'x'.

$$Mg(s) + \underset{\text{(from acid)}}{H^+(aq)} \longrightarrow Mg^{x+}(aq) + H_2(g)$$

Experiment 5.8 *To find the volume percentage of oxygen in the air and the molecular mass of oxygen*

Weigh the silica tube containing the copper before the apparatus is assembled as shown in Fig. 5.6. Starting with 100 cm³ of air in syringe A, heat the copper strongly and pass the air over it from syringe to syringe. As the oxygen

82

in the air reacts with the copper to form copper oxide, the volume of gas will gradually diminish. When there is no further diminution in volume, switch off the burner and leave the gas in one of the syringes whilst the apparatus cools back to room temperature. Read the volume of gas, largely nitrogen, that remains in the syringe and reweigh the tube that contains the copper.

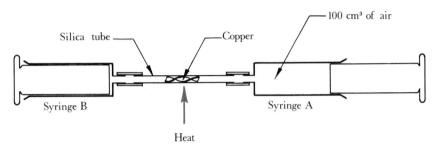

Figure 5.6   The volume percentage of oxygen in the air

From the diminution in volume of gas and the increase in mass of the tube, calculate the volume percentage of oxygen in the air and then the mass of oxygen that occupies 24 dm^3 at room temperature and pressure.

The latter value is the **molecular mass** of oxygen.

Experiment 5.9   *To determine the molecular mass of sulphur dioxide*

Thoroughly dry the apparatus shown in Fig. 5.7 and weigh it. This gives the mass of the apparatus plus that of the air it contains. Using a fume-cupboard, pass sulphur dioxide from a cylinder through the apparatus for about ten seconds, close the taps and then reweigh. Find the volume of water the apparatus will contain.

Taking the density of air at room temperature and pressure to be 1·2 g dm^{-3}, calculate the mass the flask would have if evacuated, and hence the mass of sulphur dioxide. Now calculate the mass of 24 dm^3 of sulphur dioxide, i.e., the molecular mass.

Experiment 5.10   *Investigating the reaction that occurs when sulphur burns in oxygen*

Assemble the apparatus as shown in Fig. 5.8. It does not matter if a little of the air is not replaced with oxygen during the filling process. It is helpful if the volume marker of the syringe can be set initially at 50 cm^3.

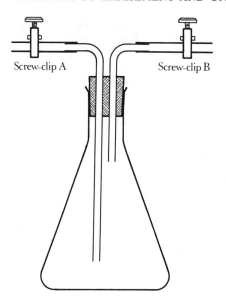

Figure 5.7   **The apparatus for weighing gases**

Apply a bunsen burner flame to the part of the boiling-tube that contains the sulphur (0.032 g), removing it when combustion commences. When the reaction is complete, allow the apparatus to regain room temperature and read the volume of gas in the syringe.

From the result, deduce a suitable value for 'y' in the equation:

$$xS(s) + yO_2(g) \longrightarrow S_xO_{2y}(g)$$

As shown in Fig. 5.9, inject into the apparatus through the rubber tube 1 cm^3 of approximately 5 M potassium hydroxide solution. Agitate the gas mixture by alternately applying mild pressure to the piston of the syringe and then releasing it. Read the volume of gas in the syringe.

Calculate the volume of product that is absorbed and hence deduce a value for 'x' in the equation.

Experiment 5.11   *To investigate the effect of pressure changes on the volume of a fixed mass of gas at constant temperature*

When the apparatus shown in Fig. 5.10 is completely horizontal, as in (*a*) of the diagram, the pressure of the gas is equal to the atmospheric pressure. It can be shown that the pressure of a column of liquid depends on its *per-*

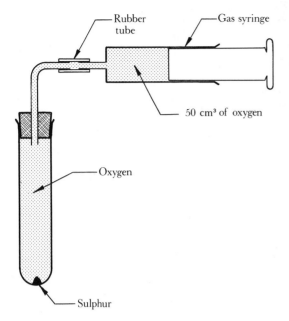

Figure 5.8 **The burning of sulphur in oxygen**

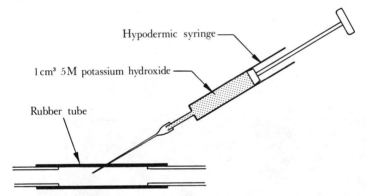

Figure 5.9 **Injection of the potassium hydroxide**

pendicular height. If the tube is tilted, the change from atmospheric pressure can be calculated from the perpendicular height of the mercury column. This can be added to or subtracted from atmospheric pressure as is appropriate. Some examples are shown in Fig. 5.10, (*b*) to (*e*).

From a suitable barometer, obtain the atmospheric pressure in mm of mercury. Use the apparatus to obtain a series of values for the length of the air column (proportional to its volume) and the corresponding pressure. Write your results as shown in Table 5.3.

Let P be the atmospheric pressure in mm of mercury

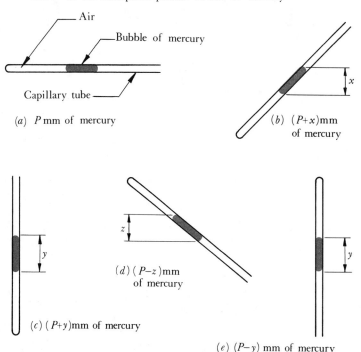

Figure 5.10   The effect of pressure on the volume of a gas

Table 5.3

Length of air column (in cm)	Perpendicular height of mercury (in mm)	Pressure of air (in mm of Hg)	$\dfrac{1}{\text{Air pressure}}$

Plot the two graphs shown in Figs. 5.11 and 5.12, using the results in your table.

This effect was originally investigated by Robert Boyle who summarized the results of his experiments in the following statement that has come to be known as **Boyle's Law**. *The volume of a given mass of gas varies inversely*

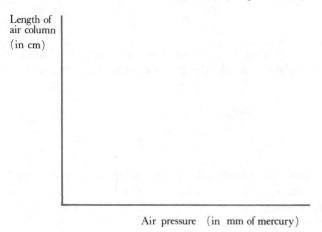

Figure 5.11

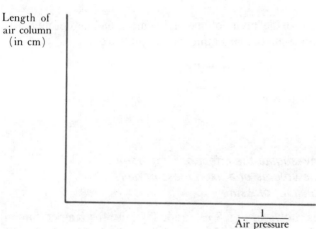

Figure 5.12

as the pressure, provided the temperature remains constant. Thus, if the volume of a fixed mass of gas is 'v' at pressure 'p', then:

$$pv = \text{constant} \quad \text{(at constant temperature)}$$

or $\quad\quad p_1v_1 = p_2v_2 \quad\quad \text{(at constant temperature)}$

where p_1 and p_2 are two values of pressure and v_1 and v_2 are the corresponding volumes, for a fixed mass of the gas.

| Are your experimental results in agreement with this?

This gives us a method of finding the new volume of a gas if the pressure conditions under which it is stored are altered.

Example 1

A cylinder with a capacity of 40 dm^3 contains carbon dioxide at 20 atmospheres pressure. What volume would the gas occupy if the pressure were 1 atmosphere?

Since
$$p_1v_1 = p_2v_2$$

$$\text{New volume of gas} = \frac{40 \times 20}{1} = 800 \text{ dm}^3$$

In the calculation above we introduced the *atmosphere* as a pressure unit. As atmospheric pressure can vary appreciably it is necessary to define a **standard atmospheric pressure** for accurate work. A pressure of 760 mm of mercury has been chosen for this purpose.

Example 2

A sample of sulphur dioxide has a volume of 40 cm^3 at 684 mm of mercury. What will be its volume at standard atmospheric pressure?

As before:
$$p_1v_1 = p_2v_2$$

Thus:
$$\text{New volume} = 40 \times \frac{684}{760} = 36 \text{ cm}^3$$

Experiment 5.12   *To investigate the effect of temperature on the volume of a fixed mass of gas at constant pressure*

Using the apparatus shown in Fig. 5.13, gradually raise the temperature of the water surrounding the tube of air and obtain a series of values for the length of air column and the corresponding temperature. It is essential that the heating is gradual and that the water is kept well stirred. If care is taken, the unit made up of thermometer, ruler and air-tube can be used as a stirrer. Enter your results as in Table 5.4.

Table 5.4

Temperature (in °C)	Length of air column (in cm)

Plot a graph of your results as shown in Fig. 5.14. Extrapolate from your graph to find the temperature at which the length of the air column would be zero.

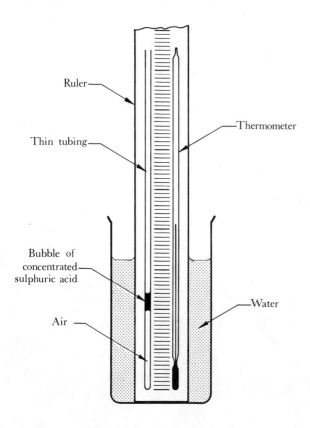

Figure 5.13   The effect of temperature on the volume of a gas

This temperature is known as **absolute zero**. Its accepted value is $-273°C$ and it is a constant for all gases. It is convenient to define a new temperature scale which starts at absolute zero and has the same increments as the Celsius scale. This is known as the **Kelvin scale** and its units are **kelvins (K)**.

Temperature (in kelvins) = °C + 273

As shown in Fig. 5.15, doubling the temperature (in kelvin) of a gas causes the volume to double. This was originally observed by the scientist Charles and is known as **Charles' Law**, normally stated as follows: *The volume of a given mass of gas is directly proportional to its kelvin temperature provided*

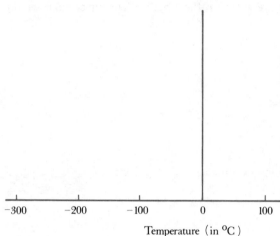

Length of air column (in cm)

Temperature (in °C)

Figure 5.14

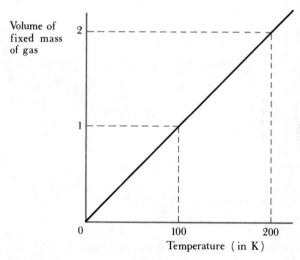

Volume of fixed mass of gas

Temperature (in K)

Figure 5.15

the pressure remains constant. Thus, if the volume of a fixed mass of gas is 'v' at kelvin temperature 'T', then:

$$\frac{v}{T} = \text{constant} \quad \text{(at constant pressure)}$$

or $$\frac{v_1}{T_1} = \frac{v_2}{T_2} \qquad \text{(at constant pressure)}$$

where v_1 and v_2 are the volumes of a fixed mass of gas at the kelvin temperatures T_1 and T_2.

As with pressure, it is convenient to have a **standard temperature** when dealing with volumes of gases. The temperature of 0°C or 273 K has been accepted for this purpose.

Example 3

A given mass of nitrogen occupies a volume of 64 cm^3 at 39°C. What volume will it occupy at standard temperature provided the pressure remains constant?

Since

$$\frac{v_1}{T_1} = \frac{v_2}{T_2}$$

$$\text{New volume of gas} = 64 \times \frac{273}{312} = 56 \text{ cm}^3$$

We can combine Charles' Law and Boyle's Law to calculate the volume changes that occur when *both* temperature and pressure conditions are altered for a gas. Thus:

$$\frac{p_1 v_1}{T_1} = \frac{p_2 v_2}{T_2} \quad \text{(for a fixed mass of gas)}$$

The most useful application of this is when we want to calculate the volume of a fixed mass of gas at standard temperature and pressure (stp), when this has been measured under other conditions.

Example 4

What will be the volume at stp of 38 cm^3 of methane measured at 880 mm of mercury pressure and at 13°C?

Since

$$\frac{p_1 v_1}{T_1} = \frac{p_2 v_2}{T_2}$$

$$\text{New volume of gas} = 38 \times \frac{880}{760} \times \frac{273}{286} = 42 \text{ cm}^3$$

Earlier in the chapter we saw that the volume of one mole of any gas at room temperature and pressure was approximately 24 dm^3. At stp the corresponding volume is taken as 22·4 dm^3.

Summary

Much experimental work is necessary before the formula of a substance, or the equation for a reaction may be written. The actual methods used will obviously vary, but in the former case involve determinations of the relative numbers of moles of atoms that are combined and in the latter the relative numbers of moles of particles taking part in the reaction.

When a reaction is carried out in solution it is necessary to know the concentrations of the reactants. A solution that contains one mole of solute in each cubic decimetre of solution is said to be 1 M.

It can be shown that the volume occupied by one mole of a gas, the **molar volume**, is approximately the same for all gases and is about 24 dm^3 at room temperature and pressure. From this fact, we can deduce **Avogadro's Law** which states that equal volumes of all gases, under the same conditions of temperature and pressure, contain the same number of molecules. Molar volume is also of use in calculating the **molecular mass** of a gas, if we know the mass of a given volume of the gas.

To the limits of our experimental accuracy we also found that gases obey **Boyle's Law** and **Charles' Law**. Boyle's Law states that the volume of a given mass of gas varies inversely as the pressure, provided the temperature remains constant. Charles' Law states that the volume of a given mass of gas varies directly as the kelvin temperature, provided the pressure remains constant. The temperature, in kelvins (K), can be calculated from degrees Celsius by adding 273.

Boyle's and Charles' Laws, singly or in combination, can be used to find the new volume occupied by a gas when the pressure and temperature conditions under which it is maintained are altered. They are particularly useful in converting volumes of gases measured at arbitrary temperatures and pressures to **standard temperature and pressure** (stp), these being 273 K temperature and 760 mm of mercury pressure. The volume of one mole of any gas (molar volume), at stp, can be taken as 22·4 dm^3.

Questions

1. An oxide of lead is found to contain 90·6 per cent lead. Calculate its formula. (Atomic masses: Pb = 207, O = 16.)

2. Red lead is an oxide said to have the formula Pb_3O_4. It is easily reduced to lead. Describe, giving practical details, how you would attempt to verify the formula. Indicate how you would use your experimental results to arrive at your conclusion. (Atomic masses: Pb = 207, O = 16.) (LN)

3. In each of the following calculate the number of moles of solute present in the solution:

    (a) 50 cm^3 of 1·0 M sodium chloride.
    (b) 20 cm^3 of 0·5 M potassium hydroxide.
    (c) 10 cm^3 of 0·2 M sulphuric acid.
    (d) 200 cm^3 of 0·01 M silver nitrate.
    (e) 80 cm^3 of 0·3 M hydrochloric acid.

4. When solutions of silver nitrate ($AgNO_3$) and potassium chromate (K_2CrO_4) are mixed a reddish-brown precipitate is formed. If 10 cm^3 of 1 M silver nitrate is taken and varying volumes of 1 M potassium chromate are added, the minimum volume of the latter to give the maximum height of precipitate is 5 cm^3. Deduce the equation for the reaction.

5. When 0·27 g of aluminium (atomic mass 27) is added to excess copper(II) sulphate solution it is found that 0·96 g of copper (atomic mass 64) is precipitated. Deduce the equation for the reaction taking place.

6. 0·25 g of calcium carbonate react with excess dilute acid to give 60 cm^3 of carbon dioxide, at room temperature and pressure.

(a) Calculate the formula mass of calcium carbonate ($CaCO_3$) from the atomic masses Ca = 40, C = 12, and O = 16.
(b) What fraction of a mole of calcium carbonate is 0·25 g?
(c) What fraction of a mole of carbon dioxide is formed?
(d) Write an equation for the reaction taking place that is consistent with these results.

7. (a) Sodium hydroxide reacts with hydrochloric acid according to the following equation:

$$NaOH + HCl \longrightarrow NaCl + H_2O$$

Calculate the volume of 0·05 M sodium hydroxide required to react exactly with 25 cm^3 of 0·2 M hydrochloric acid.

(b) Potassium hydroxide reacts with sulphuric acid according to the following equation:

$$2KOH + H_2SO_4 \longrightarrow K_2SO_4 + 2H_2O$$

Calculate the volume of 0·01 M sulphuric acid required to react exactly with 20 cm^3 of 0·04 M potassium hydroxide.

(c) Silver nitrate reacts with sodium chloride according to the following equation:

$$AgNO_3 + NaCl \longrightarrow AgCl + NaNO_3$$

Calculate the mass of silver chloride precipitated when 10 cm^3 of 0·2 M silver nitrate react with 20 cm^3 of 0·1 M sodium chloride. (Atomic masses: Ag = 108, Cl = 35·5.)

8. Phosphine is a compound of phosphorus (atomic mass 31) and hydrogen only. The density of phosphine gas at room temperature and pressure is 1·42 g dm^{-3}. Deduce the molecular mass and the formula of phosphine.

9. Correct the following gas volumes to stp.

(a) 38 cm^3 at 27°C and 800 mm of mercury pressure.
(b) 7·6 cm^3 at 91°C and 720 mm of mercury pressure.

10. What will be the volume at stp of:

   (a) 4 g of methane (CH_4)?
   (b) 42 g of carbon monoxide (CO)?

(Atomic masses: C = 12, O = 16, H = 1.)

11. 61·5 cm^3 of gas is found to weigh 0·188 g at 12°C and 765 mm of mercury pressure. What will be (a) the volume of gas at stp and (b) its molecular mass?

Rates of reaction and equilibrium

The rate of reaction

The paper on which this book is printed is slowly but steadily reacting with the oxygen in the air to form carbon dioxide and water. This is happening at so slow a rate that we cannot detect any change visually, even over several years. If we consider ways in which this change could be speeded up, the following factors would seem relevant.

(*a*) The book could be chopped into smaller pieces, thus increasing the surface area and hence the area in contact between paper and air.

(*b*) The book could be placed in pure oxygen, thus increasing the concentration of this reactant from 20 per cent to 100 per cent.

(*c*) The temperature of the book could be raised. This would obviously be the most effective method to use in this case!

Generalizing from this then, the factors that appear to affect the rate of a chemical reaction include:

(*a*) The surface area of any solid reactant.

(*b*) The concentration of liquid and gaseous reactants.

(*c*) The temperature.

In scientific work when *several factors contribute to an effect* we are attempting to measure and we wish to investigate how any *one* of these factors operates, we try to design experiments so that *the factor in which we are interested can be varied whilst the remaining factors are kept constant.* A useful reaction to use in this way is that between calcium carbonate and dilute hydrochloric acid:

$$CaCO_3(s) + 2H^+(aq) \longrightarrow Ca^{2+}(aq) + H_2O(l) + CO_2(g)$$

This reaction neither produces nor absorbs heat appreciably and so we are able to keep the temperature reasonably constant when investigating the effect of such other factors as particle size of calcium carbonate and concentration of hydrochloric acid. The rate of the reaction can be followed relatively simply by several methods, of which the most convenient is observing the change in mass with time.

Experiment 6.1 *To investigate the effect of particle size on the rate of a reaction*

Grade some marble chips (calcium carbonate) as large, medium, and small lumps and weigh out a 20 g portion of each grade on a watch-glass. Then weigh the watch-glass with the large lumps of marble together with a 100 cm³ conical flask containing 40 cm³ of 2 M hydrochloric acid and plugged with cotton wool as shown in Fig. 6.1 (*a*).

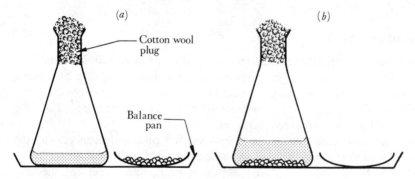

Figure 6.1 The effect of particle size on reaction rate

Add the marble chips to the acid, quickly replace the cotton wool plug and immediately start the stop-clock. Return all the previously weighed items to the balance pan and record the mass after thirty seconds. Repeat the reading of mass at thirty second intervals until there is no further loss of mass. Present your results as shown in Table 6.1.

Table 6.1

Time (in s)	Mass of apparatus (in g)	Overall loss in mass (in g)
0 30 60 90 etc.		0

To calculate the overall loss of mass at any time, subtract the mass of the apparatus at that time from its mass when the time equals zero seconds.

Repeat the experiment using the other two grades of marble chips.

Plot the results of all three experiments on the same graph using the axes shown in Fig. 6.2. The line for each experiment must be carefully labelled. Explain why there is the same final loss in mass in all three cases.

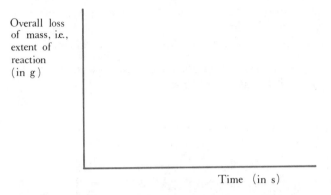

Overall loss of mass, i.e., extent of reaction (in g)

Time (in s)

Figure 6.2

At the conclusion of the experiment there will be a considerable quantity of unreacted marble still in the flask. This was arranged so that the surface area of the particles would not alter too seriously during the course of the experiment.

Experiment 6.2 *The effect of concentration on the rate of reaction*

(*a*) Repeat the previous experiment using the medium grade of marble chips in each case but with hydrochloric acid that is 1·0 M and then 0·5 M.

Tabulate the results in the same way as previously and plot them with the three concentrations of acid on the same graph axes. Label the three lines on the graph with the concentration of acid used. Why, in this case, is there not the same final loss of mass?

A reaction whose rate is easily followed or monitored is that between thiosulphate ions and hydrogen ions:

$$S_2O_3{}^{2-}(aq) + 2H^+(aq) \longrightarrow H_2O(l) + SO_2(aq) + S(s)$$

As the reaction proceeds, sulphur is thrown out of solution as a fine precipitate which changes the colourless clear solution to one that is opaque. If we place the reaction vessel on a piece of paper bearing a crayonned cross and time how long it takes for the visibility of the cross to be lost, this is the time it takes for the reaction to proceed to a definite extent under the particular conditions.

CHEMISTRY BY EXPERIMENT AND UNDERSTANDING

(b) Place 50 cm³ of a 4 per cent solution of sodium thiosulphate solution in a 250 cm³ conical flask. Add 5 cm³ of dilute hydrochloric acid and start the stop-clock. Swirl the flask continually and note the time it takes for the visibility of the cross to disappear when viewed through the reaction mixture. Repeat the experiment, altering the thiosulphate concentration as indicated in Table 6.2, which may also be used for entering the results. In each case add the acid last to the reaction mixture and time from this addition.

The rate of any process is inversely proportional to the time, hence we can use 1/time as a measure of the rate of reaction.

Table 6.2

Volume of thiosulphate (in cm³)	Volume of water (in cm³)	Time (in s)	$\frac{1}{time}$ (in s⁻¹)
50	0		
40	10		
30	20		
20	30		
10	40		

Plot a graph on the axes shown in Fig. 6.3.
How does an increase in the concentration of reactants affect the speed of the chemical change?

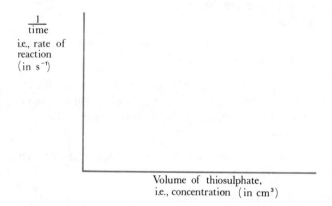

Figure 6.3

A concentrated solution contains more particles than a dilute one and hence the rate at which the reacting particles collide is increased, resulting in a faster reaction.

98

Experiment 6.3   *The effect of temperature on the rate of reaction*

We shall use the same reaction as in Experiment 6.2(*b*).

Place 50 cm³ of 1 per cent sodium thiosulphate solution in the conical flask and raise its temperature to 20°C. Add 5 cm³ of dilute hydrochloric acid and start the stop-clock. Mix the reaction mixture by continuously swirling and record the average temperature of the mixture during reaction. Find the time taken for the disappearance of the cross as in the previous experiment.

Repeat the experiment with the initial temperature of the thiosulphate solution at 30, 40, and 50°C.

| Plot a graph of your results as shown in Fig. 6.4.

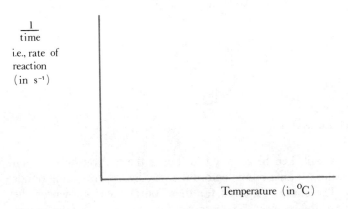

$\dfrac{1}{\text{time}}$

i.e., rate of reaction

(in s⁻¹)

Temperature (in °C)

Figure 6.4

It would seem that the increase in reaction rate with temperature can be explained because of the increase in velocity of the reacting particles. This should result in an increased rate of collision between them and hence a faster reaction. However, this factor, although contributing to the effect, is small compared with that considered below.

A reaction that has been very thoroughly studied in this connection is that between hydrogen and iodine to form hydrogen iodide:

$$H_2(g) + I_2(g) \longrightarrow 2HI(g)$$

We can visualize the reaction taking place in the steps shown in Fig. 6.5. As the hydrogen and iodine molecules approach one another, they will require a certain energy to overcome the repulsion between their electron clouds.

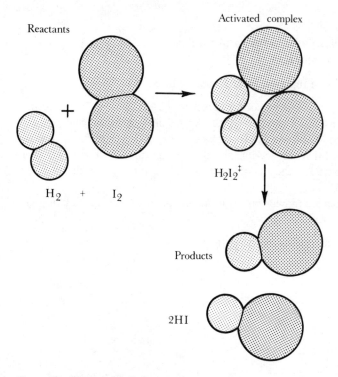

Reactants

Activated complex

$H_2I_2^{\ddagger}$

$H_2 \quad + \quad I_2$

Products

2HI

Figure 6.5   The hydrogen/iodine reaction

Additional energy will then be required to loosen the hydrogen–hydrogen bonds and the iodine–iodine bonds before the new hydrogen–iodine bonds can be formed. The energy required for these purposes is known as the **activation energy** of the reaction. The intermediate double molecule formed is known as the **activated complex**. The activated complex may either form new bonds and hence molecules of product, or reform the original bonds and thus change back into reactant molecules. The energy changes involved in the reaction between hydrogen and iodine are shown in Fig. 6.6. The 'heat of reaction' is the difference between the energy of the stable reactants and that of the stable products. If heat is given out during the reaction, the process is said to be **exothermic** and if heat is taken in the reaction is **endothermic**. Energy changes are dealt with in more detail in chapter 7.

The distribution of energy amongst the molecules of the reactants at a low temperature (T_1) and a higher temperature (T_2) is shown in Fig. 6.7. The number of molecules having the activation energy, or greater, is proportional to the shaded area under the curve in each case. There are thus more molecules with sufficient energy to react at the higher temperature and hence a faster reaction rate.

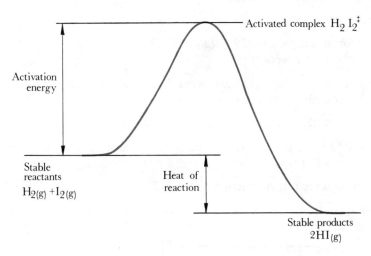

Figure 6.6 Energy changes in the reaction between hydrogen and iodine

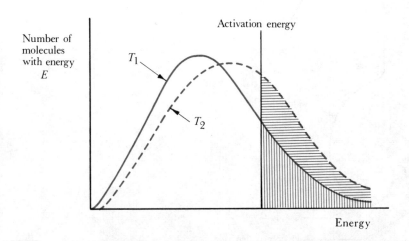

Figure 6.7 The energy distributions amongst molecules at different temperatures

Catalysts

There is one final factor that can alter the rate of a chemical change. **Catalysts** are substances the presence of which will accelerate the rate of a chemical change. *NB:* Some substances cause a slowing-down of a reaction and are known as **inhibitors**.

Experiment 6.4   *An investigation of a catalysed*
                  chemical reaction

It is difficult to believe that hydrogen peroxide is steadily undergoing decomposition according to the equation:

$$2H_2O_2(aq) \longrightarrow 2H_2O(l) + O_2(g)$$

Place a little '20-volume' hydrogen peroxide in a test-tube and examine
it carefully. Now add a small quantity of manganese(IV) oxide.

| Is any difference in the rate of reaction apparent?

A suitable apparatus for carrying out studies on the rate of this reaction is
shown in Fig. 6.8.

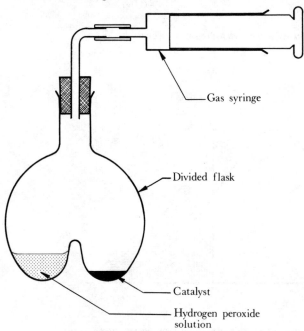

Gas syringe

Divided flask

Catalyst

Hydrogen peroxide
solution

Figure 6.8   The catalytic decomposition of hydrogen peroxide

Different groups in the class should use this apparatus, modified as required, to investigate the effect of the following factors on the rate of the
reaction:

(*a*) Concentration of hydrogen peroxide.
(*b*) Mass of catalyst.

(c) Particle size of catalyst.

(d) Temperature.

(e) Relative effectiveness of other metal oxides and other manganese compounds as catalysts.

For general guidance, hydrogen peroxide concentrations of the order of '1-volume' and catalyst masses of about 1 g are suitable. In each experiment ensure that only the factor under investigation is varied, all other factors being kept constant.

Note the volume of oxygen collected in the syringe at thirty second intervals in each case.

Present the results of each group's experiments in suitable graphical form.

Theories to explain catalytic activity

The following suggestions to explain catalytic behaviour have been postulated. It is probable that different effects or combinations of effects are responsible in particular cases.

(a) One of the reactants may be taken onto the catalyst surface, thereby making it easier for a second reactant to collide with it. In addition, the molecules so **adsorbed** may be 'activated' by becoming strained and their bonds thus weakened.

(b) A reactant may react with the catalyst forming an intermediate compound which then decomposes to form the product. In this effect one slow reaction with a high activation energy is replaced by two faster reactions with lower activation energies.

(c) Two reactant molecules may collide and their total energy, which must be conserved, may be too great for them to remain together and form a product molecule. The function of the catalyst, in such cases, is to act as a recipient for a proportion of this energy.

The extent of reaction

Some reactions are known to take place so slowly that even after millions of years they would not have occurred to any significant extent. Other reactions have been studied that are virtually complete after 10^{-9} second. It is essential to distinguish between the *rate* at which a reaction proceeds and the *extent* to which it will eventually take place. This distinction can be expressed as the difference between 'how fast' and 'how far'. The other important aspect of a reaction is 'how vigorous' and this is studied in chapter 7. In the previous part of the chapter we have been looking at the factors that affect the rate of a reaction and we shall now investigate those that influence the extent to which reactions occur.

A convenient reaction to consider first is that between iodine mono-chloride and chlorine. Your teacher will probably demonstrate this to you. Iodine monochloride is a dark-brown fuming liquid closely resembling bromine in appearance. If a sample of it is placed in a U-tube, as in Fig. 6.9, and chlorine gas passed over it, yellow crystals of iodine trichloride are formed:

$$ICl(l) + Cl_2(g) \longrightarrow ICl_3(s)$$

If the U-tube is then disconnected from the chlorine generator with the taps A and B left open, the iodine trichloride soon disappears as chlorine escapes from the apparatus and iodine monochloride is reformed. Obviously the re-action is very easily reversed:

$$ICl_3(s) \longrightarrow ICl(l) + Cl_2(g)$$

By closing taps A and B it is possible to halt the reverse reaction at such a stage that all three substances are co-existing in the tube indefinitely.

Here we have a real problem in explanation. If some of the chlorine and iodine monochloride react together, why not all? A reasonable explanation is that the reverse reaction is taking place simultaneously with the forward

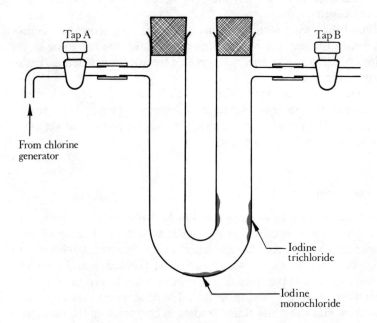

Figure 6.9 The iodine monochloride/chlorine reaction

reaction and the contents of the tube reach an equilibrium position when the rates of the forward and reverse reactions are equal.

Is there any proof that such a **dynamic equilibrium** is established? We shall investigate this in the next experiment.

If a saturated solution of lead chloride is kept in contact with excess solid lead chloride (Fig. 6.10), by definition no more solid can dissolve. There

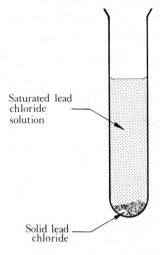

Saturated lead chloride solution

Solid lead chloride

Figure 6.10   Saturated lead chloride solution in equilibrium with solid lead chloride

could however be a dynamic *interchange* between the lead chloride already dissolved and the excess solid, or it could be that no such interchange occurs. To solve this problem it is obvious that one sample of the lead chloride must be 'labelled' in some way. We can do this by using some solid lead chloride containing a proportion of the radioactive isotope lead-212.

Experiment 6.5   *Investigating an equilibrium situation using a radioisotope labelling method*

This experiment must be performed by the teacher.

Place the saturated solution of lead chloride in a liquid counter connected to a scaler and measure the background count over a period of five minutes.

Mix the saturated lead chloride solution and the 'labelled' lead chloride solid and shake or stir for about five minutes.

Separate the mixture using a centrifuge and replace the liquid in the liquid counter and recount its activity over a five minute period.

What conclusion about the nature of the equilibrium does the comparison of the two count rates suggest?

CHEMISTRY BY EXPERIMENT AND UNDERSTANDING

Let us reconsider the iodine monochloride/chlorine reaction. It was observed that the addition of chlorine caused the system to attempt to use it up by forming iodine trichloride. When chlorine was removed from the system however, the system reacted to make some more, resulting in the disappearance of iodine trichloride and the formation of more iodine monochloride. The following analogue situation should help us to consolidate this principle.

Imagine a rodeo held in an arena of fixed dimensions. Into this are introduced a number of unbroken horses and a number of cowboys. Very soon some of the horses will have been mounted by the cowboys:

$$\text{Cowboys + horses} \longrightarrow \text{mounted horses.}$$

It will not be long, however, before some of the cowboys will be thrown from their mounts and eventually a dynamic equilibrium will be established:

$$\text{Cowboys + horses} \rightleftharpoons \text{mounted horses.}$$

What would be the effect on this equilibrium of:

(a) Introducing more cowboys into the system?
(b) Removing some of the horses from the system?
(c) Introducing more mounted horses into the system?

Let us see whether a similar principle operates in the case of some chemical systems.

Experiment 6.6 *An investigation of the effect of changing concentrations on some equilibrium systems in aqueous solution*

(a) Place sufficient solid bismuth carbonate at the bottom of a test-tube to just fill the rounded portion. Add dropwise just enough concentrated hydrochloric acid to dissolve the solid as bismuth chloride solution, carbon dioxide gas being evolved. Add some water to the tube dropwise until a precipitate just forms.

The equation for this reaction with water is:

$$Bi^{3+}(aq) + 2H_2O(l) + Cl^-(aq) \rightleftharpoons Bi(OH)_2Cl(s) + 2H^+(aq)$$

What should be the effect of adding more concentrated hydrochloric acid to the equilibrium system?

Test your prediction by experiment. If the minimum quantity of acid is added then the effect of adding further drops of water can be studied. With care the reaction can be 'see-sawed' several times.

(b) Add drops of sodium hydroxide solution to a solution of iodine in a test-tube and observe any colour change.

In an aqueous solution of iodine, the following equilibrium has been established:

$$I_2(aq) + H_2O(l) \rightleftharpoons 2H^+(aq) + I^-(aq) + IO^-(aq)$$

Any colour in the solution can be regarded as entirely due to the presence of $I_2(aq)$.

The $OH^-(aq)$ ions in sodium hydroxide solution will react with the $H^+(aq)$ ions present to form largely unionized water.

Taking this into account, explain the observed colour change. What should be added to swing the equilibrium in the opposite direction?

Carry out a test to see if this is correct.

(c) Mix together equal volumes of 0·1 M solutions of iron(III) chloride and potassium thiocyanate.

The blood-red coloration that results is due to the formation of a new ion as follows:

$$Fe^{3+}(aq) + NCS^-(aq) \rightleftharpoons FeNCS^{2+}(aq)$$

What would be the expected effect on the intensity of the blood-red colour of adding a more concentrated solution of (i) iron(III) chloride and (ii) potassium thiocyanate to separate portions of the equilibrium mixture?

Test your prediction by dividing the equilibrium mixture into two halves and observing separately the effect of adding drops of 1 M solutions of iron-(III) chloride and potassium thiocyanate.

It is obvious that such equilibrium considerations are of great importance in industrial chemistry where the economic viability of any process is directly related to the yield of product. Many industrial processes involve reactions between gases and so we shall extend our studies on equilibrium to cover that in the gaseous state.

A useful equilibrium reaction to study, that gives a visual indication of how it is balanced, is that between dinitrogen tetroxide and nitrogen dioxide:

$$\underset{\text{(light-straw)}}{N_2O_4(g)} \underset{\text{exothermic (heat given out)}}{\overset{\text{endothermic (heat taken in)}}{\rightleftharpoons}} \underset{\text{(red–brown)}}{2NO_2(g)}$$

The equilibrium mixture is prepared and collected as described in Experiment 13.13(b).

Experiment 6.7 *To investigate the effect of temperature on a gaseous equilibrium*

Use a teat-pipette to transfer a few drops of the dinitrogen tetroxide/nitrogen dioxide mixture from the tube in which it is collected to a boiling-tube. Partially close the boiling-tube with a one-holed bung. When the contents of the tube have reached equilibrium with room temperature, surround the tube in turn with a beaker containing (*a*) boiling water and (*b*) an ice and salt freezing mixture.

From the colour change of the contents of the boiling-tube determine how these temperature changes are affecting the balance of the equilibrium.

Extending the equilibrium principle to cover such cases we can observe that a temperature increase shifts the equilibrium balance in favour of the endothermically formed component whilst a temperature decrease favours the formation of more of the exothermically formed component.

Experiment 6.8 *To investigate the effect of pressure on a gaseous equilibrium*

Use a teat-pipette to transfer a few drops of the dinitrogen tetroxide/nitrogen dioxide mixture from the tube in which it is collected to a boiling-tube. Fit a one-holed bung carrying an open glass stop-cock (A) in this tube as shown

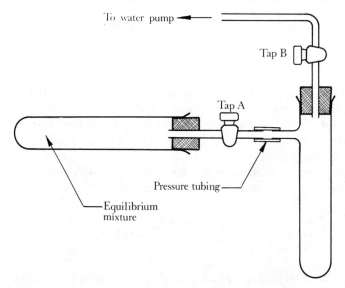

To water pump

Tap B

Tap A

Pressure tubing

Equilibrium mixture

Figure 6.11   The effect of pressure decrease on a gaseous equilibrium

108

in Fig. 6.11. When all the equilibrium mixture has vaporized and thus ex-pelled the air from the boiling-tube, close the tap and connect it to the side-arm boiling-tube. With stopcock B open, use the water pump to withdraw much of the air from the side-arm boiling-tube and then close stopcock B. If stopcock A is now opened, the equilibrium mixture expands into the additional volume and its pressure thus falls. Notice the *final* colour of the reaction mixture.

Use this observation to determine how the pressure diminution has affected the balance of the equilibrium.

As we have seen in chapter 5, if two moles of gas are formed from one mole by a chemical reaction, the volume would double. As the effect of pressure is to compress a gas, a pressure increase favours that side of the equilibrium mixture having the smaller volume, i.e., with the lower number of moles. A pressure decrease, of course, has the converse effect.

An industrial application of rates and equilibrium considerations

The solvent methanol (CH_3OH) is made industrially by the combination of carbon monoxide and hydrogen:

$$CO(g) + 2H_2(g) \rightleftharpoons CH_3OH(g)$$

The forward reaction is exothermic.

An increase in pressure will favour the formation of a greater proportion of methanol in the equilibrium mixture because the forward reaction is accompanied by a diminution in volume.

An increase in temperature will speed up both forward and reverse re-actions and so produce a faster arrival at equilibrium (see Fig. 6.12). It will at the same time, however, diminish the proportion of methanol in the

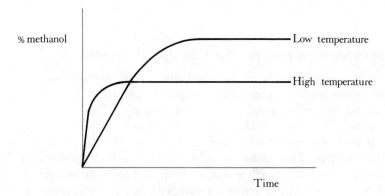

Figure 6.12   The effect of temperature on the yield of methanol

equilibrium mixture because the forward reaction is exothermic. A compromise temperature between these competing factors must therefore be employed.

A catalyst will speed up both the forward and reverse reactions and so result in a faster arrival at equilibrium. The presence or absence of a catalyst, however, does not affect the final balance of the equilibrium and hence the yield of product (see Fig. 6.13).

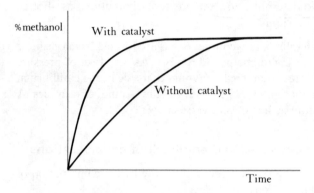

Figure 6.13   The effect of a catalyst on the yield of methanol

In the manufacture of methanol, a suitable catalyst is used at a temperature of 300°C and under a pressure of 300 atmospheres.

The higher the temperature and pressure at which a process has to be carried out, the more costly is the necessary chemical plant to build and to run. A more efficient catalyst may make it possible to operate a particular process economically at a lower temperature and pressure and much industrial research is involved with the search for new or better catalysts.

Summary

The rates of chemical reactions are affected by the following factors:

(*a*) The surface area of any solid reactant. This is because an increase in surface area results in greater contact between the reactants.

(*b*) The concentration of any liquid or gaseous reactants. The greater the concentration of these, the greater the rate of collision between reactant particles and hence the greater the rate of reaction.

(*c*) The temperature. The increase in velocity of reactant molecules with increase in temperature makes only a small contribution to the great increase in reaction rate observed. The **activation energy** is the energy required to overcome the repulsion between the electron clouds of the reactant molecules, together with that required to loosen the bonds of the reactants prior to the formation of products. The major reason for the increase in reaction rate with temperature is in the vastly increased numbers of reactant particles which then have sufficient energy to overcome the activation energy barrier.

(*d*) The presence of a **catalyst**. This will speed up the rate of a reaction that takes place slowly in its absence. Several theories have been advanced to explain how catalysts work.

A class of reactions is known in which the reactants would not be completely converted into products even after an infinite time. These are reactions that are easily reversed and thus reach a state of **dynamic equilibrium** when their composition becomes constant as the rates of the forward and reverse reactions become equal. Direct proof of the existence of such equilibria can be obtained using radioisotope labelling techniques. When a chemical system in equilibrium is subjected to a change in conditions, the equilibrium balance is shifted to best overcome the effect of the change. This may occur as follows:

(*a*) When the concentration of a component of the equilibrium is increased the balance shifts so as to use it up; when some of a component is removed the balance shifts to make some more.

(*b*) When the temperature of an equilibrium mixture is increased, the balance shifts to favour the formation of more endothermically-formed component(s); a temperature decrease favours the formation of more exothermically-formed component(s).

(*c*) A pressure increase causes a gaseous equilibrium to take up a smaller volume and hence favours the side of the equilibrium with the least number of molecules. The converse is true for a pressure decrease.

Many industrial processes depend upon equilibrium reactions and by a consideration of their effect on the rate and equilibrium position of the reaction, the optimum conditions for plant operation can be determined.

Questions

1. Imagine that you had to investigate the effect of varying the proportion of oxygen in air on the rate at which iron rusts. Describe how you would investigate this problem. You should describe the apparatus and procedure which you would use, drawing a diagram if it adds to the clarity of your answer.

You should make clear how you would ensure that any change in the rate of rusting was caused by a change in the proportions of oxygen and not by a change of any other factors during your experiment. (LN)

2. (*a*) You have been provided with a small weighed sample of zinc. How would you measure the volume of hydrogen produced when this zinc dissolves completely in dilute hydrochloric acid?

(b) What mass of zinc (atomic mass 65) would be required to produce 0·01 mole of hydrogen molecules?

(c) The addition of a little aqueous copper(II) sulphate to the zinc and hydrochloric acid is said to speed up the reaction. How would you test whether this is so? How would you decide whether the copper(II) sulphate had *catalysed* the reaction?

(d) It is thought that only one type of particle present in aqueous copper(II) sulphate is responsible for the increase in the rate of reaction. What type of particle do you think that this is? How would you test whether your suggestion is correct? (L)

3. Sodium hypochlorite solution contains the ion $ClO^-(aq)$. This undergoes slow reaction according to the equation:

$$2ClO^-(aq) \longrightarrow 2Cl^-(aq) + O_2(g)$$

The reaction is known to be catalysed by solutions of cobalt(II) nitrate. With the aid of a suitable diagram, explain how you would investigate whether the catalytic activity is due to the cobalt(II) or to the nitrate ions.

4. When carbon monoxide and steam are mixed and passed over a heated iron catalyst, they react as follows:

$$CO(g) + H_2O(g) \underset{\text{endothermic}}{\overset{\text{exothermic}}{\rightleftharpoons}} CO_2(g) + H_2(g)$$

Discuss the effect on the yield of hydrogen of:

(a) Increasing the quantity of steam.
(b) Removing the carbon dioxide.
(c) Decreasing the pressure.
(d) Increasing the temperature.

7

Energy changes accompanying chemical changes

In your previous work in the laboratory you have probably noticed that an energy change usually accompanies a chemical reaction. This can be an important supplement to visual observation in giving a clue that a chemical reaction has occurred. When, for example, water is added to white anhydrous copper sulphate it turns blue. This is accompanied by the evolution of sufficient heat energy to make the test-tube appreciably warmer. Although when many anhydrous salts react with water, heat is either evolved or absorbed, few give a colour change to provide visual evidence of reaction. As the work in this chapter develops, you will discover that by making careful measurements of such energy changes the chemist can learn very much more about the natural laws which govern chemical changes.

Let us consider a few specific chemical reactions on this basis. Your teacher may demonstrate these to you. If one mole of concentrated sulphuric acid is carefully added to sufficient water to make 1 dm^3 of solution, the temperature of the mixture rises by 17°C. In order to return to room temperature the mixture must *lose* heat. If we assume that the mixture has the same specific heat capacity as water ($4.2 \text{ kJ kg}^{-1} \text{ K}^{-1}$) we can calculate the quantity of heat that must be lost as follows:

$$\text{Heat lost} = 4.2 \times 1 \times 17 \text{ kJ} = 71 \text{ kJ}$$

The equation for the change is:

$$H_2SO_4(l) + aq \longrightarrow H_2SO_4(aq \; 1 \; M)$$

The sulphuric acid solution has *less* energy than the concentrated acid and water from which it was formed. It is usual to use the term ΔH for this change in heat content. The Greek capital delta (Δ) stands for a finite or measurable

113

change of H, the heat content or **enthalpy**. The entire experiment and result can then be summarized by the statement:

$$H_2SO_4(l) + aq \longrightarrow H_2SO_4(aq\ 1\ M); \quad \Delta H = -71\ \text{kJ mol}^{-1}$$

Before proceeding any further you should make sure that you understand completely what each part of this statement means. Another way of presenting this information is by the use of an energy level diagram as in Fig. 7.1.

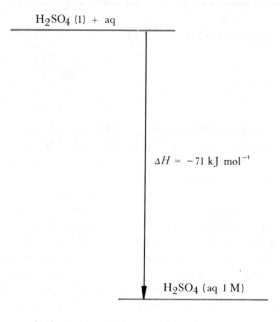

$H_2SO_4\ (l) + aq$

$\Delta H = -71\ \text{kJ mol}^{-1}$

$H_2SO_4\ (aq\ 1\ M)$

Scale: 1 cm = 10 kJ

Figure 7.1   The energy level diagram for the formation of 1 M sulphuric acid from its components

If one mole of solid ammonium nitrate is dissolved in water to make 1 dm^3 of solution, the temperature of the latter drops by 6°C. In order to return to room temperature the mixture must absorb heat from its surroundings.

$$\text{Heat absorbed} = 4 \cdot 2 \times 1 \times 6\ \text{kJ} = 25\ \text{kJ}$$

In this case the mixture has more energy than its components and so we write:

$$NH_4NO_3(s) + aq \longrightarrow NH_4NO_3(aq\ 1\ M); \quad \Delta H = +25\ \text{kJ mol}^{-1}$$

The energy level diagram for this change, using the same scale as before, is shown in Fig. 7.2.

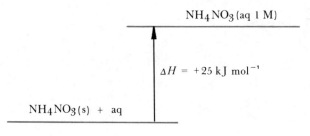

Scale: 1 cm = 10 kJ

Figure 7.2   The energy level diagram for the formation of a 1 M solution of ammonium nitrate from its components

Experiment 7.1   *To determine ΔH for some chemical reactions*

After you have carried out each of these determinations, calculate ΔH for the reaction in kJ mol^{-1} remembering to give it the correct sign. In each case draw an energy level diagram, showing the scale that you employ.

(*a*) The combustion of ethanol:

$$C_2H_5OH(l) + 3O_2(g) \longrightarrow 2CO_2(g) + 3H_2O(l)$$

Weigh the spirit lamp about half full of ethanol as shown in Fig. 7.3. With the thermometer, take the temperature of the water in the can, place the lamp under the can and light it. Stir the water with the thermometer and when the temperature has risen about 20°C extinguish the lamp and record the final temperature. Reweigh the lamp and its contents.

What are the main sources of error in this experiment? Do you think your answer is bigger or smaller than it would be if an apparatus was used that reduced these errors considerably?

(*b*) The precipitation of calcium carbonate by mixing solutions of suitable ions:

$$Ca^{2+}(aq) + CO_3^{2-}(aq) \longrightarrow CaCO_3(s)$$

Place 50 cm^3 of 2 M calcium chloride solution in a heat-insulating plastic cup, using a measuring cylinder. In a second measuring cylinder place 50 cm^3 of 2 M potassium carbonate solution. Note the initial temperature of each solution, remembering to wipe the thermometer between the measurements. Calculate the average of these initial temperatures; this is the expected temperature of the mixture assuming no chemical reaction to take place. Pour the potassium carbonate solution into the plastic cup and note the temperature of the mixture, having stirred well with the thermometer.

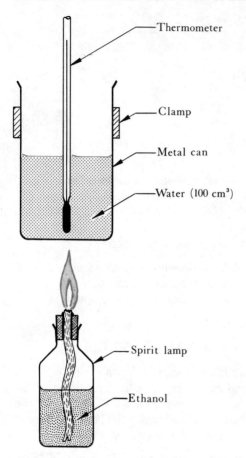

Figure 7.3   The determination of the enthalpy of combustion of ethanol

(c) The displacement of copper from a solution of its ions by zinc:

$$Cu^{2+}(aq) + Zn(s) \longrightarrow Cu(s) + Zn^{2+}(aq)$$

Place 25 cm³ of 0·2 M copper(II) sulphate solution in the bottle shown in Fig. 7.4. Insert the stopper and thermometer, turn upside down and note the initial temperature. Add about 0·5 g of zinc filings (this is about a twofold excess), shake and record the maximum temperature change occurring.

Is there any other evidence that virtually all the copper has been precipitated?

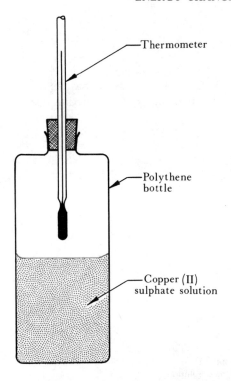

Thermometer

Polythene
bottle

Copper (II)
sulphate solution

Figure 7.4   The determination of the enthalpy of the displacement of copper by zinc

Obtaining chemical energy electrically

The last reaction in the experiment above can be regarded as occurring in two stages:

$$Zn(s) \longrightarrow Zn^{2+}(aq) + 2e^-$$

and $$Cu^{2+}(aq) + 2e^- \longrightarrow Cu(s)$$

This is utilized in the **Daniell cell** where zinc ions in contact with a zinc electrode and copper ions in contact with a copper electrode are kept in separate compartments. The electrons are transferred between the electrodes by an external circuit, thus constituting an electrical current. It should be clear that a chemical reaction such as this which *produces* electricity is the reverse of electrolysis which *uses* electricity to cause reaction.

Experiment 7.2 *Constructing and investigating a Daniell cell*

Assemble the Daniell cell as shown in Fig. 7.5. Try to ensure that the liquid heights are about the same in both compartments to avoid mixing due to liquid pressure differences.

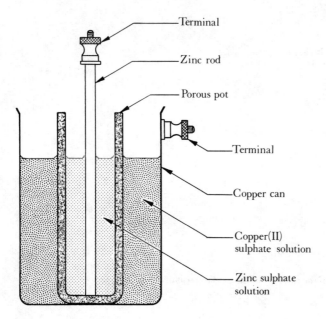

Figure 7.5 **The Daniell cell**

(*a*) Measure the cell voltage and check the polarity of the electrodes using a high-resistance voltmeter.

Is the polarity of the electrodes related to the relative reactivities of copper and zinc? Why does the partition between the compartments have to be porous? Why is the use of a 'high-resistance' voltmeter important?

(*b*) Use the cell to operate an electric motor.

If you tried to use this to determine the electrical energy obtainable from the cell reaction (in kJ mol^{-1}) what problems would you expect to encounter?

(*c*) Connect the Daniell cell into the circuit shown in Fig. 7.6, adjust the rheostat to have zero resistance and measure the cell voltage and current. Record your readings as in Table 7.1.

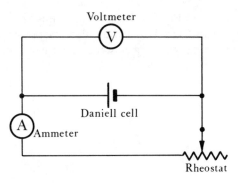

Figure 7.6   The circuit for Experiment 7.2

Table 7.1

Cell voltage (in V)	Current (in A)	Power (in W)

Increase the resistance until the cell voltage is about 0·1 V higher and note the new voltage and current in your table. Repeat the procedure with approximately 0·1 V increases until the total resistance of the rheostat is in the circuit.

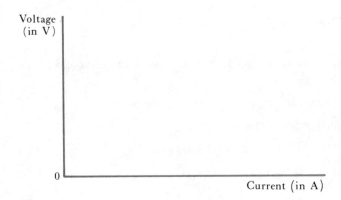

Figure 7.7

Plot a graph of voltage against current as in Fig. 7.7. From your graph, estimate the voltage when no current is drawn from the cell. Calculate the power $(V \times A)$ for each voltage reading and plot a graph of power against voltage as in Fig. 7.8. Comment on the shape of the graph.

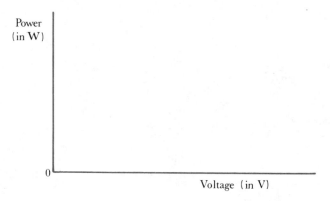

Figure 7.8

To calculate the maximum electrical energy obtainable from the reaction

This quantity is known as the **free-energy change** for the reaction and is given the symbol ΔG. We have seen that the maximum voltage obtainable from the cell is some 1·1 V, and we learned in chapter 3 that to convert one mole of copper(II) ions into atoms two faradays are required. As the Daniell cell reaction involves the conversion of one mole of copper(II) ions:

$$Cu^{2+}(aq) + Zn(s) \xrightarrow{\quad +2e^- \quad} Cu(s) + Zn^{2+}(aq)$$

$$\underset{\quad -2e^- \quad}{}$$

it must follow that $(2 \times 96\,500)$ coulombs are transferred per mole of reaction. Since:

$$\text{Energy (in joules)} = \text{volts} \times \text{coulombs}$$

the free energy transfer for the Daniell cell is

$$1\cdot1 \times 2 \times 96\,500 \text{ J mol}^{-1}$$

Hence:
$$\Delta G = -\frac{1\cdot1 \times 2 \times 96\,500}{1000} \text{ kJ mol}^{-1}$$

$$= -212 \text{ kJ mol}^{-1}$$

For this reaction:

$$\Delta H = -218 \text{ kJ mol}^{-1}$$

As can be seen, the values of ΔH and ΔG are very similar. We shall now determine both ΔH and ΔG for a further reaction to see if this is usually the case.

Experiment 7.3   *To measure ΔH and ΔG for the displacement of silver by copper*

The reaction between aqueous silver ions and metallic copper can be represented as follows:

$$2Ag^+(aq) + Cu(s) \xrightarrow{\;+2e^-\;} 2Ag(s) + Cu^{2+}(aq)$$
$$\underset{-2e^-}{\longleftarrow}$$

(*a*) To measure ΔH: use the same apparatus and method as in Experiment 7.1(*c*) but using 25 cm^3 of 0·2 M silver nitrate solution and 0·5 g of electrolytic grade copper powder.

| Calculate the value of ΔH.

(*b*) To measure ΔG: mix a suitable quantity of 'Polyfilla' using a saturated solution of potassium nitrate instead of water and use this to make a plug in the end of the inner tube of the cell as shown in Fig. 7.9. After twenty minutes this will be firm enough to complete the assembly of the cell. Use the high-resistance voltmeter to measure the cell voltage.

| Calculate the value of ΔG as shown previously.

Where does the energy liberated in a chemical reaction come from?

As the experiments we have performed show, we can carry out reactions under suitable conditions so that all the difference in chemical energy is exchanged as heat (ΔH), or so that a *proportion* of the energy is exchanged as free energy (ΔG) and the balance as heat.

The total energy change for a reaction could come from two sources:

(*a*) A difference between the bonding energy (the energy holding together the atoms making up the particles) in the reactants and products.

(*b*) The particles of the reactants could have a different kinetic energy from the particles of the products.

Consider the following data for the reaction:

$$H_2(g) + Cl_2(g) \longrightarrow 2HCl(g)$$

Temperature (in °C)	0	200	400	600
ΔH (in kJ mol^{-1})	$-183{\cdot}7$	$-184{\cdot}9$	$-186{\cdot}2$	$-187{\cdot}4$

As there is little change in ΔH with temperature even over a range of 600°C and as such a temperature change would considerably affect the kinetic energies of the particles, this evidence suggests that the factor making the greatest contribution to the value of ΔH for the reaction is the bonding energy.

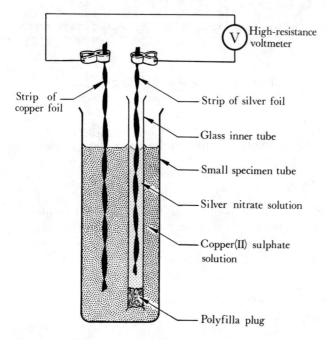

Strip of copper foil — Strip of silver foil — Glass inner tube — Small specimen tube — Silver nitrate solution — Copper(II) sulphate solution — Polyfilla plug — High-resistance voltmeter

Figure 7.9   The cell for Experiment 7.3

It has been possible to measure the bond energies involved in this reaction and they are as follows:

$$H_2(g) \longrightarrow 2H(g); \quad \Delta H = +435 \text{ kJ mol}^{-1}$$
$$Cl_2(g) \longrightarrow 2Cl(g); \quad \Delta H = +243 \text{ kJ mol}^{-1}$$
$$HCl(g) \longrightarrow H(g) + Cl(g); \quad \Delta H = +431 \text{ kJ mol}^{-1}$$

It is worth noticing that *breaking* any bond must involve the expenditure of energy whilst bond *making* is energy producing. We can insert this data into an energy cycle to show how it is related to ΔH for the reaction, as shown in Fig. 7.10.

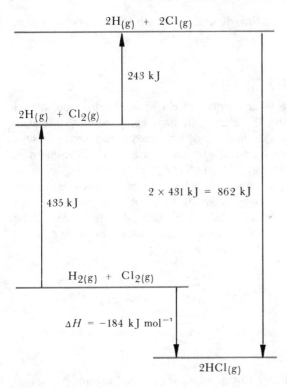

Scale: 1 cm = 100 kJ

Figure 7.10   Energy cycle for the formation of hydrogen chloride from its elements

The dissolution of ionic compounds in water

When an ionic compound dissolves in water, the process may be exothermic or endothermic, this depending on the particular solute concerned. The value of ΔH for such reactions is the algebraic sum of two factors:

$$\Delta H = + \left\{ \begin{array}{l} \text{Energy to overcome the} \\ \text{electrical attraction} \\ \text{between the ions in the} \\ \text{crystal lattice} \end{array} \right\} - \left\{ \begin{array}{l} \text{Energy liberated when} \\ \text{the ions attract an} \\ \text{indefinite number of} \\ \text{water molecules around} \\ \text{them, anions attract-} \\ \text{ing the positive end} \\ \text{of a water molecule} \\ \text{and cations the} \\ \text{negative end} \end{array} \right\}$$

123

The *sign* of ΔH for the reaction thus depends on which of these two quantities of energy is the larger.

The tabulation of energy data

The painstaking work of a large number of chemists has produced a vast quantity of data concerning the energy changes accompanying chemical reactions. It is obvious that this data is best presented in tabular form. One useful way in which this can be done is to quote such values as **enthalpy of formation** (ΔH_f) and **free energy of formation** (ΔG_f) for a variety of compounds. These are the enthalpy and free energy changes involved when one mole of the compound is formed from its elements. By convention, all reactants and products are taken to be in their normal states at 25°C. The enthalpies and free energies of formation of elements are arbitrarily taken as zero. As an example, consider the reaction:

$$C(s) + O_2(g) \longrightarrow CO_2(g); \quad \begin{cases} \Delta H = -393 \cdot 7 \text{ kJ mol}^{-1} \\ \Delta G = -394 \cdot 6 \text{ kJ mol}^{-1} \end{cases}$$

Thus ΔH_f and ΔG_f for carbon dioxide are $-393 \cdot 7$ and $-394 \cdot 6$ kJ mol^{-1} respectively.

NB: The determination of ΔG values for reactions that cannot be carried out in an electrolytic cell involves methods beyond the scope of this book.

Values of ΔH_f and ΔG_f for some typical substances are shown in Table 7.2.

Table 7.2 Enthalpies and free energies of formation

Substance	Formula	ΔH_f	ΔG_f
		(in kJ mol^{-1})	
Ethanol	$C_2H_5OH(l)$	-278	-175
Chloride ion	$Cl^-(aq)$	-167	-131
Iron(II) ion	$Fe^{2+}(aq)$	-88	-85
Iron(III) ion	$Fe^{3+}(aq)$	-48	-10
Water	$H_2O(l)$	-286	-237
Magnesium ion	$Mg^{2+}(aq)$	-477	-456
Lead ion	$Pb^{2+}(aq)$	$+5$	-24
Lead sulphate	$PbSO_4(s)$	-916	-812
Sulphate ion	$SO_4^{2-}(aq)$	-908	-741
Zinc ion	$Zn^{2+}(aq)$	-152	-147

Chemical data books are available that contain much more information of this type.

How can this data be used to determine ΔH and ΔG for other reactions?

If we require, for example, to use the data in Table 7.2 to calculate the enthalpy of combustion of ethanol we can do this by constructing a suitable energy cycle, shown in principle in Fig. 7.11 and in detail in Fig. 7.12.

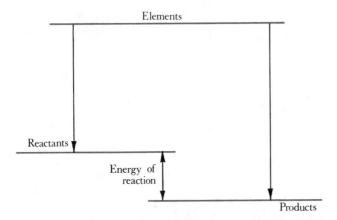

Figure 7.11　**Energy cycle for calculating energies of reaction from energies of formation**

If the free energy change for this reaction is required, an energy cycle with the appropriate free energy data should be constructed.

If the energy cycle is drawn carefully to scale, the sign of the energy change is immediately apparent.

Can we use energy changes to predict the feasibility of a chemical change taking place?

Consider the mechanical systems shown in Fig. 7.13. If the 'trigger' is released there is little difficulty in predicting the final state of each assembly. If you were required to state on what basis you made your decision, you might reply 'in the final state the potential energy (PE) of the system will be at a minimum'. Try to think of some similar situations and see if this seems to be generally applicable. Another way of stating the rule would be 'if free to do so, a mechanical system will tend to change spontaneously so that the change in potential energy (ΔPE) is negative'. It would obviously be useful to find a similar criterion for *chemical* changes. ΔH might be considered as a possibility, but we have already met a spontaneous chemical change (the dissolution of ammonium nitrate in water) for which ΔH is positive. Thus

125

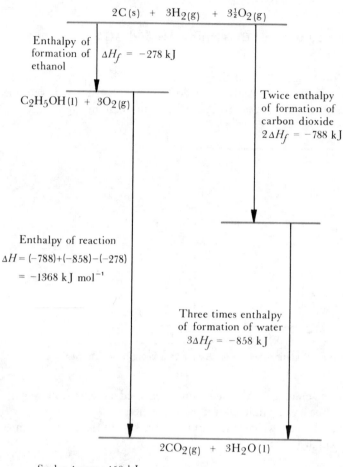

Scale: 1 cm = 150 kJ

Figure 7.12   Energy cycle for the combustion enthalpy of ethanol

ΔH will not do, but what about ΔG? It has been found that *for all reactions in which ΔG is negative, the change will take place spontaneously.*

The simplest type of reaction we can consider can be represented as:

$$X \longrightarrow Y$$

Let us consider three possible ways in which the free energy can change for reactions of this type (Fig. 7.14).

(*a*) This reaction goes virtually to completion, the minimum value for free energy being when there is almost 100 per cent Y.

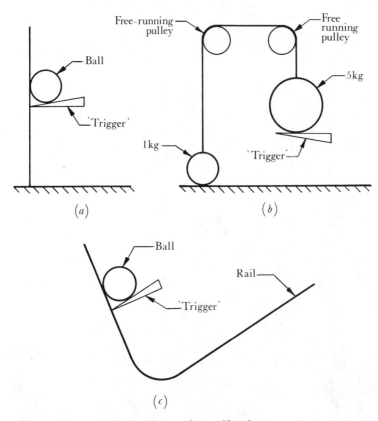

Figure 7.13   Some mechanical systems for consideration

(b) This reaction hardly goes at all, the free energy being at a minimum when hardly any of X has reacted.

(c) This is an equilibrium reaction, the minimum value of free energy being when appreciable amounts of both X and Y are present. Such reactions have values of ΔG between $+40$ and -40 kJ mol^{-1}.

Experiment 7.4   *Using ΔG to predict the feasibility of some reactions*

For each of the reactions represented by the following equations, construct energy cycles to obtain values for ΔG, using data from Table 7.2.

(a) $Pb^{2+}(aq) + SO_4^{2-}(aq) \longrightarrow PbSO_4(s)$
(b) $Mg^{2+}(aq) + Pb(s) \longrightarrow Mg(s) + Pb^{2+}(aq)$
(c) $2Fe^{2+}(aq) + Cl_2(g) \longrightarrow 2Fe^{3+}(aq) + 2Cl^-(aq)$

From the sign of ΔG, predict the feasibility of the reaction.

127

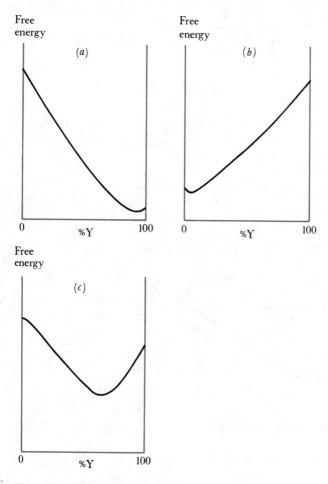

Figure 7.14   Free energy changes for three reactions

Devise and carry out an experiment in each case to test your prediction.

It is important to notice that ΔG only predicts the feasibility of a reaction taking place; it tells us nothing about the *rate* at which the reaction would proceed. If a hydrogen and oxygen mixture is kept indefinitely at room temperature and without the presence of a catalyst, it has been calculated that it would take millions of years before any observable quantity of water would be formed.

$$2H_2(g) + O_2(g) \longrightarrow 2H_2O(l); \quad \Delta G = -474 \text{ kJ mol}^{-1}$$

After a very, very long time, however, the reaction would be virtually complete.

Chemicals as fuels

We have previously determined a value of ΔH for the combustion of ethanol. The energy liberated in this reaction may be used to do useful work. You may possess a small steam engine that operates on methylated spirit, an impure form of ethanol. Consider the energy changes involved in using such an engine to drive a dynamo:

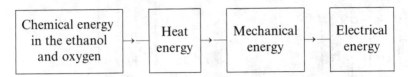

Even using very well-designed machines we would not be likely to obtain more than 20 per cent of the total energy available as useful electrical energy. If the oxidation of such a fuel could be carried out in an electrolytic cell, we would expect to get a much more favourable proportion of the energy as useful electricity. A device which uses a conventional fuel in this way is known as a **fuel cell**.

Experiment 7.5 *To make a simple fuel cell*

Set up the electrolysis cell as shown in Fig. 7.15(*a*). Connect the cell to a 6 V d.c. supply and let electrolysis continue until the tube above the anode is filled with oxygen and that above the cathode with hydrogen, as in (*b*) of the diagram. Disconnect the low-voltage supply. The assembly is now ready to act as a fuel cell. Connect a high-resistance voltmeter across the electrodes.

As we have seen in Experiment 7.2(*c*), the voltage of electrolytic cells falls as an increasing current demand is placed upon them. The fuel cell, unfortunately, shows this effect very markedly. If sufficient current to operate most appliances is demanded of the cell its voltage drops to almost zero. This cell will, however, operate a small transistor radio if its input resistance is fairly high. Much current research is being undertaken to try and overcome this problem but most attempts have so far resulted in apparatus that is both costly and bulky, as for example shown in Fig. 7.16. Acceptable fuel cells have, however, already been utilized in artificial satellites to operate communications equipment where relatively small currents are required over a long time period. From the equation:

$$2H_2(g) + O_2(g) \longrightarrow 2H_2O(l); \quad \begin{cases} \Delta H = -572 \text{ kJ mol}^{-1} \\ \Delta G = -474 \text{ kJ mol}^{-1} \end{cases}$$

129

which refers to the overall reaction taking place at the electrodes, it will be seen that about 80 per cent of the total energy change is theoretically available as electrical energy. This is obviously a most attractive prospect!

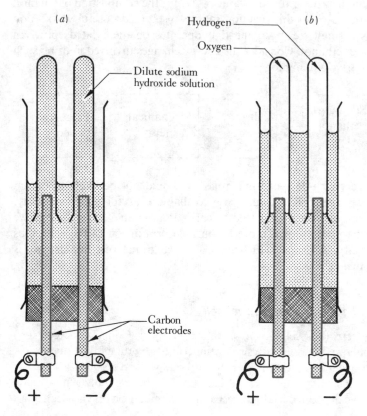

Figure 7.15   A simple fuel cell

Summary

When a chemical reaction takes place it is usually accompanied by the evolution or absorption of heat energy. We can show this change in **enthalpy** (ΔH) by quoting the energy increase or decrease of the products compared to the reactants, the usual units being kJ mol^{-1}. The information can also be presented in the form of an energy level diagram. We can sometimes determine the maximum electrical energy obtainable from such reactions using a suitable electrical cell, this quantity being known as the **free energy** change (ΔG). The maximum energy of such cells is obtained when the current drawn from them is close to zero, but they operate most efficiently (as measured by the power available) at about half of this maximum value. The main factor

Figure 7.16   A methanol fuel cell providing power for an electric hammer

contributing to the total energy change for a reaction (ΔH) is the difference between the bonding energy (the energy holding together the atoms making up the particles) in the reactants and products.

When ionic compounds dissolve in water, ΔH for the reaction is the algebraic sum of the energy to overcome the electrostatic attraction between the ions in the crystal lattice and the energy liberated when the now free ions attract around them an indefinite number of water molecules (a process called **solvation**).

Energy data is normally tabulated as **enthalpy of formation** (ΔH_f) and **free energy of formation** (ΔG_f). Other energies of reaction can be obtained from such data by the construction of a suitable energy cycle.

ΔG is useful in predicting the feasibility of a reaction; if the value is negative, the reaction is likely to take place spontaneously.

The use of fuels in combustion engines is a highly inefficient process. A comparison of ΔH and ΔG for the combustion reactions of conventional fuels prove that it would be much more efficient to 'burn' these in a suitable **fuel cell**. Fuel cells currently available will not produce enough current for most applications without showing a crippling deterioration in voltage and much current research is being undertaken to overcome this difficulty.

Coal, petroleum, and natural gas, or products obtained from them (see chapter 12) supply man with much of his energy requirements. Other

131

sources of importance are hydroelectric energy (energy from water), atomic energy (see chapter 1), and solar energy (energy from the sun).

Questions

1. The specific heat capacity of water is $4 \cdot 2$ kJ kg^{-1} K^{-1}. Explain what this statement means. How much heat is required to raise the temperature of (a) 1 dm^3 of water from 20°C to 28°C and (b) 250 cm^3 of water from 18°C to 35°C?

2. 100 cm^3 of water was placed in a plastic cup and its temperature found to be 18°C. $0 \cdot 1$ mole of ammonium chloride crystals was added and the temperature fell to 14°C. Calculate ΔH for the reaction:

$$NH_4Cl(s) \longrightarrow NH_4Cl(aq)$$

Draw an energy level diagram for the reaction.

3. Draw energy level diagrams for the reactions below:

(a) $Ag^+(aq) + Cl^-(aq) \longrightarrow AgCl(s); \quad \Delta H = -58 \cdot 6$ kJ mol^{-1}
(b) $C_2H_6(g) + 3\frac{1}{2}O_2(g) \longrightarrow 2CO_2(g) + 3H_2O(l); \quad \Delta H = -3080$ kJ mol^{-1}
(c) $C(s) + 2S(s) \longrightarrow CS_2(l); \quad \Delta H = +106$ kJ mol^{-1}

4. Carbon monoxide and carbon dioxide gases have ΔH_f values of -110 and -394 kJ mol^{-1} respectively. Use this information to determine ΔH for the reaction:

$$CO(g) + \frac{1}{2}O_2(g) \longrightarrow CO_2(g)$$

5. (a) Describe how you would attempt to find by experiment the quantity of heat liberated when 1 g of the liquid methanol, CH_4O, is burnt in air.
(b) The table shows the heat liberated when 1 g of each of three alcohols is burnt in air.

Alcohol	Heat evolved (in kJ)
Methanol, CH_4O	$22 \cdot 6$
Ethanol, C_2H_6O	$29 \cdot 7$
Propanol, C_3H_8O	$33 \cdot 4$

For each of these alcohols, calculate the heat of combustion in kJ mol^{-1}. (Atomic masses: C = 12, H = 1, O = 16.)
(c) From your results in (b) estimate the heat of combustion of butanol, $C_4H_{10}O$, in kJ mol^{-1}.
(d) The substance dimethyl ether has the same molecular formula, C_2H_6O, as ethanol, but its heat of combustion is different. Suggest a reason for this difference. (L)

6. A cell consisting of a zinc electrode dipping into zinc sulphate solution and a porous partition separating these from an iron electrode dipping into a solution of iron(II) sulphate has a measured emf of $0 \cdot 32$ V. Calculate ΔG for the reaction:

$$Zn(s) + Fe^{2+}(aq) \longrightarrow Zn^{2+}(aq) + Fe(s)$$

Explain carefully how you would determine ΔH for this reaction.

Two patterns of chemical change—
(a) Acidity and alkalinity
(b) Oxidation and reduction

As both sections of this chapter develop, you will be introduced to theories formulated by chemists of the past to explain patterns in chemical behaviour that they observed. You will see how such theories often had to be drastically modified, or even abandoned, as further experimental evidence was obtained and required accommodation in the theory. It is a useful lesson to learn that a scientific theory is only acceptable on such a temporary basis.

Acidity and alkalinity

The term **acid** was introduced into chemistry to classify that group of chemical substances which affected certain coloured materials in a distinctive way and which had a sour taste. **Alkalis** were recognized as substances that had an opposite effect on the coloured materials and which 'cured' the sourness of acids. This is merely saying what acids and alkalis *will do*, without attempting to say *what they are* or to explain why they exhibit this type of behaviour.

Experiment 8.1   *Is there a pattern in the acidity or alkalinity*
                  of oxides in aqueous solutions?

This experiment should be carried out by the teacher.

Carry out this experiment with the elements magnesium, calcium, carbon, and sulphur. Place a little of each solid element in turn in the tube shown in Fig. 8.1, pass in a slow stream of oxygen from a cylinder and heat gently with a small burner. When the reaction is complete, stop heating and allow the tube and contents to cool. Add just sufficient water to dissolve the oxide that has been produced, followed by a few drops of Universal Indicator (pH) solution.

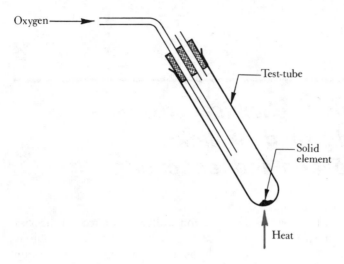

Figure 8.1   The preparation of oxides

> What theory could be advanced to distinguish between those oxides that give acids and those that give alkalis in aqueous solution?

Test the theory by preparing and testing the oxides of sodium and phosphorus by the same method.

Lavoisier first proposed the theory that the oxides of non-metallic elements are acidic and those of metallic elements are alkalis. Many oxides, however, are insoluble in water but dissolve in acids or alkalis.

Experiment 8.2   *Reactions of acids and alkalis on some oxides that are insoluble in water*

Test the solubilities of small quantities of each of the oxides listed in Table 8.1 in turn, in (*a*) dilute nitric acid and (*b*) sodium hydroxide solution. If there is no immediate reaction, warm the tubes with their contents. Enter your results in the table.

Oxides that are insoluble in water but which will dissolve in acids to give salts are called **basic oxides**. The term alkali is reserved for those oxides that are soluble in water. Those oxides that will give salts with *both* acids and alkalis are known as **amphoteric oxides**.

Table 8.1

Oxide	Solubility in dilute nitric acid	Solubility in sodium hydroxide
Copper(II) oxide (CuO) Zinc oxide (ZnO) Lead(II) oxide (PbO) Aluminium oxide (Al$_2$O$_3$) Silicon oxide (SiO$_2$)		

When sodium and magnesium oxides dissolve in water to give alkaline solutions, the equations for the reactions taking place are:

$$Na_2O(s) + H_2O(l) \longrightarrow 2Na^+(aq) + 2OH^-(aq)$$
$$MgO(s) + H_2O(l) \longrightarrow Mg^{2+}(aq) + 2OH^-(aq)$$

| Write the equation for the reaction between calcium oxide (CaO) and water.

When carbon dioxide dissolves in water to give an acid, the equation for the reaction taking place is:

$$CO_2(aq) + H_2O(l) \rightleftharpoons HCO_3^-(aq) + H^+(aq) \rightleftharpoons CO_3^{2-}(aq) + 2H^+(aq)$$

Phosphorus oxide dissolves in water to form phosphoric acid (H$_3$PO$_4$):

$$P_4O_{10}(s) + 6H_2O(l) \longrightarrow 4H_3PO_4(aq)$$

which then reacts further with water:

$$H_3PO_4(aq) + H_2O(l) \rightleftharpoons H_2PO_4^-(aq) + H^+(aq) \rightleftharpoons HPO_4^{2-}(aq) + 2H^+(aq)$$

| Write the equation for the reaction between sulphur dioxide (SO$_2$) and water.

When copper and aluminium oxides dissolve in acids, the equations for the reactions are:

$$CuO(s) + 2H^+(aq) \longrightarrow Cu^{2+}(aq) + H_2O(l)$$
$$Al_2O_3(s) + 6H^+(aq) \longrightarrow 2Al^{3+}(aq) + 3H_2O(l)$$

| Write the equations for the reactions between acids and, respectively, zinc oxide (ZnO) and lead(II) oxide (PbO).

When zinc and aluminium oxides dissolve in alkalis, the equations for the reactions are:

$$ZnO(s) + H_2O(l) + 2OH^-(aq) \longrightarrow Zn(OH)_4^{2-}(aq)$$
(the zincate ion)

$$Al_2O_3(s) + 3H_2O(l) + 2OH^-(aq) \longrightarrow 2Al(OH)_4^-(aq)$$
(the aluminate ion)

Write the equation for the reaction between lead(II) oxide and alkali. (The name given to the complex lead ion produced is the plumbite ion, $Pb(OH)_4{}^{2-}$.)

Finally, when silicon oxide dissolves in alkalis, the equation for the reaction is:

$$SiO_2(s) + 2OH^-(aq) \longrightarrow SiO_3{}^{2-}(aq) + H_2O(l)$$
(the silicate ion)

The ionic theory of acids and alkalis

As seen in chapter 3, water is considered to ionize to a limited extent into hydrogen and hydroxide ions:

$$H_2O(l) \longrightarrow H^+(aq) + OH^-(aq)$$

In pure water therefore, there are the same numbers of hydrogen and hydroxide ions. If you review the equations given above you will see that a reasonable interpretation of the nature of acids and alkalis in terms of the Ionic Theory is contained in the following statements:

(*a*) Acids are substances that when dissolved in water give rise to more hydrogen ions than hydroxide ions.

(*b*) Alkalis are substances that when dissolved in water give rise to more hydroxide ions than hydrogen ions.

(*c*) Neutral substances, such as water, contain equal numbers of hydrogen and hydroxide ions.

The pH scale

Table 8.2 shows how the balance between the concentrations of hydrogen and hydroxide ions in an aqueous solution is related to its pH.

Experiment 8.3 *Do acids having the same concentration have the same pH?*

Find the pH of 0·01 M solutions of hydrochloric, ethanoic (acetic) and nitric acids using a pH meter which has been correctly set up in accordance with the manufacturer's instructions. Between each determination carefully rinse the electrodes with distilled water. (If a pH meter is not available, Universal Indicator (pH) solution or paper may be used.)

If each of these acids ionizes in water according to the equation:

$$HX(aq) \longrightarrow H^+(aq) + X^-(aq)$$

use Table 8.2 to find the expected value for pH. What possible explanation can there be for any variation from this expectation?

Table 8.2   The pH Scale

pH	Concentration (in mol dm^{-3})	
	H$^+$(aq)	OH$^-$(aq)
0	1	10^{-14}
1	10^{-1}	10^{-13}
2	10^{-2}	10^{-12}
3	10^{-3}	10^{-11}
4	10^{-4}	10^{-10}
5	10^{-5}	10^{-9}
6	10^{-6}	10^{-8}
7	10^{-7}	10^{-7}
8	10^{-8}	10^{-6}
9	10^{-9}	10^{-5}
10	10^{-10}	10^{-4}
11	10^{-11}	10^{-3}
12	10^{-12}	10^{-2}
13	10^{-13}	10^{-1}
14	10^{-14}	1

Experiment 8.4   *Comparing the properties of solutions of hydrogen chloride in water and toluene*

NB: All test-tubes and other glassware you use in this experiment must be thoroughly dried beforehand.

(*a*) Moisten the end of a thermometer bulb with toluene, note its reading and hold it in a jar of dry hydrogen chloride gas. Note any change in the temperature. Repeat the experiment with water instead of toluene.

Apart from their characteristic effect on Universal Indicator (pH) paper, other reactions that we associate with acids are:

(*i*) The liberation of carbon dioxide from a carbonate.

(*ii*) The evolution of hydrogen gas on reaction with magnesium metal.

(*b*) Judged against these criteria, compare for acidic properties the reactions of a solution of hydrogen chloride in water with a solution of hydrogen chloride in toluene. Test the electrical conductivity of the two solutions. Record your results as in Table 8.3.

Several important conclusions should emerge from these tests.

(*a*) When hydrogen chloride dissolves in toluene no ionization reaction occurs. We conclude this because there is no temperature change associated with the dissolution, the solution is a poor electrical conductor and it gives none of the reactions we associate with solutions that are rich in hydrogen ions.

CHEMISTRY BY EXPERIMENT AND UNDERSTANDING

Table 8.3

	Hydrogen chloride in water	Hydrogen chloride in dry toluene
(i) Effect on dry Universal Indicator (pH) paper		
(ii) Effect on dry solid sodium carbonate		
(iii) Effect on dry magnesium ribbon		
(iv) Electrical conductivity		

(b) When hydrogen chloride dissolves in water however, the properties of the resulting solution lead us to conclude that it is ionized. We might consider writing the following equation to represent the ionization reaction:

$$HCl(g) + aq \longrightarrow H^+(aq) + Cl^-(aq)$$

but as we have seen in Experiment 8.4(a), this reaction is *exothermic* whereas this equation implies that it is a *bond-breaking* process. The English chemist Lowry and the Danish chemist Brönsted simultaneously proposed a theory in an attempt to explain this discrepancy. According to the Lowry–Brönsted Theory, *an acid is a proton (hydrogen ion) donor* and *a base is a proton acceptor*. In terms of this theory, the *acid* hydrogen chloride is considered to give a proton to the *base* water to form the hydronium ion (H_3O^+):

$$HCl(g) + H_2O(l) \longrightarrow Cl^-(aq) + H_3O^+(aq)$$

Such a reaction can be exothermic if the energy required to break the hydrogen-chlorine bond is less than that provided by the formation of the new hydrogen-oxygen bond.

Experiment 8.5   *Comparing the reactions of glacial ethanoic acid with those of an aqueous solution of ethanoic acid*

Carry out the tests suggested in Experiment 8.4(b) on ethanoic acid when glacial (containing no water) and on a 2 M aqueous solution. Display your results as in Table 8.3.

Write an equation for the reaction of glacial ethanoic acid with water that is consistent with *all* the experimental data we have obtained during work so far in this chapter. (The formula of ethanoic acid may be taken as HAc for this purpose.)

138

Experiment 8.6 *To find the enthalpies of neutralization of some acids and alkalis*

Place 50 cm^3 of 2 M sodium hydroxide solution in a heat-insulating plastic cup, using a measuring cylinder, and note its temperature. Place 50 cm^3 of 2 M hydrochloric acid in another measuring cylinder and note its temperature, wiping the thermometer carefully between each measurement. Add the acid to the alkali in the plastic cup and note the maximum temperature change.

Calculate the enthalpy change of the neutralization reaction as explained in chapter 7.

The experiment should now be repeated on a class co-operative basis so that every combination of reaction between each of the acids and each of the alkalis in Table 8.4 is covered by at least one group. Pool the results.

Table 8.4

	Sodium hydroxide (aq)	Potassium hydroxide (aq)
Hydrochloric acid Nitric acid Ethanoic acid		

Write an ionic equation for the reaction between hydrochloric acid and sodium hydroxide, omitting any ions not taking part in the reaction. From the results obtained in Experiment 8.3 and the above experiment, which of the reactions investigated could not be represented by the same ionic equation? Can you suggest an explanation for the failure of any of these substances to fit the general pattern of behaviour?

Strong and weak acids

The term *concentrated* as applied to acids should strictly be used only to imply that there is a large quantity of acid in a small amount (if any) of water. What we call concentrated hydrochloric acid is a saturated solution of hydrogen chloride in water. Concentrated sulphuric, nitric, and ethanoic acids are the pure substances and contain no water. A *strong* acid, on the other hand, is one which is virtually completely dissociated into ions in solutions that are 1 M or less. The converse of concentrated is *dilute* whilst that of strong is *weak*. It is essential that these terms are not confused; a 1 M solution of hydrochloric acid can be described as dilute and strong whereas a 1 M solution of ethanoic acid can be described as dilute and weak.

It is important to realize that the reverse of the reaction between ethanoic acid and water is also an acid-base reaction in terms of the Lowry–Brönsted Theory:

$$HAc(aq) + H_2O(l) \rightleftharpoons Ac^-(aq) + H_3O^+(aq)$$

Acid 1   Base 2   Base 1   Acid 2

The ethanoate ion is known as base 1 because it is formed when the ethanoic (acid 1) loses a proton. There is a similar relation between base 2 and acid 2. The balance of the equilibrium, as we have seen earlier, lies well over on the side of ethanoic acid and water. In this competition for protons it is obvious that the ethanoate ions are beating the water molecules and must therefore be considered the stronger base.

Let us now consider the corresponding reaction with hydrogen chloride and water:

$$HCl(aq) + H_2O(l) \rightleftharpoons Cl^-(aq) + H_3O^+(aq)$$

Acid 1   Base 2   Base 1   Acid 2

Here the equilibrium is balanced so that there is almost no hydrogen chloride and water. Thus water is a stronger base than the chloride ion. The bases then, in order of strength, are ethanoate ion, water, and lastly chloride ion. Now water has protons which it could give to a suitable base, in which case it would function as an acid:

$$X^-(aq) + H_2O(l) \rightleftharpoons HX(aq) + OH^-(aq)$$

Predict which of the two bases, chloride ion or ethanoate ion, would be the more effective as $X^-(aq)$ in such a reaction.

Experiment 8.7   *To test our prediction about the relative strengths of chloride ions and ethanoate ions as bases*

Find the pH of a 1 M solution of sodium chloride and of a 1 M solution of sodium ethanoate using Universal Indicator (pH) paper.

Is the result of these tests in agreement with your prediction?

NB: When it is not important to show the hydration of protons in a chemical equation, for the sake of simplicity $H^+(aq)$ is often still written instead of $H_3O^+(aq)$.

Oxidation and reduction

The first usage of the term oxidation was to describe reactions where an element reacted with oxygen to form its oxide. If lead, for example, is heated in oxygen it reacts according to the equation:

$$2Pb(s) + O_2(g) \longrightarrow 2PbO(s)$$

The lead is said to be **oxidized**.

If lead oxide is heated in a stream of hydrogen, it loses its oxygen:

$$PbO(s) + H_2(g) \longrightarrow Pb(s) + H_2O(g)$$

In this reaction the hydrogen has been oxidized and the lead is said to have been **reduced**. If lead oxide is melted and electrodes are placed in it when connected to a suitable electrical supply, a current flows through the melt with lead being liberated at the cathode and oxygen at the anode. This makes it clear that lead oxide is ionic.

In our examples, therefore, the changes taking place to the lead can be summarized as:

$$Pb(s) \underset{\text{reduction}}{\overset{\text{oxidation}}{\rightleftharpoons}} Pb^{2+}(s) + 2e^-$$

Thus in modern terms, *oxidation is defined as the loss of electrons* and, conversely, *reduction is the gain of electrons*. Chemical substances that bring about oxidation are called **oxidizing agents**; when they react in this way they are themselves reduced. Substances that bring about reduction are called **reducing agents**; when these react in this way they are themselves oxidized.

Experiment 8.8   *Examining the relative oxidizing and reducing powers of some metals*

Into the indentations of a tile place a few drops in each case of one of the following solutions:

Copper(II) nitrate, 1 M with respect to Cu^{2+} ions.
Lead nitrate, 1 M with respect to Pb^{2+} ions.
Iron(II) sulphate, 1 M with respect to Fe^{2+} ions.
Magnesium nitrate, 1 M with respect to Mg^{2+} ions.
Zinc nitrate, 1 M with respect to Zn^{2+} ions.
Tin(II) chloride, 1 M with respect to Sn^{2+} ions.

Into each solution place a small length of magnesium ribbon and see which of these metal ions is displaced by the magnesium. If no displacement seems to occur after a few minutes, remove the magnesium and scrape the surface gently to see if there is any deposit.

Repeat the experiment using, in turn, small pieces of copper, lead, iron, zinc, and tin in place of the magnesium. Enter your results as shown in Table 8.5.

Table 8.5

Metal \ Ion in solution	Cu^{2+}	Pb^{2+}	Fe^{2+}	Mg^{2+}	Zn^{2+}	Sn^{2+}
Copper						
Lead						
Iron						
Magnesium						
Zinc						
Tin						

Key: $\checkmark$ = displacement occurs; × = no displacement occurs.

Now examine the table for consistency. If, for example, metal X displaces ions of metal Y, it is not possible for metal Y to displace ions of metal X. You may need to repeat some of the tests to ensure consistency.

Make a list of the metals so that any one will displace all those below it from solutions of their salts.

Because metals characteristically react by *losing* electrons to form ions, this list places them in order of their *reducing* power. This list is known as the **activity series** of these metals.

Experiment 8.9 *An electrical method of comparing the reducing power of some metals*

Record the voltmeter readings when strips of copper, lead, iron, magnesium, zinc, and tin are used in turn as metal 'M' in the apparatus shown in Fig. 8.2.

Make a list of the metals in order of voltage observed, placing that giving the highest voltage in first place. Is the list in accordance with your results for Experiment 8.8?

Figure 8.3 shows a cell constructed by Alesandro Volta of Italy in 1800. It consists of alternate discs of zinc and silver separated by paper strips soaked

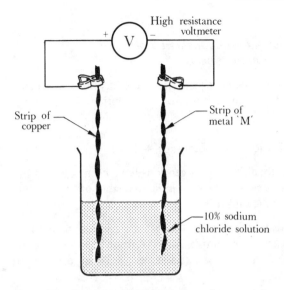

Figure 8.2   Comparing the reducing power of some metals

Figure 8.3   The cell designed by Volta

in salt water. A copy of this cell constructed at the Royal Institution was used by Michael Faraday in his experiments on electrolysis.

143

Experiment 8.10 *Some reactions of iron considered on an oxidation-reduction basis*

(*a*) Into two 100 cm^3 beakers place 40 cm^3 portions of dilute sulphuric acid. Add iron filings to each until there is no further evolution of hydrogen.

The reaction:

$$Fe(s) + 2H^+(aq) \longrightarrow Fe^{2+}(aq) + H_2(g)$$

obviously ceases when virtually all the hydrogen ions have been replaced by Fe^{2+} ions. Iron as the metal is said to have an **oxidation state** of zero. After the reaction its oxidation state is said to be $+2$.

Filter both solutions separately to remove the excess iron and any carbon present as an impurity. Transfer one sample of the solution to an evaporating basin, cover with a piece of filter-paper, and leave it aside for crystals to separate out.

The salt that forms is known as iron(II) sulphate:

$$Fe^{2+}(aq) + SO_4^{2-}(aq) + 7H_2O(l) \longrightarrow FeSO_47H_2O(s)$$

NB: The oxidation state of the metal is shown by the (II).

(*b*) To the second portion of iron(II) sulphate solution from the experiment above, add a further 20 cm^3 portion of dilute sulphuric acid. Next add drops of '20-volume' hydrogen peroxide solution with continuous stirring until there is no further observable change in colour. Transfer the solution

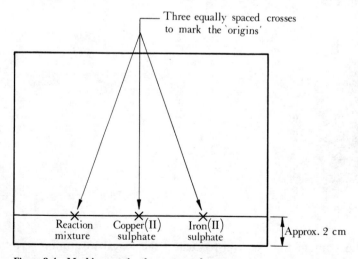

Figure 8.4 **Marking-out the chromatography paper**

to an evaporating basin, cover with filter-paper and leave it aside for crystals to separate out.

The reaction taking place when the hydrogen peroxide is added is:

$$Fe^{2+}(aq) - e^{-} \longrightarrow Fe^{3+}(aq)$$

On crystallization, the salt that forms is known as iron(III) sulphate:

$$2Fe^{3+}(aq) + 3SO_4^{2-}(aq) + 9H_2O(l) \longrightarrow Fe_2(SO_4)_3 9H_2O(s)$$

(c) To a solution of iron(III) chloride in a test-tube, add a small quantity of copper powder, stopper the tube and leave it to stand for at least twenty-four hours.

Using a pencil, mark out a piece of chromatography paper as shown in Fig. 8.4. (The size of the paper is not important.) Using a piece of glass tubing drawn out to a very fine point, apply a small spot of the above solution to the appropriate mark (the origin) on the chromatography paper as in Fig. 8.5. Do not dip the tube too deeply into the solution and wipe the out-

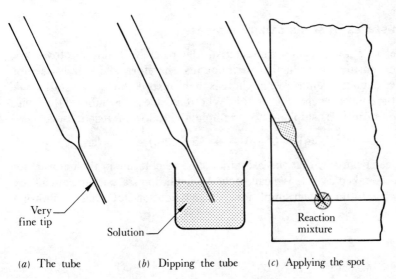

(a) The tube   (b) Dipping the tube   (c) Applying the spot

Figure 8.5 Applying the spot

side of the tube before attempting the application. In this way, with a little practice, you should be able to produce the size of spot required. Dry the spot (with a hair-dryer, if available) and then repeat the procedure to apply a second spot of the *same solution* to the *same place*. This is to build up the concentration of the sample without allowing the spot to become too large, which it would do if the same total volume of solution were applied in a single operation. It is advisable to apply at least three spots, drying fully between

145

each application, in order to ensure that there is sufficient concentration present. Using the same technique, apply spots of the aqueous solutions of copper(II) sulphate and iron(II) sulphate provided to the other two origins.

Develop the chromatogram in a solution consisting of 85 volumes of propanone, 5 volumes of distilled water and 10 volumes of concentrated hydrochloric acid. At the end of the run (i.e., when the solvent has risen as far up the paper as time allows and preferably as near the top as possible), remove the paper from the tank, dry it, and expose it to ammonia fumes until the smell of hydrogen chloride fumes has gone. In order to locate the spots, dip the paper in (or spray it with) a 0·1 per cent solution of dithio-oxamide (rubeanic acid) in ethanol, expose it to fumes from 0·880 ammonia solution, and then hang it to dry.

> What does the resulting chromatogram tell you about the reaction between iron(III) ions and copper metal? Construct an equation for this reaction showing the changes involved in the oxidation states of the iron and the copper.

Oxidation states of some other elements

As we have seen, metals characteristically react by losing electrons and forming positive ions. In their compounds, therefore, they always exhibit positive oxidation states. We might reasonably expect that non-metals would show the converse behaviour to this. When chlorine gas is bubbled through a solution of iron(II) sulphate, for example, the following reaction occurs:

$$2Fe^{2+}(aq) + Cl_2(g) \longrightarrow 2Fe^{3+}(aq) + 2Cl^-(aq)$$

It is clear from this that the oxidation state of chlorine in the chloride ion should be taken as -1. We can show the oxidation states that elements exhibit when forming such simple ions, on an oxidation state chart as shown in Fig. 8.6.

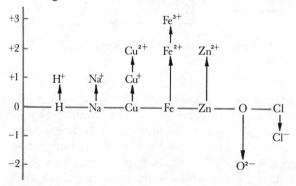

Figure 8.6 An oxidation state chart

Sometimes, however, the assignment of oxidation numbers is not so simple. When chlorine dissolves in alkaline solutions, for example, the reaction taking place is:

$$Cl_2(g) + 2OH^-(aq) \rightleftharpoons Cl^-(aq) + ClO^-(aq) + H_2O(l)$$

The following rules should be applied to determine the oxidation states of elements in such chemical species as the hypochlorite ion (ClO^-):

(a) The oxidation state of elements in the unreacted state is zero.

(b) The oxidation state of oxygen in compounds can normally be taken as -2 and that of hydrogen as $+1$.

(c) The sum of the oxidation states of all components of an ion is equal to the charge on the ion, or in the case of molecules is equal to zero.

Applying rules (b) and (c) to the hypochlorite ion it can be seen that the oxidation state of chlorine in it is $+1$.

These more difficult examples of oxidation state are often met in connection with the anion present in a salt. Potassium chlorate, for example, has the formula $KClO_3$. In attempting to assign an oxidation state to chlorine in this salt, it is helpful to realize that it consists of two types of ions, K^+ and ClO_3^-. Application of the rules now enables us to identify the oxidation state of chlorine as $+5$.

Calculate the oxidation state of chlorine in each of the following compounds and construct an oxidation state chart of the type shown previously, for this element.

$$HCl, \ KCl, \ ClO^-, \ ClO_3^-, \ ClO_4^-, \ Cl_2O_7, \ Cl_2O, \ ClO_2.$$

As we have seen previously, the oxidation state of a constituent element can be useful in giving a name to a compound. This extended use of the oxidation state concept is also helpful in this connection. FeO and Fe_2O_3 are two oxides of iron. By applying the rules outlined above we obtain the names iron(II) oxide and iron(III) oxide respectively, for them.

Some metals also form more complicated ions than simple positively charged ones. A common ion containing manganese, for example, is the permanganate ion (MnO_4^-). In these cases the oxidation states are always positive; in this example manganese is $+7$.

Experiment 8.11 *Investigating the reaction between iron(II) ions and permanganate ions in acidic conditions*

(a) Set up the experiment illustrated in Fig. 8.7.

What evidence is there that the reaction proceeds by means of electron transfer?

147

(b) Pipette 25 cm³ of a solution which is 0·1 M with respect to iron(II) ions into a conical flask. Add about 10 cm³ of dilute sulphuric acid, this constituting a suitable excess of hydrogen ions. Find the volume of 0·025 M potassium permanganate solution that must be added from a burette until the permanganate is just in excess. The reaction is self-indicating because the purple permanganate is changed to a near colourless product. One drop of excess permanganate, therefore, will colour the reaction mixture purple.

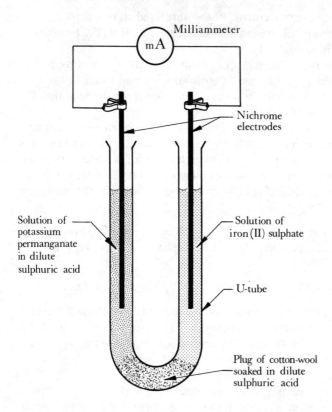

Figure 8.7   The potassium permanganate/iron(II) sulphate reaction

From your results, calculate how many moles of iron(II) ions react with one mole of permanganate ions. As the iron is changed to the +3 oxidation state, what must be the oxidation state change of the manganese? Balance the equation below, both in terms of atoms and charges, in a way that is consistent with the results of this experiment, inserting a suitable value for 'n'.

$$Fe^{2+}(aq) + MnO_4^-(aq) + H^+(aq) \longrightarrow Fe^{3+}(aq) + Mn^{n+}(aq) + H_2O(l)$$

Balancing oxidation-reduction equations

In simple cases all that is required is to add together the half-equations for the oxidation and the reduction processes involved. It should be noted that in all cases such as those that follow, appropriate tests must be carried out to identify the products before the equations can justifiably be written.

Example 1

Bromine water will oxidize iron(II) ions to iron(III) ions and is itself reduced to bromide ions.

$$Fe^{2+}(aq) - e^- \longrightarrow Fe^{3+}(aq)$$
$$Br_2(aq) + 2e^- \longrightarrow 2Br^-(aq)$$

When these are added together in such proportions that there is a common number of electrons in both, we get the overall equation:

$$2Fe^{2+}(aq) + Br_2(aq) \longrightarrow 2Fe^{3+}(aq) + 2Br^-(aq)$$

Example 2

Sulphite ions will reduce iron(III) ions to iron(II) ions and are themselves oxidized to sulphate ions.
Dealing first with the reducing agent:

(*a*) Write the formulae of the reactant and product:

$$SO_3^{2-}(aq) \longrightarrow SO_4^{2-}(aq)$$

(*b*) Supply the necessary amount of extra oxygen to the reactant as water:

$$SO_3^{2-}(aq) + H_2O(l) \longrightarrow SO_4^{2-}(aq)$$

(*c*) Free any excess hydrogen on the products side as hydrogen ions:

$$SO_3^{2-}(aq) + H_2O(l) \longrightarrow SO_4^{2-}(aq) + 2H^+(aq)$$

(*d*) Balance the charge by subtracting an appropriate number of electrons from the reactants side:

$$SO_3^{2-}(aq) + H_2O(l) - 2e^- \longrightarrow SO_4^{2-}(aq) + 2H^+(aq)$$

The half-equation for the oxidizing agent is simpler:

$$Fe^{3+}(aq) + e^- \longrightarrow Fe^{2+}(aq)$$

When these are added in the correct proportions to eliminate electrons, we have as the overall equation for the reaction:

$$SO_3^{2-}(aq) + H_2O(l) + 2Fe^{3+}(aq) \longrightarrow SO_4^{2-}(aq) + 2H^+(aq) + 2Fe^{3+}(aq)$$

149

Example 3

In acid conditions, bromate ions (BrO_3^-) will oxidize iodide ions to iodine molecules and they are themselves reduced to bromide ions.

The reaction of the reducing agent, in this case, is the simpler:

$$2I^-(aq) - 2e^- \longrightarrow I_2(aq)$$

The method for dealing with the oxidizing agent is the converse of that used for the reducing agent in the previous example:

(*a*) Write the formulae of the reactant and product:

$$BrO_3^-(aq) \longrightarrow Br^-(aq)$$

(*b*) Remove excess oxygen from the reactant as water:

$$BrO_3^-(aq) \longrightarrow Br^-(aq) + 3H_2O(l)$$

(*c*) Supply the necessary amount of extra hydrogen to the reactant as hydrogen ions:

$$BrO_3^-(aq) + 6H^+(aq) \longrightarrow Br^-(aq) + 3H_2O(l)$$

(*d*) Balance the charges by adding an appropriate number of electrons to the reactants side:

$$BrO_3^-(aq) + 6H^+(aq) + 6e^- \longrightarrow Br^-(aq) + 3H_2O(l)$$

Adding the two half-equations so that the electrons cancel gives:

$$BrO_3^-(aq) + 6H^+(aq) + 6I^-(aq) \longrightarrow Br^-(aq) + 3H_2O(l) + 3I_2(aq)$$

Although this method of balancing oxidation-reduction equations seems rather difficult, it is worth acquiring, for by its use, quite sophisticated equations can be written which are difficult to balance by any other method.

Summary

Lavoisier proposed the theory that the oxides of metallic elements are alkaline whilst those of non-metals are acidic when dissolved in water. Oxides that are insoluble in water will often dissolve in acidic or alkaline solutions and form salts. Oxides that are soluble in both acids and alkalis are said to be **amphoteric**.

According to the Ionic Theory, acids are substances that contain more hydrogen than hydroxide ions, while alkalis contain more hydroxide than hydrogen ions. In water and neutral solutions there are equal concentrations of hydrogen and hydroxide ions. The pH scale enables us to make a numerical comparison of the balance between hydrogen and hydroxide ions.

Nitric, hydrochloric, and sulphuric acids are known as **strong** acids because they are virtually completely ionized in solutions that are 1 M or less. Strong alkalis, such as sodium and potassium hydroxides, are completely ionized in solution. Ethanoic acid is a **weak** acid, its ionization reaction being an equilibrium one with the balance well on the side of the reactants. A similar situation arises with weak alkalis, one of which, ammonia solution, is studied in chapter 13. The enthalpy of neutralization of strong acids by strong alkalis is constant because an identical reaction takes place in each case, i.e.,

$$H^+(aq) + OH^-(aq) \longrightarrow H_2O(l)$$

However, in the case of weak acids or weak alkalis, some energy is required to ionize the molecules so that the ions may react, and thus the enthalpy of neutralization is lower in those reactions involving such compounds.

A solution of hydrogen chloride in toluene shows none of the chemical properties we associate with acids. Such properties are exhibited by aqueous solutions of hydrogen chloride. There is no heat change detectable when hydrogen chloride dissolves in toluene but on the dissolution of hydrogen chloride in water the reaction is *exothermic*. The Lowry-Brönsted Theory was proposed to reconcile the apparent paradox that such a reaction appears to involve bond breaking and so should be *endothermic*. This theory defines an acid as a proton (hydrogen-ion) donor and a base as a proton acceptor.

Glacial (anhydrous) ethanoic acid does not show the properties we associate with acids. When water is added to it, however, it partially ionizes by proton transfer to the water and the hydronium ions (H_3O^+) formed then confer on it these properties. The sodium salts of weak acids dissolve in water to form alkaline solutions because their anions are effective in acting as Lowry-Brönsted bases.

Oxidation is now defined as the removal of electrons and **reduction** is defined as the gain of electrons. Metals react characteristically as reducing agents and their relative reducing powers can be compared by displacement reactions or by making pairs of such metals the electrodes in electrolytic cells. The resulting order is called the **activity series** of metals. Those metals that lose electrons readily to form positive ions are powerful reducing agents and are placed high in the series. Some of the most reactive metals are not conveniently investigated by the techniques used in Experiments 8.8 and 8.9 but are included in Table 8.6 for comparative purposes. It should be clear from the experiments carried out with potassium and sodium in chapter 9, with calcium in chapter 10 and with aluminium in chapter 11 that all of these do in fact readily form positive ions and are thus correctly placed in the activity series as shown in Table 8.6. A summary of the properties of the metals in relation to their positions in the activity series is given in Table 11.6.

In the reacted state, it is possible to assign an **oxidation state** to elements.

The oxidation states of elements in simple ions such as Fe^{2+} and Cl^- are the charges on the ions. There is a set of rules for assigning oxidation states in more complicated cases. It is often helpful to make an oxidation state chart for elements.

Table 8.6   The activity series of metals based on displacement reactions

Metal	
Potassium	
Sodium	↑
Calcium	
Magnesium	Reducing
Aluminium	power
Zinc	increases
Iron	
Tin	
Lead	
Copper	

Oxidation-reduction equations are often best balanced by adding together the half-equations for the separate oxidation and reduction processes.

Questions

1. Lemon juice may be considered to be a dilute aqueous solution of citric acid. If you had a bottle of lemon juice, how would you show experimentally that citric acid is a weak acid? How do you explain the fact that hydrochloric acid is a strong acid and citric acid is a weak acid? (LN)

2. 'All acids contain oxygen' (Lavoisier).
'Acids are substances that produce hydrogen ions in solution' (Arrhenius).
'Acids are proton donors' (Brönsted).
Discuss each of these statements, pointing out the extent it is satisfactory, and where it is inadequate. (LN)

3. Oxidation may be defined in terms of electron transfer. Discuss the application of this definition to the following:

(a) Dissolving a metal in acid.
(b) Burning lead in chlorine.
(c) The change in oxidation state of a metal ion.
(d) The rapid corrosion of a galvanized iron water tank when a copper water pipe is connected to it. (LN)

4. The chemist can convert iron atoms into their ions and also bring about the reverse processes as shown by the following scheme:

$$Fe(s) \rightleftharpoons Fe^{2+}(aq) \rightleftharpoons Fe^{3+}(aq)$$

Describe how these changes may be brought about in a school laboratory and how the presence of each species may be tested for. How does the scheme relate to our ideas of oxidation and reduction and how might part of the scheme be used (in conjunction with other apparatus and chemicals) to show that electron transfer can take place at a distance?   (LN)

5. When acidified potassium permanganate solution is mixed with aqueous potassium iodide, a reaction takes place which may be represented as:

$$MnO_4^-(aq) + 8H^+(aq) + 5e^- \longrightarrow Mn^{2+}(aq) + 4H_2O(l)$$
$$2I^-(aq) \longrightarrow I_2(aq) + 2e^-$$

This reaction may be carried out without allowing the solutions to come into direct contact. Describe how you would do this and explain what happens. Give a sketch of your apparatus.   (LN)

6. Write an essay on the chemistry of simple cells, with particular reference to the Daniell Cell $(Zn:Zn^{2+}(aq)::Cu^{2+}(aq):Cu)$.   (LN)

9

Elements and the periodic table

We know that matter is made up of atoms, of which there are many different types. Before the discovery of isotopes (see chapter 1), it was assumed that all the atoms of a particular element were identical, an **element** being described as a substance which could not be broken down to a simpler substance by any chemical process. The modern definition of an element is more precise because of our understanding of the structure of the atom (see chapter 1). *An element is composed entirely of atoms all having the same number of protons in their nuclei.* Thus all atoms with the same atomic number (i.e., number of protons) will be of the same element, irrespective of their masses, which may vary due to differing numbers of neutrons in the nucleus.

There are 103 confirmed elements and two more the existence of which has been claimed. Of these, approximately 90 occur naturally in the earth's

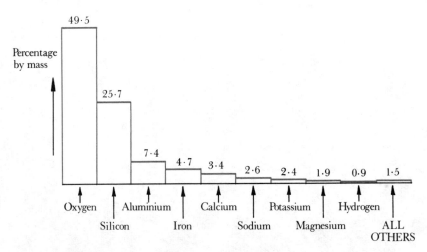

Figure 9.1   The relative abundance of elements in the earth's crust

crust or its atmosphere, the remainder having been made artificially by the use of nuclear processes. It is quite probable that more artificial elements will be made in the future, although they may have very short lives as they will be highly radioactive. It is possible that some radioactive elements not now found on earth may have been present at an earlier time but their half-lives were such that they have long since decayed into lighter elements.

As can be seen in Fig. 9.1, approximately 86 per cent of the earth's crust, including the atmosphere and the waters of the earth, is made up of just *four* elements, oxygen, silicon, aluminium, and iron. Together with the other five shown, the figure is 98·5 per cent so that the remaining elements (about 80) account for only 1·5 per cent of the mass!

Experiment 9.1   *To investigate some reactions of the elements lithium, sodium, and potassium*

These elements are potentially dangerous to handle and will be dispensed by the teacher into your test-tube or other apparatus. On no account should you touch the sample with your hands.

Carry out the following experiments with each of the elements in turn.

(*a*) Appearance. Observe the sample very carefully as it is being dispensed to you. Report on the initial appearance and on any changes that you observe.

(*b*) The effect of heat. Take a piece of asbestos paper, hold it with a pair of tongs and when your sample has been placed on it, heat in a medium, non-luminous (but not roaring) bunsen flame, holding the tongs well away from you. When any reaction has finished test the residue, when cool, with moist Universal Indicator (pH) paper.

What can you deduce about the nature of the elements as the result of this test?

(*c*) The effect on water. Take a small crystallizing dish or beaker and half fill it with water. The sample will be placed directly onto the water. **From a reasonable distance**, observe carefully what happens. When the reaction is complete, test the remaining liquid with Universal Indicator (pH) paper.

Did you see a gas being evolved? If so, what do you think it was?
Was the element more or less dense than water?
Did your result with Universal Indicator (pH) paper confirm the results in test (*b*)? Explain your answer, and suggest what the remaining liquid might be.

These three elements are called **alkali metals**.

Do you think, in view of your experiments, that this is an appropriate name? Explain your answer.

You will probably have noticed that the elements are stored in oil. Why is this necessary?

Is there any similarity in the reactivities of these elements? Which was the most reactive?

Copy and complete Table 9.1, writing the elements in order of reactivity, with the least reactive first, looking up the necessary additional information in the table at the back of this book. Comment on the reactivities relative to the atomic numbers.

Table 9.1

Element	Atomic number	Atomic mass	Physical appearance

Experiment 9.2   *To investigate some reactions of the elements chlorine, bromine, and iodine*

(a) Chlorine

These experiments must be performed by the teacher as chlorine gas is extremely toxic if inhaled.

(*i*) Bubble some chlorine through some water contained in a test-tube and then test the liquid with Universal Indicator (pH) paper. This liquid is called **chlorine-water**.

(*ii*) Add a small quantity of sodium hydroxide solution to the chlorine-water obtained in (*i*) and again test with Universal Indicator (pH) paper.

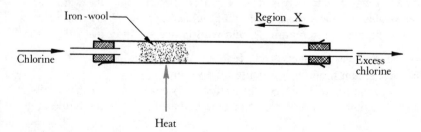

Figure 9.2   The reaction of chlorine with hot iron

What property of the chlorine-water is altered by the addition of the sodium hydroxide solution?

(*iii*) Pass a stream of chlorine over some heated iron-wool using the apparatus shown in Fig. 9.2.

What type of reaction takes place between the iron and the chlorine? Try to name the product of the reaction. Describe carefully what you see in the cool part of the tube, i.e., region X in the diagram.

(b) Bromine

(*i*) **This experiment should be performed by the teacher as bromine is a very corrosive liquid with a toxic vapour.**

Add a few cubic centimetres of liquid bromine to some water in a flask and shake well. The liquid thus obtained is called **bromine-water**.

(*ii*) Take a small quantity of the bromine-water prepared by the teacher in a test-tube, examine it and then test with Universal Indicator (pH) paper.

(*iii*) Add a small quantity of sodium hydroxide solution to the sample of bromine-water, observe carefully and then test once more with Universal Indicator (pH) paper.

(*iv*) Obtain from the teacher a few drops of liquid bromine in an ignition-tube held in an ignition-tube holder. Place a small tuft of iron-wool in the neck of the tube and heat the iron-wool until it glows red-hot.

Have you observed any significant differences in the reactions of chlorine and bromine in the above experiments?

(c) Iodine

(*i*) Take a small crystal of iodine in a test-tube, add some water and shake. Test the liquid with Universal Indicator (pH) paper.

(*ii*) Add some sodium hydroxide solution to the liquid obtained in (*i*) and test once more with Universal Indicator (pH) paper.

(*iii*) Take a small crystal of iodine in an ignition-tube held in an ignition-tube holder, place a small tuft of iron-wool in the neck of the tube and heat the iron-wool until it glows red-hot.

How do the reactions of iodine compare with those of chlorine and bromine? Which of the three elements is the most reactive?

These elements are called **halogens** (from the Greek meaning 'salt-maker'). There is a fourth halogen called fluorine but this is an even more dangerous gas than chlorine and so cannot be conveniently used in the laboratory. The halogens are studied further in chapter 15.

CHEMISTRY BY EXPERIMENT AND UNDERSTANDING

Experiment 9.3 *Further evidence of the relative reactivity of the halogens*

(*a*) The reactions of chlorine-water with solutions of potassium halides, i.e., salts of potassium and the halogens.

Take 5 cm³ of respectively potassium chloride, potassium bromide, and potassium iodide, all in aqueous solutions, in three test-tubes together with a fourth test-tube containing 5 cm³ of water to act as a standard. Add to each tube in turn a few drops of chlorine-water. Carefully compare the tubes that contained the potassium halides with each other and with that containing the water.

(*b*) The reactions of bromine-water with solutions of potassium halides.

Take fresh samples of the three solutions as used in (*a*) and, as before, another test-tube containing an approximately equal volume of water. Add to each of the four tubes in turn a few drops of bromine-water. Again using the water as a standard, compare the contents of the various tubes.

Was there an obvious reaction in every case? What do you think were the products of the reactions?

In reactions such as these, the more reactive element displaces the less reactive element from its compound.

In view of this, arrange the halogens in order of reactivity. Does this order agree with that obtained in Experiment 9.2? Copy and complete Table 9.1, this time for the halogens, again writing the elements in order of reactivity (you may include fluorine, if you wish), with the least reactive first. Comment on the reactivities relative to the atomic numbers. Does the order of re-activities relative to atomic numbers show the same trend for the halogens as it does for the alkali metals? Taking this answer into consideration, which combination of halogen and alkali metal would you expect to react most vigorously together, assuming that they do in fact react?

Experiment 9.4 *To investigate the reactions between chlorine and the alkali metals*

This experiment should show if your predictions in the last experiment were correct.

This experiment must be carried out by the teacher.

Cut a small piece of lithium, dry off as much of the oil as possible and place the metal in the tube shown in Fig. 9.3. Pass in a slow stream of chlorine from a cylinder or a generator and heat the tube gently in a bunsen flame.

158

Observe carefully and when the reaction is complete, disconnect the chlorine supply, allow the tube to cool and examine the product.

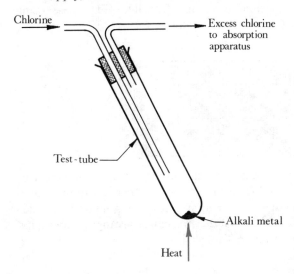

Figure 9.3 **The reaction of chlorine with the alkali metals**

Is ΔH for this reaction positive or negative? What is the product of the reaction?

Repeat the experiment with similar pieces of sodium and then potassium, using a fresh tube in each case.

How do these reactions compare with that with lithium? Do the results confirm your findings for the earlier experiments?

The classification of elements

If all the elements are arranged in order of increasing atomic number, it can be seen that elements with similar properties such as the alkali metals and the halogens occur at regular intervals of 8, 18, or 32 elements, as shown in Fig. 9.4.

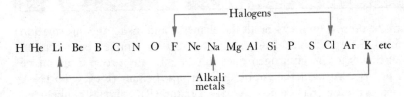

Figure 9.4

159

The number of elements occurring between successive alkali metals and successive halogens can be seen in Table 9.2, which includes the much less common rubidium (Rb), caesium (Cs), and francium (Fr), these being alkali metals, and astatine (At) which is a halogen.

Table 9.2

Alkali metals			Halogens		
Lithium	→ Sodium	8	Fluorine → Chlorine		8
Sodium	→ Potassium	8	Chlorine → Bromine		18
Potassium	→ Rubidium	18	Bromine → Iodine		18
Rubidium	→ Caesium	18	Iodine → Astatine		32
Caesium	→ Francium	32			

If our list of elements is now split up so that all the alkali metals appear in one vertical column and the halogens in another, the 'classification' begins to take shape (Fig. 9.5). These vertical columns are called **groups**. It is found, by a study of all the other elements, that they too can be arranged into groups as shown in some examples given in Table 9.3.

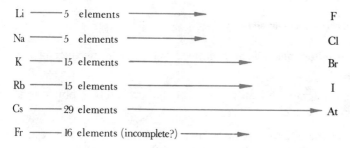

Figure 9.5

Table 9.3   Some groups of elements

Beryllium	Be	Boron	B	Scandium	Sc	Titanium	Ti	Copper	Cu
Magnesium	Mg	Aluminium	Al	Yttrium	Y	Zirconium	Zr	Silver	Ag
Calcium	Ca	Gallium	Ga	Lanthanum	La	Hafnium	Hf	Gold	Au
Strontium	Sr	Indium	In						
Barium	Ba	Thallium	Tl						
Radium	Ra								

Look up the atomic numbers of all the elements and, using the information given in Fig. 9.5 and Table 9.3 as a guide, construct a complete classification of the elements. (*NB:* Hydrogen does not fit into any group and can be written on its own, and the 'noble gas' group, helium (He), neon (Ne), argon (Ar), krypton (Kr), xenon (Xe), and radon (Rn), should be included after the halogen group.)

The horizontal rows of elements are called **periods** and the name given to the whole classification of elements is the **Periodic Table**.

The first serious classification of the elements was carried out by Dimitri Mendeleev in 1869, although important work had also been done by Lothar Meyer. The fact that the Mendeleev table is very similar to that in use today alone illustrates the achievement of his work but in addition, because of gaps in his table, he was able to predict the existence and properties of some elements that at that time had not been discovered. One such gap was between silicon and tin in the carbon group. This was filled fifteen years later by the discovery of germanium. Mendeleev actually used atomic masses as the basis of his classification because the concept of atomic numbers was not then known and, because of this, several elements did not fit by mass the positions indicated by their properties. This situation arose because of the presence of heavy isotopes in the natural element, e.g., tellurium (atomic mass 127·6) and iodine (atomic mass 126·9). Tellurium however has a lower atomic number (52) than iodine (53) and must therefore precede it in the table. It is for reasons such as this that the modern table is based on atomic numbers rather than atomic masses.

A row of ten elements that has no counterpart in earlier periods appears in Period 4. This is called a **transition period** and the elements are **transition elements**, most of them being metals. There are similar transition periods in Periods 5 and 6 but in the latter yet another sequence of elements appears, this time fourteen in number, between elements number 57 (lanthanum) and 72 (hafnium). This is called an **inner transition period** and the elements, which are very uncommon, are called the **rare earth elements** or **lanthanides**. A second inner transition period starts after element number 89 (actinium). These elements are all radioactive and are called the **actinides**. The actinide series is completed with element number 103 (lawrencium), this being the last confirmed element. Period 7 will presumably continue with the transition period starting at actinium, with the next element (number 104) in the titanium-hafnium group.

As we have found, there are great similarities in the properties of elements within a **non-transition group**, such as the alkali metals or halogens. The elements in a **transition group**, such as titanium, zirconium and hafnium, do not show such marked similarities and there is, in fact, a greater likeness between the elements within a **transition period**.

Experiment 9.5 *To compare the properties of some transition elements with those of the alkali metals*

Samples of some transition elements will be given to you. Carry out the following tests and write down the results in tabular form as in Table 9.4.

(*a*) Appearance.

(b) Physical properties. Handle the samples and see how easy, or otherwise, they are to bend, break, and scratch.

(c) Holding with tongs, heat the samples strongly and observe carefully when hot and when they have cooled.

(d) Add some water to a small piece of each sample in turn, contained in a test-tube. If no reaction is visible, heat until the water boils.

Table 9.4

Element	Appearance	Melting point	Physical properties	Effect of heat	Effect of water
Copper Zinc etc. Lithium Sodium Potassium					

Complete your results table by adding your observations for the alkali metals (from Experiment 9.1) and looking up the melting points of the elements. Do you think that there are any similarities between the alkali metals and transition elements? What important points of difference have you observed?

Experiment 9.6 *To compare some properties of transition element and alkali metal compounds*

(a) Examine the samples shown to you. These will include some compounds of as many different transition elements as possible and also some alkali metal compounds. Tabulate your results as in Table 9.5.

Table 9.5

Compound	Colour	Effect of ammonia solution on an aqueous solution of the compound	
		Colour of precipitate (if any)	Colour of solution (if soluble in excess)

(b) Make an aqueous solution of each of the samples or use the solutions provided (you will only need a few cubic centimetres). Add slowly, drop by drop, some ammonia solution to each of the solutions in turn. Observe carefully to see whether any precipitate forms. If it does, continue adding the ammonia solution to see whether any further change occurs. (There may be a colour change or the precipitate may dissolve, or both.) Record all your observations in the results table.

In general, was the appearance and the behaviour (in the ammonia solution test) of the alkali metal and transition element compounds similar, or otherwise?

When a precipitate was formed this was the insoluble hydroxide of the element and if this dissolved in excess ammonia solution a **complex ion** was produced. A complex ion occurs when a simple ion, such as the copper(II) ion (Cu^{2+}), is able to form strong chemical bonds with other particles such as molecules of ammonia (NH_3). In this case, four molecules of ammonia bond through the nitrogen atoms to one copper(II) ion and the resulting complex ion is called, logically, the *tetrammine copper(II) ion*. This is shown in Fig. 9.6, the square brackets signifying that it is a complex ion.

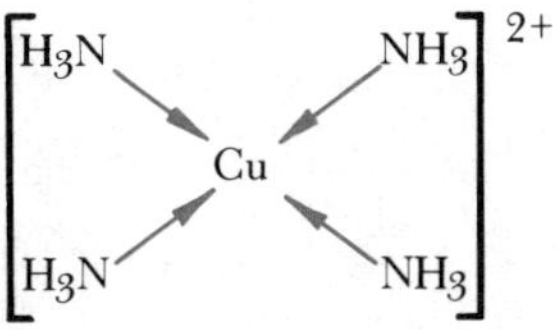

Figure 9.6   The tetrammine copper(II) ion

From your experiments, which type of element, alkali metal or transition, seems the more likely to form complex ions?

Experiment 9.7   *To prepare a sample of a compound containing a complex ion—tetrammine copper(II) sulphate,* $[Cu(NH_3)_4] SO_4 . H_2O$

Take 20 cm³ of 1 M copper(II) sulphate solution in a 100 cm³ conical flask and add slowly, with shaking, 2 M ammonia solution until the precipitate that first forms has just redissolved. Add 30 cm³ of ethanol to precipitate the complex and cool well, preferably with an ice-bath. When crystals have formed, filter or centrifuge and dry the crystals with filter-paper.

Compare your product with some crystals of copper(II) sulphate penta-hydrate, $CuSO_4 . 5H_2O$.

| By comparing the formulae of the two compounds, can you suggest how the molecules of water in the pentahydrate might be arranged?

Experiment 9.8 *To investigate some reactions of chromium compounds*

Heat, in a 250 cm³ conical flask, a mixture of 10 cm³ of 1 M potassium dichromate solution with 15 cm³ of concentrated hydrochloric acid. Boil for several minutes to drive off dissolved air and then cool slightly. Add about 3 g of granulated zinc and fit the flask with a bunsen valve, as shown in Fig. 9.7. Swirl the contents of the flask occasionally, observe carefully and note any colour changes.

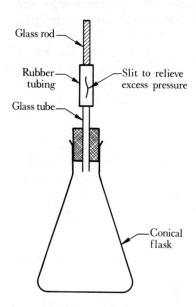

Glass rod

Rubber tubing

Glass tube

Slit to relieve excess pressure

Conical flask

Figure 9.7   The bunsen valve

When the mixture is blue, decant off the liquid into a second flask and look for any colour change. That which you see is brought about simply by atmospheric oxidation. Then add dilute potassium hydroxide solution until a permanent precipitate is formed. Warm the mixture gently but do not boil, while adding 30 cm³ of '20 volume' (2 M) hydrogen peroxide. Having brought the contents of the flask to the boil for a few minutes, cool and then filter.

Compare the colour of the filtrate with that of the original potassium dichromate solution.

Chromium can exist in its compounds in three different oxidation states (see chapter 8), $+2$, $+3$, and $+6$, each of which has a different colour. These are respectively blue, green, and yellow (or orange in acid solution) as you have seen in the experiment just completed. You have also seen how easy it is to convert one oxidation state to another. To summarize:

$$\text{Dichromate} \underset{\text{oxidation}}{\overset{\text{reduction}}{\rightleftharpoons}} \text{Chromium(III)} \underset{\text{oxidation}}{\overset{\text{reduction}}{\rightleftharpoons}} \text{Chromium(II)}$$

Dichromate	Chromium(III)	Chromium(II)
(orange)	(green)	(blue)
$+6$	$+3$	$+2$

Which of the two oxidation states chromium(III) or chromium(II) is the more stable?

The ability to exist in several oxidation states, often with distinctive colours, is a characteristic of transition elements. In the first transition period (scandium to zinc) this is true of all the elements with the exception of the first and last, i.e., scandium and zinc. Both of these have colourless compounds and only one oxidation state, respectively $+3$ and $+2$.

Construct a table showing the oxidation states for as many transition elements as you can, giving the colours where possible.

The Periodic Table and electronic structure

The electronic structure of the elements can be built up by consideration of the Periodic Table and the order in which orbitals (see chapter 1) are filled with electrons (which is not necessarily the most obvious sequence) as shown in Table 9.6.

The simplest atom, hydrogen, has its single electron in the first shell, i.e., the K-shell (see chapter 1), and the electronic structure is designated as $1s^1$. In a similar way the helium atom will have an electronic structure of $1s^2$, with two electrons in the $1s$ orbital.

The K-shell is now full and so the first element in Period 2, lithium, must have the structure $1s^2 2s^1$ in which the third electron is found in the next available orbital, which is the $2s$ orbital in the L-shell. The next element is beryllium ($1s^2 2s^2$) followed by boron ($1s^2 2s^2 2p^1$) in which the $2p$ orbital starts to fill. This progressive build-up continues with electrons successively filling each orbital in turn in the sequence shown in Table 9.6.

It can be seen by reference to the Periodic Table printed inside the back cover of this book that the build-up of s and p orbitals occurs in *non-transition* (**s** and **p block**) elements, that of d orbitals in *transition* (**d block**) elements and that of f orbitals in *inner transition* (**f block**) elements.

All s and p block elements within the same group have the same number of electrons in their outermost shell. This is illustrated in Table 9.7 for Group I (the alkali metals) and Group VII (the halogens) and accounts for the

Table 9.6 The sequence of orbitals within the atom

Orbital	Period
1s	1
2s 2p	2
3s 3p	3
4s 3d 4p	4
5s 4d 5p	5
6s 5d 4f 6p	6
7s 6d 5f	7

similarities of elements *within a group*, since it is these electrons that are most responsible for the chemistry of the elements.

Table 9.7 Outermost electron shell structure; non-transition elements

Alkali metals Group I		Halogens Group VII	
Lithium	$2s^1$	Fluorine	$2s^2 2p^5$
Sodium	$3s^1$	Chlorine	$3s^2 3p^5$
Potassium	$4s^1$	Bromine	$4s^2 4p^5$
Rubidium	$5s^1$	Iodine	$5s^2 5p^5$
Caesium	$6s^1$	Astatine	$6s^2 6p^5$
Francium	$7s^1$		

The *d* block elements within a given period also have, with few exceptions, the same numbers of electrons in the outermost shell and this is why transition elements *within a period* have similar properties, the differences that do exist being due to differing numbers of *d* electrons in the penultimate (i.e., last but one) shell (see Table 9.8).

Table 9.8   Outermost and penultimate shell structure;
             transition elements

Transition element	Structure
Scandium	$3s^23p^63d^14s^2$
Titanium	$3s^23p^63d^24s^2$
Iron	$3s^23p^63d^64s^2$
Nickel	$3s^23p^63d^84s^2$
Zinc	$3s^23p^63d^{10}4s^2$

A similar situation exists with the inner transition elements, which differ only in their numbers of f electrons, the f orbitals being deep within the atom and thus having little effect on the chemistry of the elements.

In general, *those elements with few electrons in their outermost shells are metals*, e.g., *s*, *d*, and *f* block elements, and *these form compounds in which they exhibit positive oxidation states*.

Those elements with a large number of electrons in their outermost shells are non-metals, e.g., Groups VI and VII, and these either *gain electrons to form negative ions* or *share electrons by forming covalent bonds*. In the case of these latter elements, the tendency towards metallic behaviour increases with increasing atomic number, so that the non-metals form a triangular block at the top right-hand side of the Periodic Table.

Summary

An **element** is a substance composed entirely of atoms all having the same number of protons in their nuclei. There are about ninety naturally-occurring elements but others have been made artificially and more will probably be discovered in a similar way. Most naturally-occurring elements are found in very small quantities, the bulk of the earth's crust consisting of just a few elements, notably oxygen, silicon, aluminium, and iron.

Some elements show very similar reactions to one another. Two such 'families' are the **alkali metals** and the **halogens**, all of which are very reactive. The alkali metals rapidly oxidize in air and burn with flames of characteristic colours. They dissolve quickly, and sometimes violently, in water liberating hydrogen and forming an alkaline hydroxide in solution. The halogens are only slightly soluble in water, forming a solution (sometimes coloured) with bleaching properties, but dissolve readily in alkalis. They react exothermically with iron to form the iron(III) halides (with the exception of iodine which forms iron(II) iodide; iron(III) iodide does not exist) and with the alkali metals to form the alkali metal halides. The most reactive alkali metal is that with highest atomic number, francium, but the most reactive halogen is that of lowest atomic number, fluorine. Thus the reaction between these

167

two elements would be expected to be the most vigorous of all the combinations possible.

The **Periodic Table**, first devised by Mendeleev, arranges the elements in ascending order of atomic mass so that those elements with similar properties are in vertical columns called **groups**. The resulting horizontal rows are called **periods**. The Table in use today is modified only to the extent that it is based on atomic number, as this is a more fundamental property of the atom than atomic mass.

The reasons for periodicity lie in the regular build-up of electrons within the atom with increasing atomic number. Elements in which s and p orbitals are being filled with electrons are called **non-transition elements**, those in which d orbitals are being filled are called **transition elements**, and those in which f orbitals are being filled are called **inner transition elements**.

Non-transition elements within a group have similar properties because they have the same number of electrons in the outermost shell of the atom, but the elements in successive groups differ because of the increasing number of electrons in the outermost shell. Successive transition elements, however, differ little in properties since the build-up of electrons in these atoms is in the penultimate (i.e., last but one) and not the outermost shell.

These similarities in the properties of transition elements can be seen by consideration of the first transition period, scandium to zinc:

(*a*) All are metals with generally high melting points and ductility and relatively low chemical reactivity.

(*b*) Most of their compounds are coloured, with the exceptions of those of scandium and zinc, the first and last members.

(*c*) They readily form **complex ions**.

(*d*) They can exist in several oxidation states (except scandium and zinc).

These properties are often referred to as 'transitional characteristics' since, for the most part, they are peculiar to transition elements. To illustrate this point, an interesting comparison with the properties of the alkali metals, which is a typical group of non-transition metals, can be made.

In general, those elements with few electrons in their outermost shell have the properties of metals and exhibit positive oxidation states in their compounds, while those with a large number of electrons in their outermost shell are non-metals and either form negative ions or covalent bonds in their compounds.

Questions

1. For each of the pairs of elements (*a*) sodium and potassium, (*b*) chlorine and bromine, give **three** properties that illustrate their chemical similarity.

Suggest an electronic explanation for this similarity. (O & C)

2. What experimental evidence could you collect in a school laboratory and what other data could be referred to in order to show that the elements have periodic variations in their properties?

Describe clearly how this evidence could be presented to others. (LN)

3. Mendeleev stated that '(some) properties of the elements are a periodic function of their atomic masses'.

Describe some periodic functions of the elements, choosing as far as you are able both from 'chemical' properties and 'physical' ones. What is the connection between these properties and the structure of the atoms? (LN)

Metallic elements and their compounds—I

The extraction of metals

When a metal reacts, each atom normally forms a positive ion by the loss of one or more electrons. Thus the atom is *oxidized* to the ion:

$$M - ne^- \longrightarrow M^{n+}$$

(where n is a small whole number). In order to extract a metal from one of its compounds, each ion must be made to accept back the electron or electrons that were given up when the compound was formed. Thus the ion must be *reduced* to the atom:

$$M^{n+} + ne^- \longrightarrow M$$

The ease of reduction obviously varies from one metal to another.

Experiment 10.1   *To investigate the ease of reduction*
                           of certain metal oxides

(*a*) **With carbon.** Make a small cavity in a charcoal-block and place in it a small sample of the oxide under test. Cause a bunsen flame to play on the sample by blowing vigorously with a blowpipe, from a position just inside the flame, as in Fig. 10.1, until it is thoroughly heated. Carry out the test on each of the oxides listed in Table 10.1 and record the results.

(*b*) **With hydrogen.** Place a small quantity of each sample in turn in the apparatus shown in Fig. 10.2. Turn on the supply of town gas, which contains a large proportion of hydrogen, and displace all the air from the apparatus. When this has been done light the gas escaping from the hole in the test-tube and adjust the flow of gas to give a small steady flame. Heat the

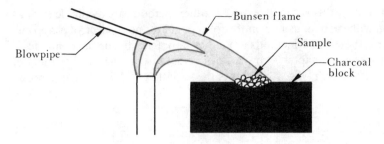

Figure 10.1   Use of the charcoal block

Table 10.1

Metal Oxide	Observations	
	Carbon	Hydrogen .
Magnesium oxide Aluminium oxide Iron(III) oxide Lead(II) oxide Copper(II) oxide		

oxide gently and observe carefully. At the end of the experiment, examine
the residue when cold.

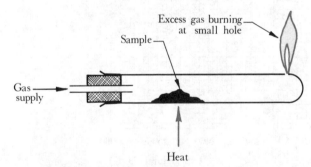

Figure 10.2   Reduction with hydrogen

Were similar effects obtained with both reducing agents? Were any of the
oxides not reduced in these experiments? Are your results consistent with
what you know about the activity series of the metals?

The principles of extraction

As reduction is the gain of electrons, the most obvious method of extraction
would seem to be electrolysis of a suitable compound in order to obtain the

metal. However, this is too expensive if other methods are available such as reduction with carbon, usually in the form of coke, and so electrolysis is only used where these other methods are either impracticable or uneconomic.

We have seen in chapter 7 how ΔG can be used to predict the feasibility of reactions. The graph (Fig. 10.3) shows the variation of ΔG with temperature

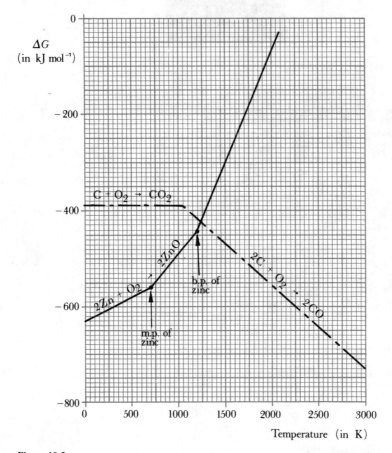

Figure 10.3

for the reactions in which oxides of zinc and carbon are formed. Below about 1000 K carbon forms carbon dioxide and above this temperature it forms carbon monoxide. Let us consider the possibility of reducing zinc oxide with carbon at two temperatures, 1000 K and 1500 K.

(a) At 1000 K. The reaction is:

$$2ZnO + C \longrightarrow 2Zn + CO_2$$

We can determine the feasibility of the reaction at this temperature by calculating ΔG.

$$C + O_2 \longrightarrow CO_2; \quad \Delta G = -390 \text{ kJ mol}^{-1} \tag{1}$$
$$2Zn + O_2 \longrightarrow 2ZnO; \quad \Delta G = -490 \text{ kJ mol}^{-1} \tag{2}$$

Subtracting (2) from (1) and rearranging gives:

$$2ZnO + C \longrightarrow 2Zn + CO_2; \quad \Delta G = +100 \text{ kJ mol}^{-1}$$

Thus at 1000 K, the reaction would only occur to a negligible extent.

(b) At 1500 K. The reaction is:

$$2ZnO + 2C \longrightarrow 2Zn + 2CO$$

Consider:

$$2C + O_2 \longrightarrow 2CO; \quad \Delta G = -470 \text{ kJ mol}^{-1} \tag{3}$$
$$2Zn + O_2 \longrightarrow 2ZnO; \quad \Delta G = -300 \text{ kJ mol}^{-1} \tag{4}$$

Subtracting (4) from (3) and rearranging gives:

$$2ZnO + 2C \longrightarrow 2Zn + 2CO; \quad \Delta G = -170 \text{ kJ mol}^{-1}$$

At this temperature, therefore, the reduction of zinc oxide with carbon is energetically feasible.

It will also be noted from the graph that zinc is above its boiling point at 1500 K and so distils out of the reaction vessel, thus assisting in its purification.

Application of similar reasoning enables us to predict the feasibility of this method of reduction for any other metal oxide. It can be seen that calculating ΔG for the reduction process involves subtracting ΔG for the formation of the metal oxide from ΔG for the formation of the appropriate oxide of carbon. Hence at the temperature where the lines intersect on the graph, ΔG for the reduction process is zero. As we have seen in chapter 7, the reaction will be an equilibrium one in that temperature region; below it the reaction will not occur appreciably and above it an acceptable yield of metal will form. It is if this temperature is too high that such a method of extraction becomes unsuitable. This is the case with those metals high in the activity series such as the alkali metals, calcium, magnesium, and aluminium, and for these an electrolytic method is used. In a similar way, it can be shown that hydrogen is also unsuitable for reducing the oxides of these metals.

The techniques of extraction

Very few metals are found in the free state (i.e., uncombined with other elements), gold being the notable exception although silver, copper, tin, lead, and mercury are sometimes found in this condition. The most reactive metals are usually found as chlorides or carbonates and the less reactive as oxides or sulphides, as shown in Table 10.2. More detailed information on metal ores is given in Table 11.5.

Table 10.2

Metal	Most common ore	Method of extraction
Potassium Sodium	Chlorides	Electrolysis of fused chloride or oxide
Calcium Magnesium	Chlorides and carbonates	
Aluminium	Oxide	
Zinc Iron Tin	Oxides and sulphides	Reduction of oxide with carbon
Lead Copper	Sulphides	Special reduction method

The metal content of many ores is very low so that much preliminary work must be done in order to concentrate the ore and so make extraction economic. This is usually carried out where the ore is found to avoid transporting large quantities of worthless material. It may take the form of simple washing, as with tin ore, or more sophisticated techniques such as **oil flotation** for zinc ores, where the ore is churned up with a mixture of oil and water to cause the necessary separation.

The ore **concentrate** may then be in a suitable condition for the extraction process, but if it is a carbonate or sulphide it is next roasted in air in order to convert it to the oxide. If electrolysis is to be used, the ore must be more extensively purified than for a reduction method since, in this case, it is not normal to subject the metal, when obtained, to further purification. The differences in procedure can be summarized as shown in Table 10.3.

Table 10.3

Reduction with carbon	Electrolytic reduction
Concentration of ore Roasting of ore Reduction Purification of metal (often by electrolysis)	Concentration of ore Extensive purification of ore Electrolysis

The method of extraction used, in relation to the positions of the metals in the activity series is shown in Table 10.2.

Lithium, sodium, and potassium

The elements do not occur naturally in the free state but their compounds, notably the chlorides, are widely distributed. The metals themselves are extracted on a relatively small scale but find important uses in a variety of fields. Lithium in certain alloys and sodium as a coolant in nuclear reactors are just two examples.

The most important properties of these alkali metals have been dealt with in detail in chapter 9 and are merely summarized here:

(a) They are all very reactive, the reactivity increasing with increasing atomic number (i.e., down the group). This reactivity is due to the ease with which the atom can lose the single electron in its outermost shell to form a positively charged ion, e.g.,

$$Li - e^- \longrightarrow Li^+$$

For this reason, the alkali metals are good reducing agents but are not easily obtained by reduction from their compounds. Thus electrolysis of the appropriate fused compound is the only practicable method of producing the free metal.

(b) They react readily with air (the free element must be kept under oil) and burn with flames of characteristic colours when heated, to form oxides that are basic.

(c) There is a vigorous reaction with water, evolving hydrogen, and producing strongly alkaline hydroxides.

(d) They react readily with most non-metallic elements to form stable compounds that are ionic in structure and usually soluble in water.

(e) The metals themselves are soft, malleable and ductile, and are a silvery colour and lustrous when freshly cut, but tarnish rapidly. They have very low densities and melting points.

Experiment 10.2   *To test for alkali metal compounds;*
                  the flame test

There are two techniques, of which the first is generally more reliable.

(a) Method I. Take a test-tube and half fill it with cold water. Dry the outside of the tube and dip the end in concentrated hydrochloric acid (contained in a watch-glass) and then in the sample under test (also contained in a watch-glass). Heat the tip of the tube and hence the sample in a non-luminous bunsen flame and observe the colour of the flame produced. Provided that heating is not continued for too long, the tube will be kept relatively cool by the water it contains, but if it does become hot, the water is easily replaced. If the flame colour is not particularly pronounced, alternate dipping of the tube in the acid and the sample can be continued until a satis-factory result is obtained. The tip of the tube is easily washed, when cool, and the procedure repeated with the next sample.

(b) Method II. In this method, the test-tube is replaced by a platinum (or nichrome, which is much cheaper) wire sealed into a length of glass rod. The wire is cleaned by dipping in concentrated hydrochloric acid and heating. The test is then carried out as before by dipping the cleaned wire into con-centrated hydrochloric acid and then into the sample and heating in a non-luminous bunsen flame. The disadvantage of this method is the difficulty of cleaning the wire after use as some substances, notably sodium compounds, give a very persistent flame.

Carry out a flame test on at least one sample of respectively a lithium, a sodium, and a potassium compound, and observe the characteristic colours produced.

What role do you think was played by the hydrochloric acid in this test?

Sodium hydroxide

Sodium hydroxide is caustic and care should be taken to avoid contact with either skin or clothing.

Experiment 10.3 *To investigate the properties of sodium hydroxide (caustic soda)*

Carry out the following tests:

(a) Appearance.

(b) Using a spatula, place a pellet or flake of sodium hydroxide on a watch-glass and leave to stand for some time, observing occasionally.

(c) Test some sodium hydroxide solution with Universal Indicator (pH) paper.

(d) Add a few drops of sodium hydroxide solution to 2 cm³ of each of the following solutions, contained in test-tubes: copper(II) sulphate, iron(II) sulphate, iron(III) chloride, zinc sulphate, lead(II) nitrate, and calcium chloride. If a precipitate forms, add more sodium hydroxide solution until present in excess.

(e) Add some sodium hydroxide solution to a spatula measure of ammo-nium chloride in a test-tube and warm gently. Test any gas evolved with moist Universal Indicator (pH) paper.

Tabulate your results and draw any general conclusions that you can about the nature of sodium hydroxide.

In test (b), the sodium hydroxide underwent **deliquescence**.

| Suggest a meaning for the term deliquescence.

The manufacture of sodium hydroxide

Sodium hydroxide is manufactured on a very large scale for use in a wide range of industries such as the manufacture of soap, paper, and viscose rayon (artificial silk) and the processing of petroleum and aluminium.

The method used for manufacture is the electrolysis of aqueous sodium chloride (brine). The problem is to prevent the chlorine also produced from recombining with the sodium hydroxide. This is achieved in several ways, the most common in the UK being the **Castner-Kellner** or **mercury cathode** process (Fig. 10.4).

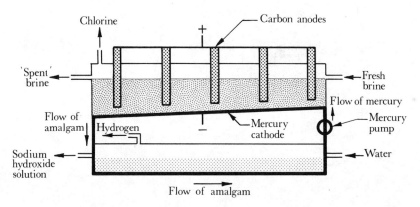

Figure 10.4   The mercury cathode cell

Brine is electrolysed in long shallow tanks with carbon rod anodes and a cathode of mercury, flowing across the floor of the cell by gravity, in a thin layer. Chlorine gas is evolved at the anodes by discharge of chloride ions:

$$Cl^-(aq) - e^- \longrightarrow Cl$$

then,
$$Cl + Cl \longrightarrow Cl_2(g)$$

At the mercury cathode, the normal order of discharge is reversed and sodium ions, not hydrogen ions, are discharged:

$$Na^+(aq) + e^- \longrightarrow Na(s)$$

The sodium atoms immediately dissolve in the mercury to form an **amalgam**, which is effectively an alloy of sodium and mercury:

$$Na(s) + Hg(l) \longrightarrow Na/Hg(l)$$

177

The liquid amalgam flows into a lower cell containing water, where it reacts to form sodium hydroxide and liberates hydrogen gas. This may be represented by the equation:

$$Na/Hg(l) + H_2O(l) \longrightarrow Na^+OH^-(aq) + \tfrac{1}{2}H_2(g) + Hg(l)$$

The mercury is re-cycled and the solution of sodium hydroxide, when sufficiently concentrated, can be removed and either used as a solution or evaporated to obtain the solid. The hydrogen and chlorine obtained are, of course, valuable by-products. A simplified reaction sequence is shown in Fig. 10.5.

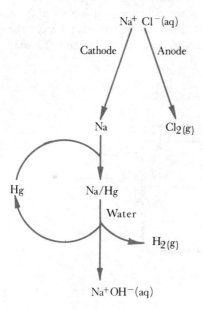

Figure 10.5   The reaction sequence

Sodium carbonate

Experiment 10.4   *To investigate the properties of sodium carbonate*

Carry out the following tests:

(*a*) Compare the appearance of anhydrous sodium carbonate (soda ash, Na_2CO_3) and hydrated sodium carbonate (washing soda, $Na_2CO_3 \cdot 10H_2O$).

(*b*) Place some crystals of washing soda on a watch-glass and leave for some time, observing occasionally.

(*c*) Add a few drops of dilute hydrochloric acid to some solid sodium carbonate and test the gas evolved.

(d) Add a few drops of aqueous sodium carbonate to 2 cm^3 of each of the following solutions, contained in test-tubes: copper(II) sulphate, iron(II) sulphate, iron(III) chloride, zinc sulphate, lead(II) nitrate, and calcium chloride.

(e) Heat some soda ash on a piece of asbestos paper.

(f) Test some sodium carbonate solution with Universal Indicator (pH) paper.

Tabulate your results and draw any general conclusions that you can about the nature of sodium carbonate.

In test (b), the washing soda is said to undergo **efflorescence**.

Suggest a meaning for the term efflorescence.

The manufacture of sodium carbonate

Sodium carbonate is used extensively for making other chemicals, notably glass, soap, and sodium hydroxide, and is thus manufactured on a very large scale.

The method used is the **Solvay** or **ammonia soda** process which uses sodium chloride as the starting material in the form of brine (i.e., a saturated aqueous solution of sodium chloride). The brine is saturated with ammonia gas and the 'ammoniated brine' is allowed to trickle down successive tall 'Solvay' towers against a current of carbon dioxide gas flowing up the towers, as shown in Fig. 10.6.

When carbon dioxide dissolves in water, the equilibrium set up lies well to the left (see chapter 8):

$$CO_2(g) + H_2O(l) \rightleftharpoons HCO_3^-(aq) + H^+(aq) \qquad (1)$$

In the presence of sodium ions from the brine, the sparingly soluble sodium hydrogen carbonate might be expected to precipitate but the concentration of hydrogen carbonate ions (HCO_3^-) is insufficient for this to happen. However, by adding ammonia, the equilibrium in equation (1) is shifted to the right by removal of protons:

$$NH_3(g) + H^+(aq) \rightleftharpoons NH_4^+(aq)$$

and the concentration of hydrogen carbonate ions is increased sufficiently for sodium hydrogen carbonate to precipitate:

$$Na^+(aq) + HCO_3^-(aq) \rightleftharpoons Na^+HCO_3^-(s)$$

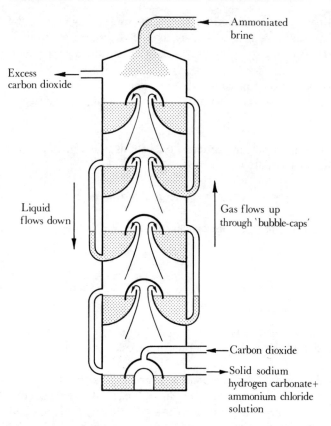

Figure 10.6   A Solvay tower

This precipitate is filtered off, washed, and heated to give anhydrous sodium carbonate, also called soda ash, the carbon dioxide evolved being re-admitted to the Solvay towers:

$$2Na^+HCO_3^-(s) \longrightarrow Na^+{}_2CO_3{}^{2-}(s) + CO_2(g) + H_2O(g)$$

The main supply of carbon dioxide for the Solvay towers is obtained by heating limestone:

$$CaCO_3(s) \longrightarrow CaO(s) + CO_2(g)$$

and the quicklime produced, after 'slaking' with water:

$$CaO(s) + H_2O(l) \longrightarrow Ca(OH)_2(s)$$

is heated with the ammonium chloride solution left after filtering off the sodium hydrogen carbonate, to regenerate ammonia gas:

$$NH_4^+(aq) + OH^-(s) \longrightarrow NH_3(g) + H_2O(l)$$

Thus, theoretically, no ammonia is used up but in practice a little is lost and must be replaced.

It can be seen that the whole process is very efficient as the only waste product is calcium chloride, all other by-products being used up.

A simplified reaction scheme is shown in Fig. 10.7.

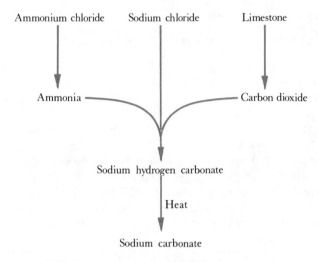

Figure 10.7   The Solvay process (simplified version)

Calcium and magnesium

These elements do not occur naturally in the free state but their compounds are widely distributed, notably in the form of the carbonates. Chalk, limestone, and marble are all forms of calcium carbonate, magnesite is magnesium carbonate, and dolomite is a mixed carbonate of calcium and magnesium.

Calcium metal is used on a relatively small scale but magnesium finds extensive and very large scale use, notably in lightweight alloys.

Both elements are in Group II (the **alkaline earth** Group) of the Periodic Table and so exist in their compounds as positive ions of the type M^{2+}. Being high in the activity series, both metals are reactive and not easily obtained by reduction of their compounds. Thus an electrolytic method must be used or alternatively a very powerful reducing agent such as silicon (in the form of ferrosilicon) which is used to reduce magnesium oxide at high temperature.

Both metals have low densities, and melting points much higher than those of the alkali metals. They are comparatively soft (although much harder than the alkali metals) and are malleable and ductile, magnesium being more so than calcium. They are silvery-white and lustrous when freshly cut but they tarnish on exposure to air, calcium doing so more rapidly than magnesium.

Experiment 10.5 *To investigate some properties of calcium and magnesium*

Carry out the following tests on suitable samples of the two metals:

(*a*) Appearance.

(*b*) The effect of heat. Hold a piece of magnesium ribbon with a pair of tongs and heat strongly, holding the tongs at arm's length and not looking directly at the sample. Examine the residue when cold and test it with moist Universal Indicator (pH) paper. Repeat this procedure, with the same precautions, using a piece of calcium.

(*c*) The reaction with water. Place a piece of magnesium into some cold water contained in a test-tube. If a gas is evolved, try to identify it and finally test the remaining liquid with Universal Indicator (pH) paper. Repeat this procedure with a piece of calcium. If there is no reaction, **your teacher** will use the apparatus shown in Fig. 10.8 to test whether there is a reaction with

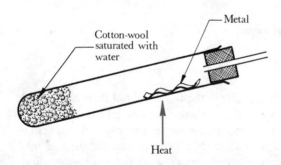

Figure 10.8   The effect of steam on a metal

steam. The cotton-wool at the bottom of the test-tube is saturated with water and the sample of metal is placed near the mouth of the tube. Heat the metal strongly. This will probably cause sufficient steam to be produced but if not, heat the cotton-wool occasionally in order to vaporize the water.

Tabulate your results and compare the reactivities of the two metals. How do these reactivities compare with those of the alkali metals? Would you expect the element barium to be more or less reactive than calcium? Explain your answer.

Experiment 10.6   *To test for compounds of calcium and magnesium*

Carry out the following tests on suitable compounds of the two metals:
(*a*) The flame test, as described in Experiment 10.2.
(*b*) To an aqueous solution of the compound add slowly, drop by drop, aqueous sodium hydroxide until present in excess.
(*c*) To a concentrated aqueous solution of the compound add dilute sulphuric acid.
(*d*) The Titan Yellow test. This is a special test for magnesium compounds. To an aqueous solution of the compound add a few drops of sodium hydroxide solution followed by a few drops of the Titan Yellow reagent.
(*e*) The Calcichrome test. This is a special test for calcium compounds. To the reagent add a few drops of sodium hydroxide solution. This should produce a deep blue colour. Add this blue liquid to an aqueous solution of the compound under test.

Tabulate your results and indicate those tests that could be used to distinguish between calcium and magnesium compounds.

Experiment 10.7   *To investigate the properties of some compounds of calcium and magnesium*

(*a*) Make a loop in a length of thick iron wire and support the wire in a clamp or on a tripod. Place a piece of marble on the loop and heat very strongly for at least fifteen minutes.
Place some powdered chalk in an ignition-tube and heat strongly for a few minutes, testing occasionally for the evolution of carbon dioxide. Repeat this part of the experiment with some powdered magnesium carbonate in a second ignition-tube.

What can you deduce about the relative stabilities of the carbonates of calcium and magnesium when heated?

(*b*) When cool, carefully place the residue left after heating the marble onto a watch-glass and add water slowly, drop by drop. Transfer the resulting powder to a small beaker, add more water, stir well and finally filter or centrifuge to obtain a clear filtrate. Test the filtrate with (*i*) Universal Indicator (pH) paper, and (*ii*) by passing carbon dioxide gas (from a generator) through it.

Does the marble undergo any change on heating? Explain your answer and attempt to write an equation if you think that there has been a reaction.

The powder obtained on first adding water to the residue is called **slaked lime** (calcium hydroxide, $Ca(OH)_2$) and the solution of it in water is called **lime-water**.

| Is slaked lime very soluble in water? As a result of test ($b(i)$), what is the nature of lime-water?

Carbon dioxide reacts with lime water to produce insoluble calcium carbonate ($CaCO_3$).

| Write an equation for this reaction.

(c) Repeat the whole procedure described in (b), using the residue left after heating the chalk.

| Compare the results obtained in (b) and (c) and explain any differences.

(d) Repeat the whole procedure described in (b), using the residue left after heating the magnesium carbonate.

| Compare the results obtained in (d) with those obtained in (c).
| Tabulate all your results, as shown in Table 10.4 to summarize the properties
| of the carbonates, oxides, and hydroxides of calcium and magnesium.

Table 10.4   Some of the properties of calcium and magnesium

Compound	Property	Magnesium	Calcium
Carbonate	Effect of heat		
	Solubility in water		
Oxide	Reaction with water		
Hydroxide	Solubility in water		
	pH of solution		
	Effect of carbon dioxide on solution		

Summary

The extraction of a metal involves the reduction of ions of the metal to atoms by acceptance of electrons:

$$M^{n+} + ne^- \longrightarrow M$$

A reactive metal such as sodium which is high in the activity series is normally more stable as the ion than as the atom. Thus the ion has little desire to accept electrons, which means that the metal is not easily obtained from its compounds. The ions of a less reactive metal such as iron will more readily accept electrons and thus the metal is easier to extract. Those metals very low in the activity series have such a strong attraction for their electrons that they are very stable as the metal and are sometimes found naturally in the 'free' or 'native' state, as for example is gold.

The cheapest reducing agent for use on an industrial scale is carbon, usually in the form of coke. It is possible, by considering the free energy changes for the reactions, to predict those metals that can be extracted by reduction of the oxide with carbon at an economically viable temperature. Such metals are low in the activity series. Where this method is unsuitable, electrolysis is normally used for extraction.

Many ores, as mined, have to be treated to remove worthless material in order to increase the metal content to a workable level. This treatment may vary from a simple washing to a chemical purification, depending on the nature of the ore and the subsequent extraction method to be used. In general, for electrolytic extraction, a very pure starting material is necessary as it is difficult and expensive to purify the metal, once obtained. With other reduction methods such particular care is neither necessary nor economic and in these cases the metal is usually refined after extraction.

Compounds of the alkali metals are very widespread in nature, one of the most important being sodium chloride which is used for the manufacture of a wide range of sodium compounds, including sodium hydroxide by the **mercury cathode** process and sodium carbonate by the **Solvay** process. Alkali metal compounds are readily detected by the flame test (see Table 10.5). This test is best carried out with the appropriate chloride (hence the use of concentrated hydrochloric acid), as these are more volatile than most other compounds and so give better flame colours.

Table 10.5   Flame colourations

Flame colour	Metal
Red	Lithium
Golden-yellow	Sodium
Lilac	Potassium
Brick-red	Calcium
Greenish-blue	Copper

Sodium hydroxide is a **deliquescent** solid, which means that it absorbs sufficient moisture from the air to dissolve itself, and has strongly alkaline properties. Thus it liberates ammonia from ammonium compounds, precipitates insoluble hydroxides of metals from their aqueous solutions and so on.

Sodium carbonate in the form of washing soda ($Na_2CO_3.10H_2O$) is **efflorescent** and *loses* water of crystallization to change from large, colourless crystals to a white powder which is the monohydrate ($Na_2CO_3.H_2O$). Sodium carbonate has alkaline properties and precipitates insoluble carbonates of some metals from their aqueous solutions.

Calcium and magnesium are not as reactive as the alkali metals. This is shown by the reaction with water which is much less vigorous, magnesium only reacting appreciably with steam. The reactivity of the alkaline earth elements (Group II) increases with increasing atomic number, as does that of the alkali metals (Group I). Calcium gives a flame of characteristic colour, unlike magnesium which is best detected by the Titan Yellow test, when a red colouration or precipitate is obtained. The compounds of calcium are generally more stable than those of magnesium, as is shown by magnesium carbonate which decomposes much more readily on heating than does calcium carbonate. This is to be expected from their relative positions in the Group.

Questions

1. In the extraction of metals a mineral has to be reduced in some way to produce the metal. Describe, with examples, the types of compounds which are reduced and the various methods of reduction available. What other factors must be considered if it is desired to make the process as cheap as possible?　　　　(LN)

2. Write an account of the methods by which common metals are extracted from their naturally occurring ores.　　　　(LN)

3. Solid sodium chloride does not conduct electricity. When melted, or when dissolved in water, the liquids are conductors. Explain these observations.
Describe the electrolytic manufacture of sodium hydroxide from sodium chloride. A simple diagram of the electrolytic cell should be given. Name **one** valuable by-product and give **one** large-scale use of this by-product.　　　　(O & C)

4. Give an account of the chemical reactions involved in the manufacture of sodium carbonate by the Solvay process. On what properties of sodium hydrogen carbonate does the success of this process depend?
Starting from solid sodium hydroxide, how would you prepare a solid sample of sodium hydrogen carbonate?　　　　(C)

11

Metallic elements and their compounds—II

Aluminium and lead

Aluminium does not occur in the free state but is the most abundant metal in the earth's crust, found mainly in clay and rocks in the form of silicates but also in large deposits of the oxide from which it is extracted, no economic method having yet been found for extraction from the silicates. Small deposits of metallic lead have been reported but these are insignificant and even lead compounds are not common, the most abundant being the sulphide.

Aluminium is used very extensively for a large variety of purposes such as alloys, cooking utensils, foil, paints, etc. Lead is also very important although used on a much smaller scale than aluminium. It finds use in alloys, accumulators, paints, radiation screening, etc.

Aluminium is in Group III of the Periodic Table and forms Al^{3+} ions, although in some compounds, notably the chloride, it forms covalent bonds. This is to be expected with elements in groups near the middle of the Periodic Table and many compounds of lead, which is in Group IV and has two oxidation states ($+2$ and $+4$), are covalent, particularly those containing the element in its higher oxidation state. The Pb^{2+} ion is common but the Pb^{4+} ion is very rare.

The positions of the two metals in the activity series (see Table 8.6) show that aluminium, which is near the top, can only be extracted by an electrolytic method (see Table 10.2), while lead, which is near the bottom, can easily be obtained by reduction of the oxide with carbon.

Whereas aluminium is light and has a relatively high melting point, lead is very dense and has a low melting point. Both metals are soft and very malleable when pure, but although aluminium is also very ductile, lead is not as it lacks the necessary strength. Aluminium is silvery-white, has a high lustre and does not tarnish under normal conditions due to a thin, very coherent layer of oxide which protects the metal from further attack by the air. Lead is grey and also lustrous when freshly cut but slowly tarnishes on exposure to air.

Experiment 11.1   *To investigate some properties of aluminium and lead*

Carry out the following tests on suitable samples of the metals:
(a) Appearance.
(b) The effect of heat. Place a small sample of each of the powdered metals in turn on a piece of asbestos paper held with tongs and heat strongly, holding the tongs at arm's length.
(c) The reaction with water. Add a piece of each metal in turn to some cold water contained in a test-tube. If there is no reaction, try the effect of steam on the metal, as described in Experiment 10.5(c) using the apparatus shown in Fig. 10.8.

Are your results consistent with the positions of the metals in the activity series given in Table 8.6?

(d) The surface of aluminium is protected by a layer of the oxide which may be removed by warming the sample of the metal (e.g., a milk-bottle top) with a solution of mercury(II) chloride. Remove the metal from the solution, wipe the surface clean and leave it exposed to the air for a few minutes. Repeat with another piece of aluminium, but after treatment to remove the oxide film, place the metal in some cold water. Identify any gas evolved.

Are these results more consistent with the position of aluminium in the activity series?

(e) The reaction with hydrochloric acid. Add a piece of each metal in turn to some concentrated hydrochloric acid in a test-tube and test any gas evolved. If there is no reaction, warm gently.
(f) The reaction with sodium hydroxide. Add a piece of each metal in turn to some concentrated sodium hydroxide solution in a test-tube, and test any gas evolved. If there is no reaction, warm gently.

Were the reactions of the two metals similar?

Metals that dissolve in both acid and alkali with the evolution of hydrogen are those that form amphoteric oxides. Aluminium forms the Al^{3+} ion and the $[Al(OH)_4]^-$ (aluminate) ion, while lead forms the Pb^{2+} ion and the $[Pb(OH)_4]^{2-}$ (plumbite) ion, when dissolved respectively in acid and alkali. (See chapter 8.)

Experiment 11.2   *Tests for aluminium and lead compounds*

Carry out the following tests on suitable compounds of the two metals:
(a) The flame test.
(b) To an aqueous solution of the compound add slowly, drop by drop, aqueous sodium hydroxide until present in excess.
(c) To an aqueous solution of the compound add dilute sulphuric acid.
(d) To an aqueous solution of the compound add potassium iodide solution.
(e) The Alizarin test. This is a special test for aluminium compounds. To an aqueous solution of the compound add a few drops of sodium hydroxide solution followed by the Alizarin reagent.

Tabulate your results and indicate those tests that could be used to identify respectively aluminium and lead in their compounds.

Experiment 11.3   *The amphoteric nature of the hydroxides*
                   of aluminium and lead

(a) Place 1 cm^3 of aqueous aluminium sulphate in each of two test-tubes and add to each just sufficient sodium hydroxide solution to give a precipitate of aluminium hydroxide. To the first tube add more sodium hydroxide solution, drop by drop, until the precipitate just disappears.

Write equations for the precipitation of aluminium hydroxide and for the formation of the aluminate ions which have been formed as the result of the reaction between aluminium hydroxide and excess hydroxide ions from the sodium hydroxide. Comment on the solubility of the aluminate ion.

To the precipitate of aluminium hydroxide in the second tube add dilute sulphuric acid, drop by drop, until the precipitate just disappears.

Why has the aluminium hydroxide dissolved this time? Write an equation to represent the reaction.

(b) Repeat the whole procedure using aqueous lead(II) nitrate instead of aqueous aluminium sulphate.

Were similar results obtained with the aluminium and the lead compounds? Explain in detail with equations, all that has happened in (b).

NB: As was shown in chapter 8, the *oxides* of aluminium and lead are also amphoteric.

The extraction of aluminium

The main ore of aluminium is **bauxite**, which is principally aluminium oxide together with silica and iron(III) oxide, both of which must be removed. This is conveniently done by using the amphoteric nature of aluminium oxide. The crude ore is treated with hot concentrated sodium hydroxide which dissolves the aluminium oxide as sodium aluminate:

$$Al_2O_3(s) + 3H_2O(l) + 2OH^-(aq) \longrightarrow 2[Al(OH)_4]^-(aq)$$

The impurities are filtered off and on cooling the solution of sodium aluminate and 'seeding' with a little aluminium hydroxide, the aluminate precipitates as aluminium hydroxide:

$$[Al(OH)_4]^-(aq) \longrightarrow Al(OH)_3(s) + OH^-(aq)$$

The precipitate of aluminium hydroxide is separated and then roasted to form very pure aluminium oxide:

$$2Al(OH)_3(s) \longrightarrow Al_2O_3(s) + 3H_2O(g)$$

Aluminium oxide has a very high melting point and is almost a non-conductor when molten. Thus it is dissolved in molten cryolite (sodium aluminium fluoride, $Na_3^+AlF_6^{3-}$) which, in addition to lowering the melting point of the aluminium oxide, is an electrolyte. This mixture (mainly cryolite with approximately 5 per cent of aluminium oxide) is electrolysed in large, shallow cells lined with graphite which acts as the cathode, and with graphite anodes (see Fig. 11.1). The working temperature of the cell, approximately 1000°C, is maintained by the very large current needed.

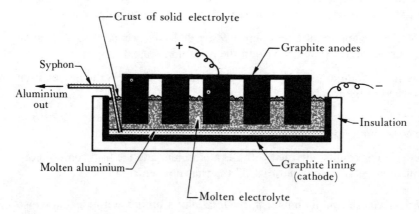

Figure 11.1   The extraction of aluminium

The reactions are complex and not fully understood but molten aluminium is formed at the cathode and is drawn off from time to time. Oxygen is given off at the anodes which, at the high temperature of the cell, burn away rapidly and must be constantly replaced.

Iron

Iron occurs in the free state only in meteorites, although the core of the earth may contain the element in large quantities. It is the second most abundant element in the earth's crust, occurring mainly as the sulphide, oxides and the carbonate. Iron is an essential component of haemoglobin, the red blood pigment responsible for distributing oxygen in the body.

Pure iron, though malleable and ductile, has little use as it is very soft and corrodes rapidly, but the presence of even very small quantities of other elements alters the properties remarkably, as will be discussed later.

Iron is placed in the first transition period in the Periodic Table and can exist as the Fe^{2+} ion and as the Fe^{3+} ion in its compounds. It appears fairly low down in the activity series and is readily obtained by reduction of the oxide with carbon (see Table 10.2).

The element is moderately dense and has a high melting point. It is white and lustrous but rusts more or less rapidly, depending on the conditions. In moist air, or in the presence of electrolytes, such as sea-water, rusting is rapid and the metal must be adequately protected, for example by paint or a covering of another metal such as zinc (galvanization).

Experiment 11.4   *Tests for iron compounds*

As the two oxidation states of iron are almost equally common, it is necessary to know tests for both forms.

(*a*) Add a little potassium hexacyanoferrate(III) solution to a few cubic centimetres of an aqueous solution of (*i*) an iron(II) compound and (*ii*) an iron(III) compound.

(*b*) Repeat these tests, but this time use a solution of ammonium thiocyanate to add to the solutions of the two iron compounds.

Which reagent is the more suitable for detection of (*i*) an iron(II) compound and (*ii*) an iron(III) compound? What other test have you met which would distinguish the two oxidation states?

The extraction of iron

The ore is normally roasted to remove moisture and to convert any other compounds of iron to the oxide. The roasted ore (three parts by weight) is

191

charged into the **blast furnace**, together with coke (two parts by weight) and limestone (one part by weight). The furnace (see Fig. 11.2) consists of a tall steel tower, lined with fire-brick. Solid materials are charged through a gas-tight 'double-bell hopper' at the top and pre-heated air is blown in through jets or 'tuyeres' near the bottom. Molten metal collects at the bottom of the furnace and the impurities, in the form of 'slag', float on top. Both are tapped off when necessary and the gases produced during the process pass out from the top of the furnace and are used for heating the in-coming air. The blast furnace is designed to run continuously for long periods, materials being added at the top and products being removed from the bottom in a definite cycle, the timing of which depends on the size of the furnace.

The coke burns in the blast of hot air to give carbon monoxide:

$$2C(s) + O_2(g) \longrightarrow 2CO(g)$$

This reaction is exothermic and the temperature reached in this part of the furnace is approximately 1600°C. The iron oxide is reduced to iron by the carbon monoxide in the middle and upper regions of the furnace:

$$Fe_2O_3(s) + 3CO(g) \longrightarrow 2Fe(s) + 3CO_2(g)$$

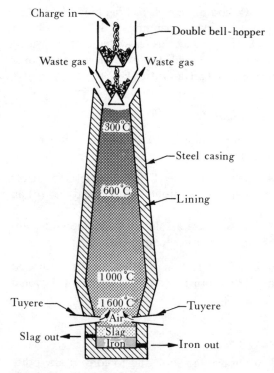

Figure 11.2   The blast furnace

The iron forms initially as a spongy mass but gradually melts as it moves down the furnace towards the hottest region.

The limestone in the charge decomposes at the temperature of the furnace to give calcium oxide (quicklime):

$$CaCO_3(s) \longrightarrow CaO(s) + CO_2(g)$$

The quicklime reacts with impurities in the ore, notably silica (sand) to form silicates, for example calcium silicate:

$$CaO(s) + SiO_2(s) \longrightarrow CaSiO_3(l)$$

These form a molten slag which, by floating on top of the molten iron, protects it from oxidation by the air-blast.

The metal produced in the blast furnace is called pig iron and contains up to 4 per cent of carbon and smaller quantities of other elements such as sulphur, phosphorus, silicon, and manganese. Pig iron is brittle and hard and although some is used for making castings, most is made into steel.

Cast iron is used for objects where no great strength is required, e.g., machinery bases, fire-grates, engine blocks, etc.

Steel

Steel is essentially the alloy of carbon with iron, but there are many different varieties with totally different properties, depending on the quantity of carbon present. In addition, other alloying elements produce a further range of steels, including stainless steel which contains chromium and nickel.

'Mild steel' contains up to 0·15 per cent of carbon and is used for many sorts of pressings, such as car bodies, because it is tough and malleable.

'Medium steel' contains up to about 1 per cent of carbon and becomes increasingly tough with increasing carbon content, but the malleability decreases. This type of steel is used for structural purposes in the form of girders and beams.

'Tool steel' has a high carbon content, up to about 1·5 per cent, and as a result is very hard. As the name suggests, it is used for tools but because of its hardness, it is very brittle and hence cannot be used for any purpose where strength is required.

In addition to the presence of carbon and other elements, the properties of a steel can be altered drastically by heat treatment. If the metal is heated to red heat, it may be cooled rapidly (quenching) to give a very hard but brittle product, or slowly (annealing) which produces a tough but comparatively soft metal. To remove brittleness, but often retain hardness, the steel is heated to a temperature of 200 to 300°C and allowed to cool slowly (tempering).

To convert pig iron to steel, the carbon content must be reduced to the required level and other undesirable impurities, notably sulphur, silicon, and phosphorus, must be removed. This is done by oxidation in either a **Bessemer converter**, **an open hearth furnace**, or an **electric arc furnace**.

The modern Bessemer converter is appreciably different to the original type. As shown in Fig. 11.3, it consists of a pear-shaped vessel, lined with a

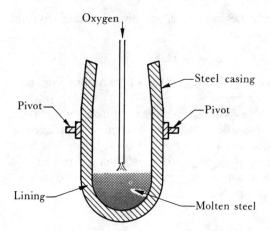

Figure 11.3   The Bessemer converter as used in the LD process

heat-resisting material, which can be rotated about a horizontal axis to allow pig iron, sometimes mixed with scrap metal, to be charged and the finished steel to be poured out. Oxidation is achieved by a blast of oxygen from an 'oxygen lance' directed onto the surface of the molten metal. This technique is known as the LD process and accounts for about 21 per cent of British-made steel. The unwanted oxides are given off if gaseous (e.g., carbon dioxide) but if solid (e.g., silica) they form a slag with the lining of the furnace or with slag-making material added to the charge.

The open hearth furnace (Fig. 11.4) consists of a large shallow trough or hearth lined with heat-resisting material. The charge is heated by gas or a petroleum product burning in pre-heated air. The hot gases leaving the furnace pass through special brick structures and when these are at a sufficiently high temperature, the direction of flow of the gases is reversed so that the hot brick heats the incoming air. The impurities are given off as gases or form a slag as in the Bessemer process. The air passing over the charge causes the oxidation to take place, but the process can be greatly speeded up by playing a blast of oxygen from a lance onto the surface of the molten metal, which has been heated in the normal way. When the steel is ready, the whole hearth is rotated for pouring. Approximately 55 per cent of British steel is made by this method.

In the electric arc process, which accounts for about 16 per cent of British

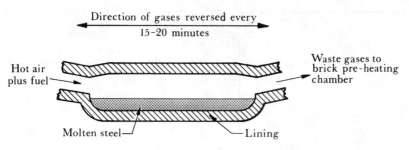

Figure 11.4 The open hearth furnace

steel, no oxidizing gases are used. Unwanted impurities are caused to enter the slag by the addition of suitable slag-making materials.

The most efficient method of using pig iron from the blast furnace is to charge it into the steel furnace while still molten. For this purpose, very large insulated containers, usually on a railway track, are used. If scrap metal is to be added to the charge, the heat from the molten pig iron will at least partially melt it.

The finished steel is cast into large 'ingots' which are normally allowed to solidify, but are then kept hot until ready for rolling or forging into their finished shape.

Experiment 11.5 *To detect the metals present in a coin by chromatography*

Dip the coin to be analysed very briefly into a small quantity of 'aqua regia' (3 volumes concentrated hydrochloric acid plus 1 volume concentrated nitric acid—**handle with extreme care**!) contained in a small beaker. This will remove a trace of the surface of the coin by converting the metals present to their soluble ions. Dilute the acid approximately twenty times with distilled water.

Mark out a piece of chromatography paper as shown in Fig. 11.5. Using the technique described in Experiment 8.10(*c*), apply to the respective origins spots of the coin solution and of 1 per cent solutions of the nitrates of silver, nickel, and copper(II), to serve as standards.

Develop the chromatogram with a solvent of propanone (85 volumes), distilled water (5 volumes) and concentrated hydrochloric acid (10 volumes). At the end of the run, remove the paper from the tank and dry it.

Locate the spots by dipping into or spraying with either water saturated with hydrogen sulphide and made alkaline with 0·880 ammonia solution, or a 0·1 per cent solution of dithio-oxamide in ethanol, followed by exposure to the fumes from 0·880 ammonia solution. Finally dry the paper and examine the spots produced.

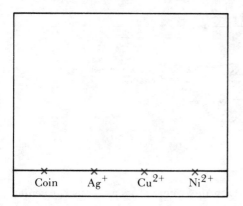

Figure 11.5 Marking out the chromatography paper

Determine which metals were present in the coin that you used, by comparison of the spots obtained from your sample with those from the standard solutions.

The modern coinage metals; copper, tin, zinc, and nickel

The traditional coinage metals are copper, silver, and gold, but owing to cost the latter two have been largely superseded (completely in the UK) by tin, zinc, and nickel. The compositions of modern British coins are shown in Table 11.1.

What characteristics must a coinage metal possess?
Why are copper, silver, and gold particularly suitable for this purpose?

Table 11.1 The composition of British coins

	Coin	Percentages by weight			
		Copper	Tin	Zinc	Nickel
Pre-decimal coins	½d; 1d	97	0·5	2·5	
	3d	79		20	1
	6d; 1/-; 2/-; 2/6	75			25
Decimal coins	½p; 1p; 2p	97	0·5	2·5	
	5p; 10p; 50p	75			25

Copper does occur in the free state but much more commonly as sulphides or the carbonate. Most copper ores contain only small proportions of copper and extraction is difficult for this reason. Simple reduction with carbon is not used because of the difficulty of obtaining a sufficiently pure oxide of copper. Instead, the sulphide ores are roasted in air to convert them to copper(I) sulphide which is decomposed by a prolonged blast of air to the metal, much of which is refined further by electrolysis.

Traces of metallic tin have been reported but the main source of the element is from the oxide, which is easily reduced by carbon.

Zinc does not occur in the free state and is found mainly as the sulphide and the carbonate. The ore, after concentration, is roasted to convert it to the oxide which is then reduced with powdered coke. The principle of this extraction was discussed in chapter 10, where it was pointed out that because of the low boiling point of zinc (907°C) the metal could be collected by condensing its vapour. An electrolytic method of extraction is also used, with an electrolyte of zinc sulphate obtained by dissolving the oxide in sulphuric acid.

Nickel does not occur in the free state and nickel ores, principally the sulphide, are low in nickel content. The sulphide is roasted to give the oxide which is then reduced with 'water-gas' (a mixture of carbon monoxide and hydrogen) to give the crude metal. Subsequent refining utilizes the fact that the metal combines with carbon monoxide at low temperatures to give a volatile compound called nickel carbonyl ($Ni(CO)_4$):

$$Ni(s) + 4CO(g) \rightleftharpoons Ni(CO)_4(g)$$

On heating to a higher temperature, the equilibrium is driven to the left and the carbonyl decomposes, depositing the metal in a pure form as pellets.

Copper finds very extensive and varied use apart from that in coins. There are many alloys, notably the brasses and bronzes, and it is used as electrical conductors, in plumbing, boiler-making, and roofing.

The most important use for tin is in coating steel to prevent corrosion and this 'tin-plate' is used very extensively for canning food and drinks. In addition, there are many important alloys of tin, such as solders and type metal.

Like tin, zinc is used on a very large scale for protecting iron or steel from corrosion by covering it with a thin coating of the metal; this is called 'galvanizing'. However, galvanized iron cannot be used for food containers as the zinc is poisonous. Another important use of zinc is in alloys, notably the brasses.

Nickel is used in a wide variety of alloys, such as stainless steel and nickel silver, and is normally plated onto iron or steel prior to chromium plating, as better adhesion of the chromium is obtained in this way. In a finely divided condition, nickel is very important as a catalyst, for example in the manufacture of margarine.

Copper, zinc, and nickel all appear in the first transition period and tin is in Group IV, above lead. Copper forms Cu^{2+} and Cu^+ ions but the former is much the more stable oxidation state. Both zinc and nickel form only one type of ion, Zn^{2+} and Ni^{2+} respectively, but nickel is known in other oxidation states, although these are rare. Tin, like lead, has two oxidation states ($+2$ and $+4$) but the only common ion is Sn^{2+}. Many tin compounds, in both oxidation states, are covalent.

Of the four metals, zinc is the highest in the activity series, the other three being low down and hence not very reactive under most conditions.

Copper has a characteristic pink to brown colour with a lustrous appearance. It is comparatively soft, is very malleable and ductile, and has a high density and melting point.

Tin is a soft, silvery-white, and lustrous metal. It is malleable but not ductile, with a low melting point and fairly high density.

Zinc is a moderately hard, bluish-white, lustrous metal which tarnishes to a dull grey colour. It is fairly dense, with low melting and boiling points and is brittle at room temperature but becomes malleable and ductile in the range 100 to 150°C.

Nickel is a hard, white, lustrous metal, which is very malleable and ductile. It has a high density and melting point.

Experiment 11.6 *To test for compounds of copper, tin, zinc, and nickel*

(*a*) Carry out a flame test on each of the compounds given.

(*b*) Carry out the following tests on aqueous solutions of compounds of the four metals. In each case use approximately 2 cm³ of the solution under test.

(*i*) Add sodium hydroxide solution slowly, drop by drop, until finally present in excess.

In each case, name the precipitate formed and write equations for the reactions concerned.

The precipitates obtained when using the tin and zinc compounds dissolved in excess alkali because the soluble stannite, $[Sn(OH)_4]^{2-}$, and zincate, $[Zn(OH)_4]^{2-}$, ions were respectively formed.

What can you deduce about the nature of tin and zinc as a result of these experiments? Write equations to show the reactions between the original precipitates and the excess alkali in these two cases.

(*ii*) Add ammonia solution slowly, drop by drop, until finally present in excess.

In each case, name the precipitate formed. Why did the precipitate obtained from the copper compound dissolve in excess ammonia solution? Which of the other metals formed complex ions with the ammonia solution?

(*c*) The following tests are specifically for the metals named.

(*i*) Tin. To a solution of the tin compound in a test-tube add a few drops of mercury(II) chloride solution. A white precipitate turning grey indicates the presence of a tin(II) compound.

The tin(II) ion has changed to tin(IV) and the mercury(II) ion has changed to mercury(I).

What type of reaction is this? Write an equation for it.

(*ii*) Nickel. To a solution of the nickel compound in a test-tube add 0·880 ammonia solution, followed by a few drops of dimethylglyoxime.

Describe tests that you would perform to distinguish the following pairs of metal ions:
(*a*) lead(II) and tin(II),
(*b*) copper(II) and nickel,
(*c*) magnesium and aluminium.

Summary

Aluminium, the most abundant metal in the earth's crust, is extracted by the electrolysis of bauxite, but the metal appears to be much more stable than its position in the activity series would suggest, due to a protective coating of the oxide. If this is removed, the metal becomes very reactive. Aluminium and lead, in the form of the metals, oxides, or hydroxides will dissolve in both acid and alkali to give complex ions. Neither aluminium nor lead gives a characteristic flame but the two ions can easily be distinguished by the Alizarin test for aluminium, which gives a red precipitate, and the general insolubility of lead compounds (see Table 11.2).

Iron, the second most abundant metal in the earth's crust, is extracted by reduction of the oxide with carbon in the **blast furnace**. The **pig iron** produced is converted to **steel**, an alloy of iron and carbon, in either the **open hearth furnace**, the **Bessemer converter**, or the **electric arc furnace**. The properties of the steel vary according to (*a*) the carbon content, (*b*) the heat treatment, and (*c*) the presence of other alloying elements.

Chromatography can be used to detect very small quantities of metal ions by suitable development and location techniques.

The metals present in modern British coins are copper, tin, zinc, and nickel. Tin and zinc are amphoteric and copper, zinc, and nickel all form soluble complex ions with ammonia, called **ammines**. The tin(II) ion is a powerful reducing agent.

Tables 11.2, 11.3, 11.4, 11.5, and 11.6 summarize general information on the metals studied in chapters 10 and 11.

Table 11.2 Solubilities in water of some common salts
(all are soluble unless shown otherwise)

Cation	Anions			
	Chloride	Nitrate	Sulphate	Carbonate
Lithium				O
Potassium				
Sodium				
Calcium			O	×
Magnesium				×
Aluminium				Does not exist
Zinc				×
Iron(II)				×
Nickel				×
Tin(II)				Does not exist
Lead(II)	×		×	×
Copper(II)				×

Key: × = insoluble; O = sparingly soluble.

Table 11.3 Insoluble hydroxides and carbonates

Cation	Colour	
	Hydroxide	Carbonate
Calcium	White	White
Magnesium	White	White
Aluminium	*Colourless	
Zinc	*White	White
Iron(II)	Green	Brown
Iron(III)	Brown	
Nickel	Green	Pale green
Tin(II)	*White	
Lead(II)	*White	White
Copper(II)	Blue-green	Green

* amphoteric.
Those carbonates left blank do not exist.

Table 11.4 The effect of heat on some metal compounds

Cation	Anions				
	Chloride	Nitrate	Sulphate	Carbonate	Hydroxide
Potassium		Nitrite + Oxygen			
Sodium					
Calcium		Oxide	Oxide	Oxide	Oxide
Magnesium		+	+	+	+
Zinc		Nitrogen	Sulphur	Carbon	Water
Iron(II)		dioxide	trioxide	dioxide	
Lead(II)		+			
Copper(II)		Oxygen			

 not decomposed by heat.

Notes: (*a*) The sulphate and carbonate of calcium only decompose at high temperature.

(*b*) Iron(II) compounds that do decompose leave a residue of *iron(III) oxide*, as iron(II) oxide is not stable in air.

(*c*) Some sulphates give off sulphur dioxide as well as the trioxide.

Table 11.5   The main commercial sources and physical properties of some important metals

Metal	Main commercial source	Appearance of metal	Density (in $g\ cm^{-3}$)	Melting point (in°C)
Lithium	Petalite, $(Li, Na)AlSi_4O_{10}$	Silvery, tarnishing rapidly in air	0·53	180
Potassium	Carnallite, $KCl.MgCl_2.6H_2O$		0·86	63·5
Sodium	Brine, NaCl(aq)		0·97	97·8
Calcium	Calcium chloride, $CaCl_2$	Silvery-white, lustrous, tarnishing in air	1·55	851
Magnesium	Sea-water, $MgCl_2$(aq)		1·74	650
Aluminium	Bauxite, $Al_2O_3.xH_2O$	Silvery-white, lustrous	2·70	660
Zinc	Blende, ZnS	Bluish-white, lustrous, tarnishing in air	7·13	419
Iron	Haematite, Fe_2O_3 Siderite, $FeCO_3$	White, lustrous	7·86	1530
Nickel	Pentlandite, $(Ni, Fe)_9S_8$	White, lustrous	8·90	1455
Tin	Cassiterite, SnO_2	Silvery-white, lustrous	7·28	232
Lead	Galena, PbS	Grey, lustrous, tarnishing in air	11·30	327
Copper	Chalcopyrite, $CuFeS_2$	Pink, lustrous, tarnishing in air	8·94	1083

All the pure metals are soft, malleable, and ductile, with the exception of (a) tin and lead which are soft and malleable but not ductile, (b) nickel which is hard, malleable, and ductile and (c) zinc which at room temperature is moderately hard and brittle but in the range 100 to 150°C becomes malleable and ductile.

Table 11.6 The activity series and chemical properties

Metal	Displacement of metal from aqueous solution	Ease of reduction of oxide	Action on cold water	Action on steam	Action on hydrochloric acid
Potassium	(Hydrogen displaced from water present)		Hydrogen displaced		
Sodium				Hydrogen displaced	
Calcium					
Magnesium					
Aluminium	Order of displacement	Increases	No reaction		Hydrogen displaced
Zinc					
Iron					
Tin				No reaction	
Lead					
Copper					No reaction

NB: The reactions of the metals with respectively chlorine and oxygen are consistent with their positions in the series, potassium being the most reactive and copper the least. (See chapters 9, 10, 11, 14, and 15.)

Questions

1. (*a*) Name the raw materials used in the manufacture of iron and give an account of the chemical reactions taking place in the blast furnace. (*No* diagram is required.)

(*b*) What elements, other than iron, are present in (*i*) mild steel, (*ii*) stainless steel?

(*c*) For **each** of **two** of the following alloys, (*i*) name the metals present in the alloy, and (*ii*) give **one** reason why the alloy is used in preference to the pure metals it contains.

Brass, solder, type-metal, duralumin. (C)

2. Outline the extraction of aluminium from *purified* bauxite. Give **two** important uses of this metal.

From the position of aluminium in the activity series, what would you expect its reaction to be with (*a*) hydrochloric acid, and (*b*) oxygen?

Describe **two** tests which would enable you to distinguish between crystals of sodium sulphate and crystals of aluminium sulphate. (O & C)

3. (*a*) Describe the essential steps by which you would convert: **either** a copper(II) salt to a sample of a copper(I) compound, **or** metallic iron to a sample of an iron(II) salt.

(*b*) Copper and iron are both called 'Transition Metals'. Indicate two or three ways in which the properties of these two metals and their compounds resemble each other.

(c) When dry ammonia gas was passed over 16·0 g of anhydrous copper(II) sulphate, 24·5 g of a violet solid was produced which was thought to have the formula $CuSO_4.5NH_3$. Do you think that the experimental observations are consistent with this formula for the violet solid?   (L)

4. Some metals form compounds in more than one 'oxidation state'; e.g., copper forms both copper(I) and copper(II) compounds. Select another metal known to you which forms compounds in two oxidation states, and discuss the methods by which:
    (a) the metal may be converted into compounds of the lower oxidation state;
    (b) compounds in the lower oxidation state may be converted into compounds in the higher oxidation state;
    (c) the changes in (a) and (b) may be reversed.   (LN)

5. Some metals are used as the pure element, but often an alloy of two or more metals is to be preferred. Describe some common alloys and discuss how alloying alters the properties and usefulness of the parent metals.   (LN)

6. Draw a diagram to show how you would dry hydrogen gas and use it to reduce a metallic oxide. State the reason for one safety precaution necessary in this experiment.
    Which of the following oxides can be reduced by hydrogen: calcium oxide, copper(II) oxide, lead(II) oxide, magnesium oxide, zinc oxide?
    Choosing **one** of these oxides which can be reduced,

    (a) give the equation for the reaction,
    (b) state what you would see when the reduction is complete,
    (c) give **one** test to confirm that the solid product is a metal.

    How is the ease of reduction of a metallic oxide related to the method chosen for the extraction of a metal from its ore? Illustrate your answer by briefly referring to the extraction of iron and aluminium.   (JMB)

Non-metallic elements and their compounds—I

Group IV—carbon and silicon

Experiment 12.1   *The action of heat on substances of plant and animal origin*

On pieces of asbestos paper, heat small samples of each of the substances listed below. Note particularly the appearance of the final product.
Starch, sugar (sucrose), rice, cheese, wood, meat, hair, nail clippings.

Experiment 12.2   *The effect of heating some substances of plant and animal origin with dry copper(II) oxide*

Mix approximately equal masses of copper(II) oxide and one of the substances listed for use in Experiment 12.1. Place the mixture in an ignition-tube and heat strongly. Remove some of the gas in the part of the tube above the mixture and test it with lime-water, as shown in Fig. 12.1.

What conclusion can be reached from the results of these experiments?

The carbon formed in Experiment 12.1 is known as **graphite**. Carbon can also exist as **diamond**, formed in nature by the enormous pressure which occurs in parts of the earth's crust. Diamond is unstable and undergoes a very slow but steady conversion to graphite. These two forms of carbon consist of nothing other than carbon atoms, the difference between them being in the way the atoms are arranged. X-ray diffraction studies (see chapter 4) have shown that in graphite the atoms are arranged in hexagonal planes, whilst in diamond each carbon atom is at the centre of a regular tetrahedron which has four more carbon atoms at its corners (see Fig. 12.2). When an element can exist in more than one physical form it is said to exhibit **allotropy**. Diamond and graphite are the **allotropes** of carbon.

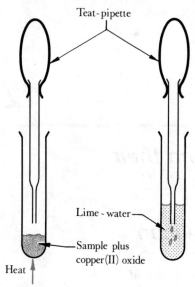

Teat-pipette

Lime - water

Sample plus
copper(II) oxide

Heat

Figure 12.1   The lime-water test in Experiment 12.2

Experiment 12.3   *Making models of the crystal structures of graphite and diamond*

(*a*) Graphite. Make a jig by drawing a circle the diameter of the spheres on a piece of cardboard. Divide the radius into the circumference (it fits exactly six times) and cut out the disc enclosed by the line. Mark thirteen of the polystyrene balls at 120° around their equators using every other one of the radius markings on the jig. Assemble into three rings by joining the spheres in the positions marked using short lengths of pipe-cleaner. You will notice that there are only three bonds between each atom and the others. The extra electron is donated to a general 'plasma' above and below the plane of the atoms. This 'plasma' keeps the different layers apart because of the mutual repulsion of like charges and the similarity to metallic structures accounts for the good electrical conducting properties of graphite.

(*b*) Diamond. Make a jig by drawing a circle 0·93 times the diameter of the spheres on a piece of cardboard. Mark off the circumference into six, as previously, and cut out the disc. Mark fourteen spheres by sitting them in the jig so that the edge of the cardboard is parallel to the equator of the sphere and make three marks at 120° intervals on this 'line of latitude'. The fourth position for the tetrahedron is at the 'north pole'. Join the spheres with short lengths of pipe-cleaner. As in this case four bonds are formed between each atom and its nearest neighbours, the structure is not a good electrical conductor.

Would you expect diamond or graphite to have the higher density? Check your answer using a data book. Diamond is the second hardest substance known while graphite is used as a lubricant; can you suggest any explanation for this difference? See if you can find out what is the hardest substance known, and suggest the kind of structure it might have.

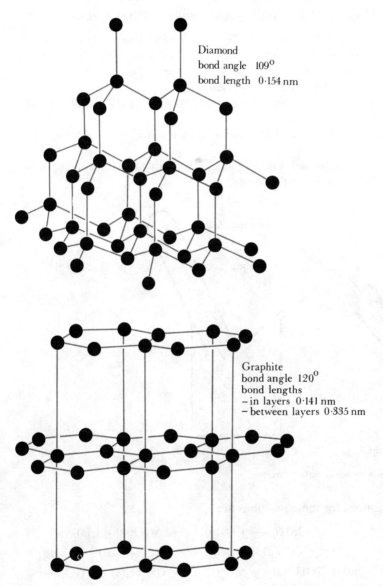

Diamond
bond angle 109°
bond length 0·154 nm

Graphite
bond angle 120°
bond lengths
– in layers 0·141 nm
– between layers 0·335 nm

Figure 12.2   The structure of carbon

CHEMISTRY BY EXPERIMENT AND UNDERSTANDING

Experiment 12.4 *The laboratory preparation of carbon dioxide*

The most convenient reaction is that between marble (calcium carbonate) and hydrochloric acid:

$$CaCO_3(s) + 2H^+(aq) \longrightarrow Ca^{2+}(aq) + CO_2(g) + H_2O(l)$$

Using the apparatus shown in Fig. 12.3 collect three tubes of carbon dioxide for tests (*a*) to (*c*) and then use gas directly from the generator for test (*d*).

(*a*) Plunge a lighted splint into the gas.

(*b*) Plunge a piece of burning magnesium attached to the end of a spatula into the gas.

(*c*) Add some Universal Indicator (pH) solution to the tube of gas and shake.

(*d*) Pass the gas through a tube of lime-water until no further change takes place and then boil the final mixture.

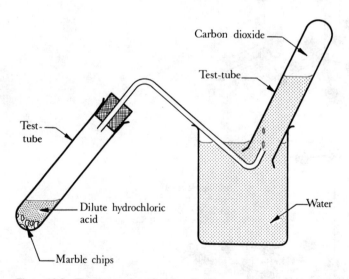

Figure 12.3 **The preparation of carbon dioxide**

The equations for these reactions are:

(*b*) $2Mg(s) + CO_2(g) \longrightarrow 2MgO(s) + C(s)$

(*c*) $CO_2(g) + H_2O(l) \rightleftharpoons HCO_3^-(aq) + H^+(aq)$

(*d*) $\underbrace{Ca^{2+}(aq) + 2OH^-(aq)}_{\text{Lime-water}} + CO_2(g) \longrightarrow CaCO_3(s) + H_2O(l)$

then:

$$CaCO_3(s) + CO_2(g) + H_2O(l) \rightleftharpoons Ca^{2+}(aq) + 2HCO_3^-(aq)$$

Find out some of the industrial uses of carbon dioxide paying particular attention to those physical and chemical properties of the gas that make it suitable for each use.

Experiment 12.5 *The preparation and properties of carbon monoxide*

Carbon dioxide can be reduced to carbon monoxide by the action of red-hot charcoal, using the apparatus shown in Fig. 12.4:

$$C(s) + CO_2(g) \longrightarrow 2CO(g)$$

This preparation must be carried out by the teacher as carbon monoxide is extremely poisonous.

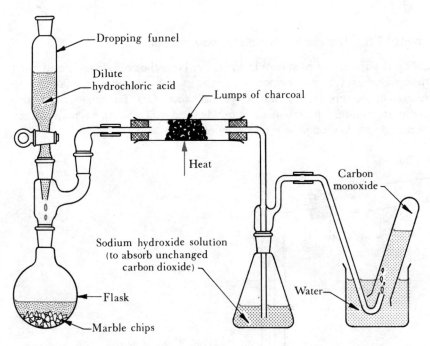

Figure 12.4   The preparation of carbon monoxide

Each group will be provided with four tubes of gas for testing:

(*a*) Apply a lighted splint to the mouth of the tube and shake any product with a little lime-water.

209

(b) Investigate the effect of burning magnesium on a sample of gas.
(c) Find out the effect of the gas on Universal Indicator (pH) solution.
(d) See what effect the gas has on lime-water.

Construct equations for any reactions that take place. Find out some of the industrial uses of carbon monoxide and correlate these with the physical and chemical properties of the gas.

Coal

An important source of carbon compounds is coal. Apart from coal gas (which is steadily being superseded in the UK as a source of domestic energy by North Sea gas and other natural gases), coal tar can be separated and processed to yield products as diverse as fertilizer and dyestuffs, plastics and drugs.

Experiment 12.6   *The destructive distillation of coal*

Set up the apparatus as shown in Fig. 12.5. Heat the coal strongly and burn the coal gas at X, as it is formed. When the reaction is complete, examine the residue in the tube (coke) and the distillate (coal tar). The coal tar is a very complex mixture of carbon compounds, and compounds of many other elements are also found in it to a smaller extent.

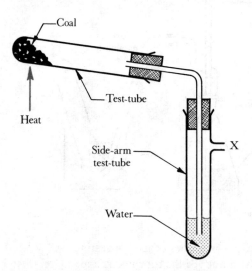

Figure 12.5   The destructive distillation of coal

Petroleum oil

The second source of carbon compounds we shall consider is petroleum oil. This consists largely of compounds that contain only carbon and hydrogen, the **hydrocarbons**. The simplest of these is the gas methane, the main constituent of **natural** (or **North Sea**) **gas**, whose structure was studied in chapter 4.

$$
\begin{array}{c}
H \\
| \\
H-C-H \\
| \\
H
\end{array}
$$

If two carbon atoms are joined together and the remaining bonds joined to hydrogen atoms, the result is ethane:

$$
\begin{array}{c}
H \quad H \\
| \quad | \\
H-C-C-H \\
| \quad | \\
H \quad H
\end{array}
$$

It is important to appreciate that although we represent this by a 'squashed' formula on paper, in three dimensions ethane has the shape of two tetrahedra joined at a corner. If three carbon atoms are joined with the remaining bonds going to hydrogen atoms the result is propane, and with four carbon atoms butane. There are two ways in which the four carbon atoms in butane can be joined, giving rise to two different substances that have the same molecular formula, C_4H_{10}, but different chemical and physical properties. Such compounds are known as **isomers**.

$$
\begin{array}{c}
H \quad H \quad H \quad H \\
| \quad | \quad | \quad | \\
H-C-C-C-C-H \\
| \quad | \quad | \quad | \\
H \quad H \quad H \quad H \\
\text{Butane}
\end{array}
\qquad
\begin{array}{c}
H \quad H \quad H \\
| \quad | \quad | \\
H-C-C-C-H \\
| \quad | \quad | \\
H \quad CH_3 H \\
\text{2-methyl propane}
\end{array}
$$

2-methyl propane is so named because there is a methyl group, CH_3- (from methane), attached to the *second* carbon atom in a propane molecule. Methane, ethane, propane, and butane can all be represented by the general formula C_nH_{2n+2}, where n equals 1, 2, 3, and 4 respectively. Such a series of compounds is called an **homologous series**. This particular series is named the **alkanes**. The early members of this series, having relatively light molecules, are gases at room temperature but as the value of n increases they become liquids and eventually solids.

Write the formulae and give names to all the isomers of hexane (where $n = 6$).

Another homologous series of hydrocarbons is known that has the general formula C_nH_{2n}. This series is named the **alkenes** and the first two members are the gases ethene (sometimes called ethylene) and propene (sometimes called propylene).

Ethene   Propene

A third series, known as the **arenes** are derivatives of benzene and contain a ring of six carbon atoms.

Benzene   Toluene

As we shall see later, compounds containing such carbon-to-carbon double bonds show a particular type of chemical behaviour. This behaviour is not shown by the arenes and therefore it is preferred to show the extra bonds not between particular carbon atoms in the molecules (as above) but shared between all six carbon-carbon linkages:

Benzene   Toluene

Crude oil is a complicated mixture of hydrocarbons belonging to all three series. If we are to make use of these compounds it is first necessary to separate them. The technique used for doing this is **fractional distillation**.

Experiment 12.7   *The fractionation of crude oil*

Using the apparatus shown in Fig. 12.6, carry out fractional distillation of the crude oil, collecting the distillate in four fractions:

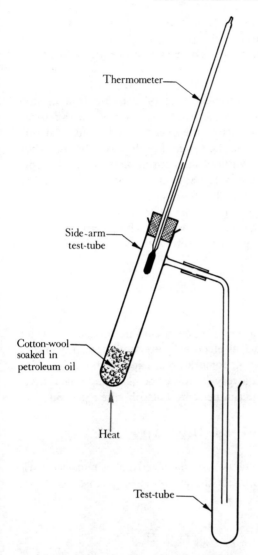

Figure 12.6   The fractionation of crude petroleum oil

(a) That distilling between room temperature and 70°C.
(b) That distilling between 70°C and 120°C.
(c) That distilling between 120°C and 170°C.
(d) That distilling between 170°C and 220°C.

Compare each of the fractions in terms of:
(a) Colour.

(b) Viscosity. Pour each sample in turn over an upturned crystallizing dish standing on an asbestos mat.

(c) Inflammability. Try to ignite each sample in turn as it flows over the crystallizing dish during test (b).

On an industrial scale, fractionation of crude oil is carried out in huge fractionating towers as illustrated on the front inside cover. In this tower all but the very heaviest components of the crude oil are converted into vapour by heating and thus travel up the tower. The dissolved hydrocarbon gases reach the top of the tower without condensing and the liquids condense at different heights up the tower due to differences in their boiling points because of their varying molecular masses.

Coal, natural gas, and oil are formed in the earth by the degradation of dead plant and animal matter. The compounds of which they are composed, therefore, owe their origin to the photosynthetic activities of plants.

Photosynthesis

This is the process by which green plants convert carbon dioxide and water into oxygen and simple sugars, such as glucose, by utilizing the energy in sunlight. It is essentially the reverse of, for example, paper burning in which energy is liberated. The process is a very complex one involving many stages of reaction but the overall change can be represented by the equation:

$$6CO_2(g) + 6H_2O(l) \longrightarrow C_6H_{12}O_6(aq) + 6O_2(g)$$

Glucose is one of several simple sugars known collectively as **monosaccharides**. The arrangements of the atoms in the molecule of glucose and in its isomer fructose are:

Glucose

Fructose

You will no doubt be relieved to know that you would not be expected to remember these formulae at this level! We will represent them in future by the symbol:

The **disaccharide** sucrose (cane sugar) is formed when a molecule of glucose and one of fructose join together, with the elimination of a molecule of water. Another important disaccharide, maltose, is made when two glucose molecules join in a similar fashion. When many monosaccharide molecules join together in this way to form a long chain compound, the result is a **polysaccharide** such as starch.

Experiment 12.8 Comparing the reactions of glucose, fructose, maltose, sucrose, and starch

(*a*) Boil a little of each substance in turn with some Fehling's solution (made by mixing equal volumes of Fehling's solutions I and II).

Fehling's solution contains copper(II) ions. If a red (or orange) precipitate forms this is due to the formation of copper(I) oxide:

$$Cu^{2+}(aq) \longrightarrow Cu_2O(s)$$

Checking the oxidation state change for copper shows this to be a reduction reaction. Sugars bringing about this change are known as **reducing sugars**.

(*b*) Add some of each to separate portions of iodine solution.

(*c*) Boil some sucrose with dilute sulphuric acid for two minutes. Cool the mixture and add portions of solid anhydrous sodium carbonate until no further effervescence occurs. Carry out Fehling's test on the product.

On the Venn diagram outlined in Fig. 12.7, classify glucose, fructose, maltose, and sucrose.

Experiment 12.9 Can starch be broken down into anything simpler?

The breakdown of polysaccharides into mono- and disaccharides is one of the important changes that take place in our food as it passes through our digestive system. It is acted upon by enzymes such as ptyalin in saliva and amylase in the stomach to bring about this change.

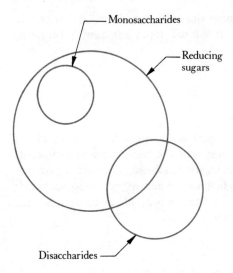

Figure 12.7

(*a*) Fill a test-tube to about 1 cm depth with saliva and add about 4 cm³ of starch solution. Leave the mixture to stand for at least fifteen minutes, then take a portion of it and carry out a Fehling's test.

(*b*) Add a few drops of concentrated hydrochloric acid to about 5 cm³ of starch solution in a small beaker, and boil for fifteen minutes taking care not to lose much of the beaker's contents by splashing. As water is boiled away,

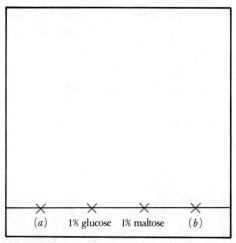

(*a*) Starch treated with saliva
(*b*) Starch treated with acid

Figure 12.8   Chromatography of starch-breakdown products

keep the volume reasonably constant by the addition of fresh distilled water. When this stage is completed, boil away about two-thirds of the water to concentrate the solution. Neutralize the mixture by adding solid, anhydrous sodium carbonate until no further effervescence occurs. Carry out a Fehling's test on a portion of the mixture.

Both of these processes should have brought about the breakdown of the starch:

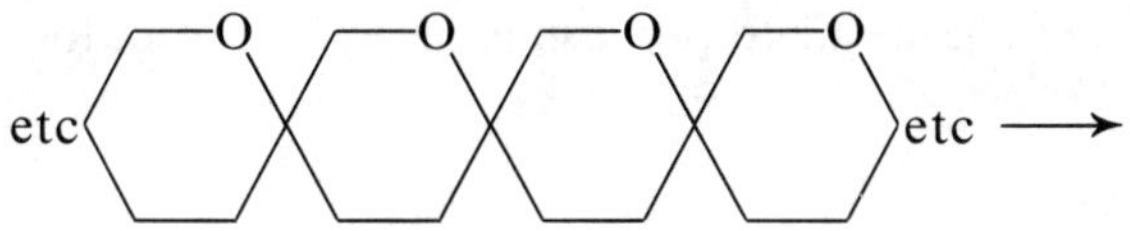

Starch

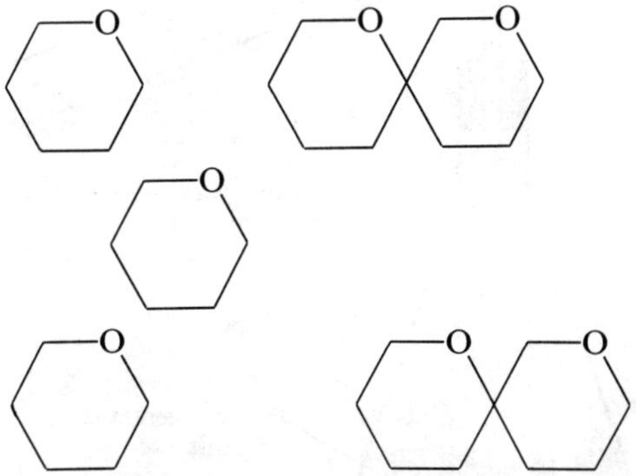

Monosaccharides   Disaccharides

We can investigate the products of each of these breakdowns further using paper chromatography. Mark out a sheet of chromatography paper as illustrated in Fig. 12.8 and apply spots of the various solutions shown, as described for Experiment 8.10(c).

Develop the chromatogram in a solvent of propan-2-ol (60 volumes), glacial ethanoic acid (20 volumes), and distilled water (20 volumes). Locate the colourless spots by spraying with or dipping in the following locating agent, which must be mixed immediately prior to use:

2% solution of phenylamine (aniline) in propanone (5 volumes)
2% solution of diphenylamine in propanone (5 volumes)
85% aqueous orthophosphoric acid (1 volume).

Hang the paper to dry in air and then heat it in an oven at 100°C for two or three minutes. As the spots quickly fade, they should be ringed round in pencil immediately after they are formed.

Compare the location of the spots above the origins for mixtures from (a) and (b) with those above the standards, and hence identify the sugars in each.

Experiment 12.10   *Breaking down glucose to ethanol*
                   by fermentation

The apparatus is shown in Fig. 12.9 and the fermentation mixture is made up as follows. Dissolve 12 g of glucose in 50 cm^3 of boiling water whilst stirring well. Add a pinch of each of ammonium phosphate and potassium nitrate and dilute to about 200 cm^3. Then add about 10 g of yeast made into a paste with a little water, fit the air-trap and stand in a warm place for about one week.

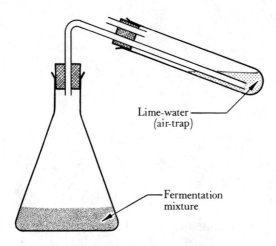

Lime-water
(air-trap)

Fermentation
mixture

Figure 12.9   The fermentation of glucose

The reaction is brought about by enzymes present in the yeast:

$$C_6H_{12}O_6(aq) \longrightarrow 2C_2H_5OH(aq) + 2CO_2(g)$$

Experiment 12.11   *Making a solution of alcohol in water*
                   stronger in alcohol

Decant and filter the mixture obtained by fermentation in the previous experiment. Place the filtrate in the distillation apparatus shown in Fig. 12.10 and collect four fractions each of about 40 cm^3.

The fermentation mixture contains about 15 per cent of ethanol. Ethanol boils at 79°C and has a density of 0·79 g cm^{-3}. What trend in the composition of the four fractions would this data lead you to expect?

Test your predictions by comparing the inflammability of each fraction and if time is available find the density of each.

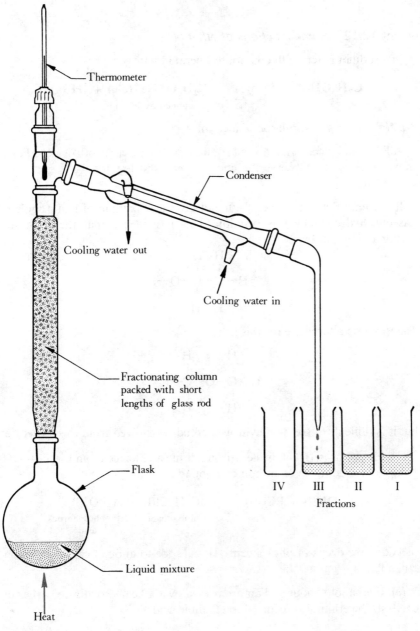

Figure 12.10   Fractional distillation

It is not possible to completely separate a mixture of ethanol and water by fractionation alone.

Experiment 12.12   *Some reactions of ethanol*

(*a*) Sodium reacts with ethanol to liberate hydrogen:

$$C_2H_5OH(l) + Na(s) \longrightarrow C_2H_5O^-Na^+(alc) + \tfrac{1}{2}H_2(g)$$
Sodium ethoxide

NB: (alc) represents solution in alcohol.

Add a small piece of freshly cut sodium to about 1 cm depth of *dry* ethanol in a *dry* test-tube. Observe the effervescence and test for the evolution of hydrogen.

It is found that one mole of ethanol gives a maximum of half a mole of gaseous hydrogen by this reaction. This is evidence that the structural formula of ethanol is:

$$\begin{array}{ccccc} & H & & H & \\ & | & & | & \\ H - & C & - & C & - O - H \\ & | & & | & \\ & H & & H & \end{array}$$

The isomeric alternative for this is:

$$\begin{array}{ccccc} & H & & H & \\ & | & & | & \\ H - & C & - O - & C & - H \\ & | & & | & \\ & H & & H & \end{array}$$

but it is difficult to see how hydrogen could be evolved from this structure.

(*b*) Phosphorus(III) chloride will substitute a chlorine atom for an —OH group in a wide range of carbon compounds:

$$3C_2H_5OH(l) + PCl_3(l) \longrightarrow 3C_2H_5Cl(l) + H_3PO_3(l)$$
Chloroethane   Orthophosphorous
acid

Add a few drops of phosphorus(III) chloride to about 1 cm depth of *dry* ethanol in a *dry* test-tube.

(*c*) If ethanol vapour and air are passed over a heated platinized asbestos catalyst, the ethanol is oxidized to ethanoic acid:

$$C_2H_5OH(g) + O_2(g) \longrightarrow CH_3COOH(g) + H_2O(g)$$

Carry out the reaction using the apparatus shown in Fig. 12.11. Divide the condensed product into three portions and test these as follows:

(*i*) Observe the effect of Universal Indicator (pH) paper.
(*ii*) Observe the effect of solid magnesium carbonate.
(*iii*) Observe the effect of a small piece of clean magnesium ribbon.

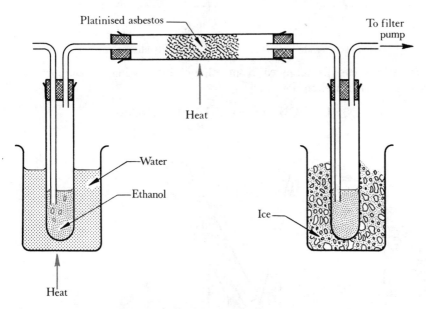

Figure 12.11   The oxidation of ethanol to ethanoic acid

Compare the results of these tests with those obtained using an equivolume mixture of ethanol and water.

The oxidation of ethanol to ethanoic acid is also brought about by the enzymes secreted by 'Bacterium Aceti' when wine is turned into vinegar.

(*d*) Ethanoic acid and ethanol react together to form the ester ethyl ethanoate:

$$CH_3COOH(l) + C_2H_5OH(l) \rightleftharpoons CH_3COOC_2H_5(l) + H_2O(l)$$

The proportion of ester in the equilibrium mixture can be increased by adding concentrated sulphuric acid to remove the water.

Warm together ten drops each of glacial ethanoic acid and ethanol with two drops of concentrated sulphuric acid for two or three minutes. Cool the mixture and pour into a beaker containing a little sodium carbonate solution. This will neutralize the excess acid and allow the characteristic smell of the ethyl ethanoate to be detected.

The structures of ethanoic acid and ethyl ethanoate are:

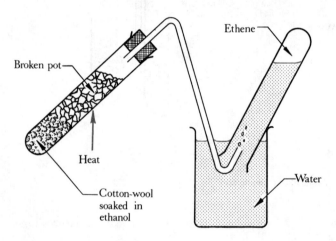

Ethanoic acid   Ethyl ethanoate

(e) Water can be removed from ethanol by passing its vapour over strongly heated broken pot:

$$C_2H_5OH(g) \longrightarrow C_2H_4(g) + H_2O(g)$$
$$\text{Ethene}$$

Ethene

Broken pot

Heat

Cotton-wool
soaked in
ethanol

Water

Figure 12.12 The dehydration of ethanol

Set up the apparatus as shown in Fig. 12.12 and heat the part of the tube containing the broken pot. The ethanol will be heated by conduction and slowly vaporizes. Collect at least two tubes of ethene and test them as follows:

(i) Apply a lighted splint to the mouth of the tube.

(ii) Add some bromine-water (an aqueous solution of bromine) to the gas and shake the tube.

The reaction with bromine water is:

$$\underset{\substack{\text{(colourless)}}}{\overset{\displaystyle H}{\underset{\displaystyle H}{}}C=C\overset{\displaystyle H}{\underset{\displaystyle H}{}}} + \underset{\substack{\text{(reddish} \\ \text{--brown)}}}{Br_2} \longrightarrow \underset{\substack{\text{(colourless)}}}{H-\overset{\displaystyle H}{\underset{\displaystyle Br}{C}}-\overset{\displaystyle H}{\underset{\displaystyle Br}{C}}-H}$$

The decolourization of bromine water by compounds containing carbon-to-carbon double bonds is a useful test for such compounds. Substances giving positive results for this test are said to be **unsaturated**.

Industrial production of carbon compounds

The graph shown in Fig. 12.13 shows clearly how an increasing quantity of carbon compounds is being obtained from oil while the supplies from coal and fermentation are tending to decline. Ethene, for example, is nowadays a most important industrial raw material and as such is required in considerable quantities. It would obviously not be practicable to go through the sequence:

$$starch \rightarrow glucose \rightarrow ethanol \rightarrow ethene$$

to obtain these bulk supplies. Ethene is present to a very limited extent in petroleum oil. Fortunately a process is available for the conversion of saturated hydrocarbons, such as hexane, into unsaturated ones. The process is known as **cracking**:

Hexane   Ethane   Ethene

NB: This example shows just one of the ways in which hexane may be 'cracked'; there are many other possibilities.

Experiment 12.13   *Cracking a saturated hydrocarbon to give unsaturated products*

Heat the tube shown in Fig. 12.14 in the region of the iron-wool and the oil will vaporize by conduction. Use the bromine water test to investigate the unsaturated nature of the product.

The discovery of Polythene

A team of chemists working for ICI in 1935 obtained a white, waxy solid by subjecting ethene to a pressure of 2000 atmospheres at a temperature of 170°C. It was discovered that the wax was formed by a reaction in which

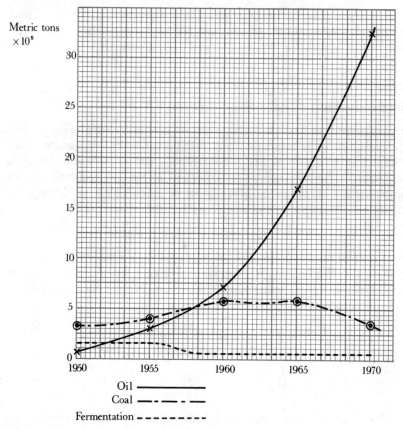

Oil ——————

Coal —— — — . — —

Fermentation — — — — — — — —

Figure 12.13　Sources of carbon compounds

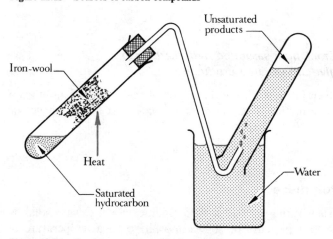

Figure 12.14　Cracking a saturated hydrocarbon

the double bonds open up and the molecules join together in chains, a process known as **polymerization**.

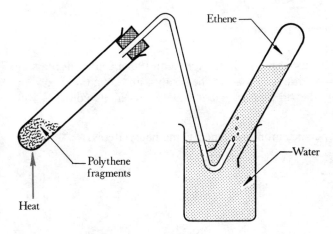

Unfortunately, the polymerization of ethene is beyond the resources of a school laboratory, but we can study the reverse process quite easily. In addition, the polymerization of styrene, a molecule similar to ethene, is carried out in Experiment 12.16.

Experiment 12.14   *Cracking Polythene*

Heat the Polythene strongly in the apparatus shown in Fig. 12.15. Collect one or two tubes of product and test with bromine water.

The waxy substance also formed is partially cracked Polythene.

Ethene

Polythene
fragments

Water

Heat

Figure 12.15   Cracking Polythene

Investigation of some other polymers

The substances from which polymers, or plastics, are obtained by poly-merization are known as **monomers**. The polymerization of many monomers is much easier than the polymerization of ethene.

Experiment 12.15   *The breakdown and repolymerization of perspex*

The experiment should be carried out in a fume-cupboard or a well-ventilated laboratory as the monomer fumes are toxic.

Heat some perspex chips carefully in the apparatus shown in Fig. 12.16, taking care to cause the minimum of carbonization as this will inhibit the subsequent repolymerization.

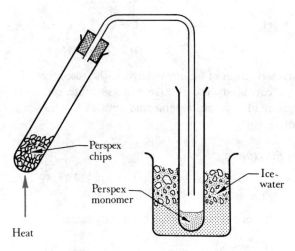

Figure 12.16   The depolymerization of perspex

To repolymerize the monomer, add *no more* than 10 per cent of its mass of benzoyl peroxide as a catalyst. Dissolve the catalyst and plug the tube with cotton wool. Stand the tube in an oven at 95°C, when its contents will harden after about an hour.

The formula for perspex monomer, methyl methacrylate, is:

$$\underset{H}{\overset{H}{\diagdown}}C=C\underset{C}{\overset{CH_3}{\diagup}}\overset{O}{\diagdown}OCH_3$$

Its resemblance to ethene is responsible for its undergoing polymerization by a similar reaction.

Experiment 12.16   *The polymerization of styrene*

Method I

Place a few cm^3 of styrene in a test-tube and add *not more* than 10 per cent of benzoyl peroxide as a catalyst. Dissolve the catalyst and plug the tube with cotton wool. Heat in an oven at 95°C until the solid polymer is formed.

Method II

Mix equal volumes of styrene and paraffin oil, place them in the apparatus shown in Fig. 12.17, and reflux them for at least forty minutes.

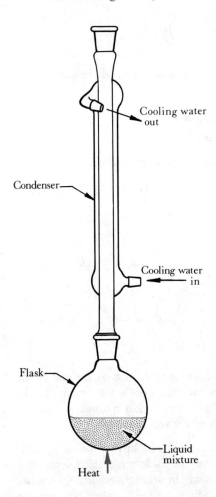

Figure 12.17   Apparatus for refluxing liquid mixtures

Refluxing means to boil a mixture of liquids and condense the vapour formed in a condenser placed vertically above the distillation vessel.

Cool the mixture and pour it into five times its own volume of methylated spirit. The polymer formed by the refluxing will be precipitated.

The formula of styrene is:

$$
\begin{array}{c}
\text{H} \qquad\qquad \text{H} \\
\diagdown \qquad\qquad \diagup \\
\text{C}=\text{C} \\
\diagup \qquad\qquad \diagdown \\
\text{H}
\end{array}
$$

Once again, the similarity in structure to ethene can easily be seen.

Experiment 12.17   *The formation of Nylon 6.6 by interfacial polymerization*

The reaction is between 1,6-diaminohexane and adipyl chloride:

$$
\underset{\text{1,6-diaminohexane}}{
\begin{array}{c}
\text{H} \quad\;\; \text{H H H H H H} \quad\;\; \text{H} \\
\diagdown \;\; | \; | \; | \; | \; | \; | \;\; \diagup \\
\text{N--C--C--C--C--C--C--N} \\
\diagup \;\; | \; | \; | \; | \; | \; | \;\; \diagdown \\
\text{H} \quad\;\; \text{H H H H H H} \quad\;\; \text{H}
\end{array}}
\;+\;
\underset{\text{adipyl chloride}}{
\begin{array}{c}
\text{O} \qquad \text{H H H H} \qquad \text{O} \\
\diagdown\diagdown \; | \; | \; | \; | \quad\;\; \diagup\diagup \\
\text{C--C--C--C--C--C} \\
\diagup \; | \; | \; | \; | \quad\;\; \diagdown \\
\text{Cl} \;\; \text{H H H H} \qquad \text{Cl}
\end{array}}
$$

$$
\downarrow
$$

$$
\begin{array}{c}
\text{H} \quad\;\; \text{H H H H H H H O H H H H} \\
\diagdown \;\; | \; | \; | \; | \; | \; | \; | \; \| \; | \; | \; | \; | \quad\;\; \text{O} \\
\text{N--C--C--C--C--C--C--N--C--C--C--C--C--C} \quad \diagup\diagup \\
\diagup \;\; | \; | \; | \; | \; | \; | \quad\;\;\;\; | \; | \; | \; | \quad \diagdown \\
\text{H} \quad\;\; \text{H H H H H H} \qquad \text{H H H H} \quad \text{Cl}
\end{array}
\;+\; \text{HCl}
$$

You will notice that this reaction leaves reactive groups on the end of the molecule which can react further with new molecules of the starting materials, thus forming long molecular chains. The name Nylon 6.6 means that six carbon atoms are contributed from each of the reactants.

Place a small quantity of a 5 per cent solution of adipyl chloride in tetra-chloromethane in a 10 cm^3 beaker and carefully add an equal volume of a 5 per cent solution of 1,6-diaminohexane in dilute sodium hydroxide solution so that it floats on top. The nylon forms at the interface between the liquids and may be gripped with a pair of forceps and coiled onto a glass rod as illustrated in Fig. 12.18.

Terylene

Another important man-made fibre made by a similar reaction is the poly-ester best known by its trade name, 'Terylene'. Here the two starting materials

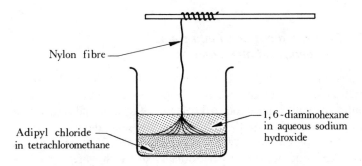

Figure 12.18   The formation of nylon

are terephthalic acid and ethan-1,2-diol. The reaction is too complicated for class practical at this level, however, the equation for the reaction being:

This also leaves a reactive group at either end of the new molecule which can react with more starting material to give a long chain polymer.

Vegetable oils

Vegetable oils, such as castor oil, are very different chemically from petroleum oil. A molecule of castor oil contains several different reactive groups of atoms that link saturated hydrocarbon chains of varying length (represented by the 'blocks' in the following formula):

These groups can be acted upon by various chemical reagents to produce several useful derivatives.

229

Experiment 12.18 *Converting castor oil into soap, detergent, and margarine*

(*a*) Mix together about 2 cm³ of castor oil and 10 cm³ of 5 M sodium hydroxide solution in a beaker and boil them together for about ten minutes, stirring continuously with a glass rod. Add 10 cm³ of a saturated solution of common salt in water to decrease the solubility of the soap and continue the boiling for a further three minutes. Cool the mixture and filter off the solid that forms. Test the lathering properties of this 'soap' with water.

The reaction can be represented by the following equation, where the 'blocks' represent the parts of the molecule linked by the reactive —COO— group:

(*b*) Place 1 cm³ of castor oil in a dry test-tube and add 2 cm³ of concentrated sulphuric acid to it dropwise. Stir the mixture with a glass rod until a viscous liquid is formed. Wash this several times with water to remove excess acid and test its lathering properties.

The equation for the reaction is as follows, where the 'blocks' represent the parts of the molecule linked by the reactive —CHOH— group:

(*c*) **This experiment must be carried out by the teacher.**

Place 100 g of castor oil in the apparatus shown in Fig. 12.19. Add 0·5 g of finely divided nickel as a catalyst and raise the temperature to about 100°C with rapid stirring. Sweep out the air from the apparatus using a carbon dioxide generator and raise the temperature to 180°C, maintaining it steadily there until the end of the experiment. Bubble hydrogen from a cylinder through the mixture for two hours, burning the excess gas at the jet. Sweep out the apparatus once more with carbon dioxide and filter the hot mixture, using a filter pump, to remove the catalyst. On cooling, the mixture should solidify into a fat.

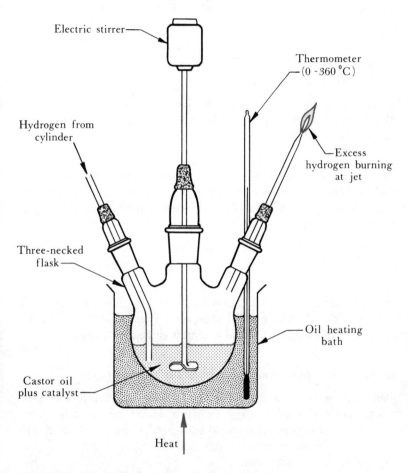

Figure 12.19   The production of margarine from castor oil

The equation for the reaction is:

The 'blocks' this time represent the parts of the molecule linked by the reactive —C=C— group.

Experiment 12.19 *How do soaps and detergents work?*

(*a*) Fill a 250 cm^3 beaker three-quarters full of water and float an aluminium disc, about 2 cm in diameter and a few millimetres thick, carefully on the surface. Now add a few drops of liquid detergent.

This demonstrates the dramatic lowering in the surface tension of water that soaps and detergents produce.

(*b*) Place a large drop of water on a small square of unused fabric. You will see that it remains almost spherical for a long time and does not spread to wet the material. Now add a small amount of detergent to the water drop.

Another important property of soaps and detergents that assists them in cleaning is the type of ion they contain. This consists of a long chain of carbon atoms that dissolves readily in grease, and an ionic 'head' that dissolves readily in water. The way in which these substances work when cleaning is shown diagrammatically in Fig. 12.20.

(*c*) In a darkened room examine a piece of bandage under an ultra-violet lamp. Now wash the bandage in a solution of a commercial detergent such as 'Tide'.

The bandage appears 'whiter-than-white' because the detergent has impregnated it with substances called **phosphors**. These absorb light in the ultra-violet region of the spectrum and re-emit it in the visible region.

Experiment 12.20 *The action of soap on waters of various types*

Place 25 cm^3 of the water to be tested in a conical flask and find out how many equal soap flakes must be added to give a lather lasting five seconds. Carry out this experiment using distilled, temporarily hard, permanently hard and tap waters. Repeat the experiment but first boil each water sample and then allow it to cool to room temperature.

Find out what solid is deposited when temporarily hard water is boiled.

Use the chemistry in the early part of this chapter to explain:
(*a*) Why temporarily hard water is softened by boiling.
(*b*) How the salts responsible for temporary and permanent hardness get into the water.

Experiment 12.21 *What ions are responsible for hardness in water?*

Find out how many equal soap flakes are required to give a lather lasting five seconds with 25 cm^3 portions of 0·2 per cent solutions of sodium chloride,

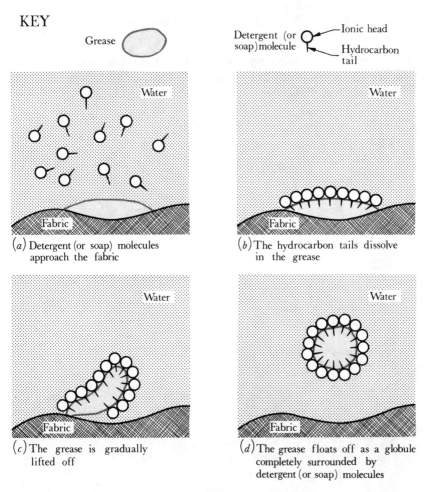

Figure 12.20 How soaps and detergents remove grease from fabrics

calcium chloride, magnesium chloride, potassium nitrate, sodium sulphate, iron(II) sulphate, magnesium sulphate, and calcium nitrate.

From the results of your experiments deduce which ions are responsible for making water hard.

Experiment 12.22 *How may hard water be softened?*

(*a*) Using washing soda (hydrated sodium carbonate). Add a measure of washing soda crystals to 25 cm³ of tap-water and see if this affects the number of soap-flakes required to produce a five second lather.

Deduce the chemical reaction occurring between washing soda and tap-water and write an equation to represent it.

(b) Using an **ion-exchange resin** such as 'Zeo-Karb' (see Fig. 12.21). Take 25 cm^3 of tap-water which has been passed through the column and find out how many soap flakes are required to give a five second lather.

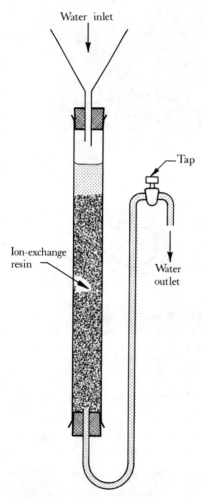

Figure 12.21   An ion-exchange column

As the hard water passes through the column, the ions it contains that are responsible for hardness are exchanged for sodium ions held on the resin. The exchange process can be represented by the equation:

$$Ca^{2+}(aq) + 2Na^+(resin) \rightleftharpoons Ca^{2+}(resin) + 2Na^+(aq)$$

When the resin is virtually exhausted of sodium ions, it can be recharged by passing a concentrated solution of sodium chloride through the column, thus reversing the reaction.

(c) The 'Calgon' process. Take 25 cm^3 of tap-water and add a measure of 'Calgon' to it. Find out how many soap flakes are required to give a five second lather.

'Calgon' contains ions that can be represented as $[Na_2X]^{2-}$. These react with the ions in water that are responsible for hardness in the following manner:

$$Ca^{2+}(aq) + [Na_2X]^{2-}(aq) \longrightarrow [CaX]^{2-}(aq) + 2Na^+(aq)$$

The complex calcium ions so formed do not react with the negative ions in the soap to form a scum.

| Why is it desirable to remove the hardness from water?

Silicon

The place of silicon in the Periodic Table is just below that of carbon. The element has the same crystal structure as that of diamond. It occurs plentifully in rocks and sand.

Experiment 12.23   *The extraction of silicon from sand*

It is essential that the sand and the ignition-tube used are thoroughly dried in an oven at 100°C prior to carrying out this experiment.

Silicon oxide (sand) can be reduced to silicon by magnesium:

$$SiO_2(s) + 2Mg(s) \longrightarrow Si(s) + 2MgO(s)$$

The reaction mixture contains a small excess of magnesium and so the product will contain this plus magnesium oxide as impurities. Both the impurities will dissolve in dilute hydrochloric acid, leaving the silicon undissolved.

Mix thoroughly together one volume of finely powdered magnesium and two volumes of *dry* purified sand. Use this mixture to one-third fill an ignition-tube and secure this in a clamp at its neck. Put on the safety goggles and heat the mixture with a bunsen burner at the end nearest the mouth of the tube.

Place about 25 cm^3 of dilute hydrochloric acid in a beaker and when the tube is cool, tip out its contents into the beaker. A small quantity of magnesium silicide is also formed and this reacts with the acid to give silicon hydrides. These gases ignite spontaneously on coming into contact with air.

(A harmless and entertaining diversion!) Heat the beaker until the contents just boil and then filter the mixture while still hot. Wash the residue of silicon with a little distilled water, transfer it to a watch glass, and dry in an oven at 100°C.

The use of silicon in solid state diodes

The silicon is carefully purified and a small, controlled quantity of another element is added to it. This new element comes either from Group III or Group V of the Periodic Table. The number of such added atoms is extremely small, about 1 to every 10^7 silicon atoms.

If a Group III element is present in the structure, this means that the crystal contains a few atoms which are each one electron *short*; the resulting silicon is known as *p* type.

If a Group V element is present in the structure, this means that the crystal contains a few atoms which have an electron in *excess*; the resulting silicon is known as *n* type.

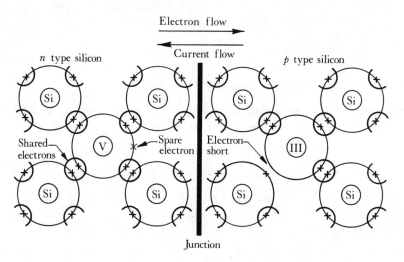

Figure 12.22   A silicon diode

In Fig. 12.22 you can see the situation that arises when a piece of *n* type and a piece of *p* type silicon are joined. Electrons can flow from the *n* type silicon to the 'holes' in the *p* type silicon, but not in the other direction. The device will thus only allow the passage of current in one direction and can therefore be used to rectify an a.c. supply.

236

Silicones

These are polymers that consist of long chains of alternating silicon and oxygen atoms:

$$
\begin{array}{ccccccc}
& \mathrm{CH_3} & & \mathrm{CH_3} & & \mathrm{CH_3} & & \mathrm{CH_3} \\
& | & & | & & | & & | \\
\mathrm{etc{-}O{-}} & \mathrm{Si} & \mathrm{{-}O{-}} & \mathrm{Si} & \mathrm{{-}O{-}} & \mathrm{Si} & \mathrm{{-}O{-}} & \mathrm{Si{-}etc} \\
& | & & | & & | & & | \\
& \mathrm{CH_3} & & \mathrm{CH_3} & & \mathrm{CH_3} & & \mathrm{CH_3}
\end{array}
$$

Experiment 12.24 *Some uses and properties of silicones*

(*a*) A comparison of silicone grease and hydrocarbon grease at elevated temperatures. Fill two ignition-tubes to a depth of about 1 cm, one with silicone grease and the other with a hydrocarbon grease such as Vaseline. With an elastic band, fasten both tubes to a thermometer (reading -10 to $110°C$), place the lower ends of the tubes and the thermometer bulb in a beaker of water (about half-full) and slowly warm the water. Note the temperature at which each grease melts.

(*b*) Make up a 1 per cent solution of the silicone MS 1107 in propanone. Immerse a piece of cotton wool in this solution, wring it out and place it in an oven at $150°C$ for fifteen minutes. After this, compare its water-repellancy with an untreated sample by holding both under a tap.

(*c*) One-quarter fill a test-tube with distilled water and add one drop of liquid detergent. Shake until a good foam is produced. Dip the tip of a glass rod in some Antifoam RD silicone and transfer a small quantity to the test-tube. Observe the effect of the silicone on the foam.

(*d*) Treat one side of a microscope slide with a solution of MS 1107 in propanone, as used in (*b*). Place the treated slide in an oven at $150°C$ for fifteen minutes. Using a 5p piece, find the minimum angle from the horizontal that the slide must be tilted before the coin will slide (*i*) on the untreated side and (*ii*) on the treated side.

Find out what you can about the commercial applications of these properties of silicones.

Summary

Carbon, an essential constituent of living organisms, can exist in two **allotropic** forms. Graphite, the stable form at all temperatures, consists of planes of hexagonally arranged atoms and is a good electrical conductor. Diamond, which has a tetrahedral structure, is extremely hard and is a poor electrical conductor. Carbon dioxide, prepared by the action of dilute acids on a suitable carbonate, does not support the combustion of a lighted splint although magnesium continues to burn in it. It gives an acidic solution in water and turns lime-water milky and then, when in excess, clear again. Carbon monoxide, which can be made by passing carbon dioxide over heated carbon, burns to form carbon dioxide but does not itself affect lime-water. It is only very slightly soluble in water, the solution being neutral.

Two important sources of carbon compounds, on an industrial scale, are coal and petroleum oil. Coal is a complex mixture of many carbon compounds. Petroleum oil consists mainly of hydrocarbons from the **alkane**, **alkene** and **arene** series. The compounds in petroleum oil are separated by fractional distillation.

Plants produce simple **monosaccharide** sugars by **photosynthesis**. For storage purposes these are converted by the plant into **disaccharides** and then **polysaccharides**. Monosaccharides and some disaccharides reduce the copper(II) ions in Fehling's solution on boiling, and are known as reducing sugars. Starch will not affect Fehling's solution but gives a blue-black colouration with iodine solution. Starch can be broken down to mono- and disaccharides by the action of enzymes such as salivary ptyalin or by boiling with a dilute acid. The breakdown products of starch can be identified using paper chromatography. Glucose can be made into a dilute solution of ethanol in water by fermentation and this solution can be concentrated by fractional distillation.

Anhydrous ethanol reacts with sodium metal to give hydrogen, with phosphorus(III) chloride to give chloroethane and with oxygen in the presence of a heated platinum catalyst, to give ethanoic acid. It can be dehydrated by passing its vapour over heated broken pot to give ethene. Ethanoic acid and ethanol react to form the ester ethyl ethanoate. An aqueous solution of ethanoic acid differs from one of ethanol in that it gives hydrogen with magnesium ribbon, carbon dioxide with carbonates and has an acidic pH. A summary chart of the reactions of ethanol is given in Fig. 12.23.

Bromine water is decolourized by substances containing carbon-to-carbon double bonds, such as ethene, and this can be used as a test for them. **Saturated** hydrocarbons can be broken down to **unsaturated** ones by **cracking**, a process that involves passing them in the vapour state over a heated catalyst such as steel-wool. At elevated temperatures and very high pressures, ethene can be **polymerized** to give Polythene. Derivatives of ethene, such as methyl methacrylate and styrene, can be more easily polymerized by gentle heating in the presence of a catalyst such as benzoyl peroxide. Other polymers can be made, such as nylon and Terylene, by reacting together alternate molecules of two suitable substances so that a simple substance is eliminated between them and a long chain is formed.

Vegetable oils, such as castor oil, contain carbon-to-carbon links across which hydrogen can be added to convert them into fats, using a catalyst of finely divided nickel. They also contain an ester linkage that can be broken down by boiling with alkalis to give a **soap** and an —OH group that reacts with cold concentrated sulphuric acid to form a **detergent**. Soaps and detergents operate by lowering the surface tension of water and so increasing its wetting power. In addition, because they contain a 'hydrocarbon tail' which dissolves in grease and an 'ionic head' that dissolves in water, they can lift grease particles from fibres.

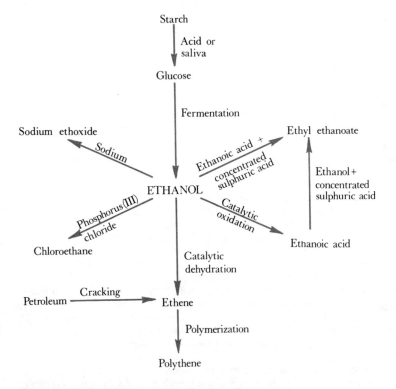

Figure 12.23 Ethanol and some related compounds

Calcium, magnesium, and to a lesser extent iron(II) ions are present in hard waters as a result of the action of rain-water on rocks containing these ions, and they react with the ions in soap to give an insoluble scum. In temporarily hard water they are chiefly present with hydrogen carbonate ions produced by the action of carbon dioxide in rain-water on carbonate rocks, and on boiling, the insoluble carbonates are precipitated and the water is thereby softened. In permanently hard water the accompanying anion is sulphate and such solutions are not affected by boiling. In general, hard water may be softened by (a) adding washing soda to precipitate ions responsible for hardness as the carbonate, (b) passing the water through an ion-exchange column which exchanges the offending ions for sodium ions, and (c) adding 'Calgon' which converts these ions into complex anions that do not react with soap. It is desirable to soften hard water to avoid wastage of soap and to prevent the formation of deposits of carbonates in boilers and hot water pipes. It should be noted that a detergent does not form a scum with hard water.

Silicon can be extracted from dry, purified sand by reaction with powdered magnesium. Silicon, with very small amounts of an impurity added from Groups III or V of the Periodic Table, is used in solid state diodes. **Silicones** are polymers consisting of chains of alternate silicon and oxygen atoms. They are used in high temperature greases, for water-proofing fabrics, as anti-foaming agents, and to reduce surface friction.

Questions

1. (a) Draw a labelled diagram of the apparatus you would use to prepare and collect carbon dioxide. Name the chemicals used and give the equation for the reaction.
    (b) Explain the following statements:
        (i) A blue flame is frequently seen above a red hot coal fire.
        (ii) It is dangerous to keep a motor car engine running in a closed garage.
        (iii) When carbon dioxide is passed into a concentrated solution of sodium hydroxide, a white precipitate is slowly formed. (C)

2. By means of a labelled diagram and an equation, show how a sample of carbon dioxide can be made and collected in the laboratory.
    Without giving any details of the apparatus used, describe briefly how you could convert carbon dioxide into pure carbon monoxide.
    A journalist in a motoring magazine wrote, 'On a busy roadway, the proportion of carbon monoxide has varied from 6 parts per million to 180 parts per million.'
    (a) At what time of day would you expect the concentration of carbon monoxide to be high?
    (b) By what reaction is the carbon monoxide formed?
    (c) What is the effect of carbon monoxide on blood, and why does this make the gas so poisonous? (JMB)

3. (a) Explain, with an example, what is meant by *fractional distillation*. Draw a diagram of an apparatus used for fractional distillation.
    (b) A sample of iron filings is contaminated with lubricating oil. Describe a method by which you would attempt to determine the percentage by weight of iron filings in the sample. (C)

4. 'Over one third of the heat and power for the world is obtained from petroleum. In addition, petroleum has become the raw material for the manufacture of many useful chemicals.'
    Illustrate this quotation by describing concisely how petroleum is treated in order

to obtain fuels and valuable chemicals. You should describe (*a*) the process whereby the components of petroleum are partly separated from each other and (*b*) the subsequent treatment of these components to obtain new and useful materials.   (LN)

5. A certain mineral water manufacturer claims that his product contains glucose. Describe, with full experimental details, how you would use chromatography to test this claim.

6. Describe how you would obtain a sample of almost pure ethanol from a sugar.
   Outline the steps by which ethanol is manufactured from petroleum oil. Name all the chemical processes involved.
   Describe **one** chemical and **one** physical test to distinguish between pure water and pure ethanol. State the result of each test on each of these substances.   (JMB)

7. Describe the laboratory preparation of ethene from ethanol, drawing a diagram of the apparatus you would use. Give the structural formulae of **two** other members of the alkene series. How does ethene react with (*a*) chlorine, and (*b*) concentrated sulphuric acid?   (C)

8.

$$\begin{array}{ccc} H & & H \\ \diagdown & & \diagup \\ & C{=}C & \\ \diagup & & \diagdown \\ H & & Cl \end{array}$$

The substance whose molecular structure is shown above is sometimes called vinyl chloride.

   (*a*) Suggest a more systematic name for the compound.
   (*b*) How would you show that vinyl chloride contains carbon-to-carbon double bonds?
   (*c*) What will be the structure of polyvinyl chloride?

9. Describe, with illustrative examples, different kinds of polymerization. How does the chemist exploit these processes to make materials having specified properties which are in common everyday use?   (LN)

10. Construct a Venn diagram to show how the sets 'hydrocarbons', 'unsaturated compounds', and 'plastic monomers' are related. Place on the appropriate part of your diagram methane, ethene, styrene, 1,6-diaminohexane, and castor oil.

11. How is hard water formed in nature? How does the chemist explain the properties of this liquid and how does he remove hardness from water?   (LN)

12. River water in many places contains calcium hydrogen carbonate and dissolved air. Explain how this happens. Explain the formation of a white precipitate when some of this water is boiled.
   River water can be *softened* by the process of *ion exchange*. Explain the meaning of the words in italics. Give **two** reasons for softening water.
   Discuss briefly the biological significance of the air dissolved in river water. (O & C)

13.

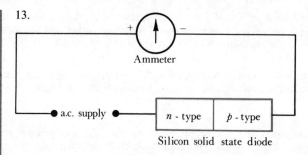

Silicon solid state diode

When the above circuit is operating, in which direction will the meter needle move?
Which of the elements zinc, indium, germanium, antimony, or lead could be present in the *n*-type silicon? Explain your answer.

Non-metallic elements and their compounds—II

Group V—nitrogen and phosphorus

Proteins

Pictures of people, particularly children, from under-developed countries who are dying of starvation are very common (Fig. 13.1). You will probably know that what they need most if they are to survive is food that is rich in **protein**, such as meat, fish, cheese, and eggs. Why are proteins so essential to a healthy life? To understand this, we first have to find out which elements they contain and then how the atoms of these elements are arranged to give the compounds their particular properties.

In earlier experiments, you will have discovered that all foodstuffs, including proteins, contain carbon and hydrogen. The next experiments should enable you to confirm the presence of another vital element.

Experiment 13.1 *Investigating proteins*

You will need small samples of substances rich in protein such as meat, fish, cheese, gelatin, milk powder, etc. (*NB:* Eggs are rather too messy for convenient use but egg powder would be quite suitable.)

Mix the sample with about twice its bulk of soda lime and place the mixture on a piece of asbestos paper. (It is obvious that powdered material is preferable to lumps of meat, etc., as it is so much easier to mix.) Holding the asbestos paper with tongs, heat the mixture. Note the odour of the fumes given off and test them with moist Universal Indicator (pH) paper. Finally, hold the stopper from a bottle of concentrated hydrochloric acid in the fumes.

NB: The laboratory will need to be well-ventilated during this experiment, for reasons that will become obvious!

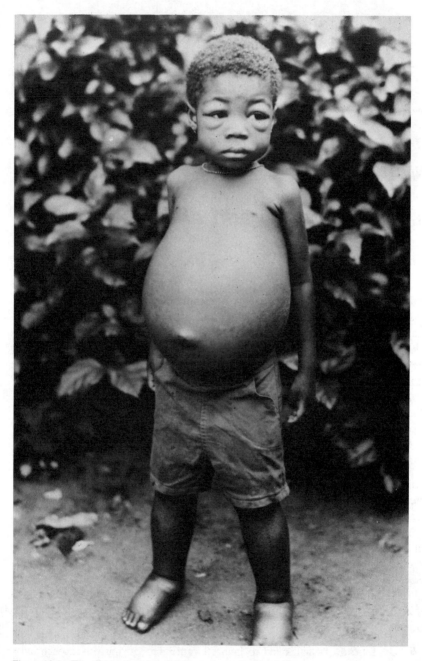

Figure 13.1   The effects of protein deficiency

Repeat the experiment with as many different samples as are available or as time allows.

| Were similar results obtained in the various experiments?

Soda lime is quicklime (calcium oxide) slaked with sodium hydroxide solution (instead of water which would give slaked lime, i.e., calcium hydroxide), the result being a mixture of sodium and calcium hydroxides and *not* a compound. When heated with the protein the soda lime causes the material to break down and give off a mixture of substances in the fumes. One of these substances, that you might be able to smell, caused the effects you will have observed with the Universal Indicator (pH) paper and the hydrochloric acid fumes.

| Write down what you regard as the most important characteristics of this compound, as far as is possible from this experiment.

The compound concerned is **ammonia**, which you may have met at home in the form of a solution in water and used as household cleaning liquid.

Experiment 13.2   *To prepare ammonia and investigate some of its properties*

Mix together approximately equal quantities of solid calcium hydroxide and ammonium chloride and half fill a test-tube with the mixture. Collect the gas given off as shown in Fig. 13.2.

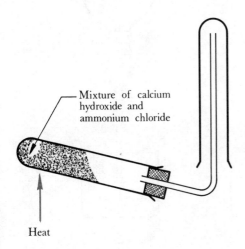

Heat

Figure 13.2   The preparation of ammonia

CHEMISTRY BY EXPERIMENT AND UNDERSTANDING

What can you deduce about the gas from the way in which the apparatus is arranged? How could you check your ideas? During the experiment, look at the reaction tube occasionally, when you should be able to see one of the other products of the reaction. Bearing this in mind, at the end of the experiment write an equation for the reaction between calcium hydroxide and ammonium chloride.

Warm the mixture gently and carry out the following tests on the gas evolved:

(a) Test the gas issuing from the delivery-tube with moist Universal Indicator (pH) paper.

How can this test assist you when collecting tubes of the gas?

(b) Appearance.
(c) Odour.
(d) Hold the stopper from a bottle of concentrated hydrochloric acid near the mouth of a test-tube full of the gas.

(These three tests can all be carried out, in order, on one test-tube of gas.)

From the tests carried out so far, does the gas that you have prepared have similar properties to that present in the fumes obtained in Experiment 13.1?

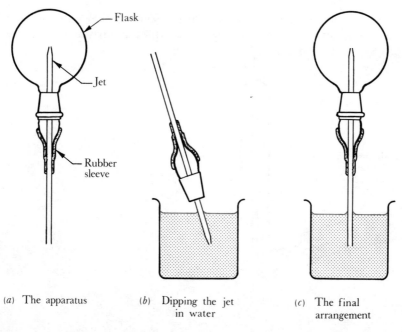

(a) The apparatus

(b) Dipping the jet in water

(c) The final arrangement

Figure 13.3   The 'Fountain Experiment'

(e) Plunge a burning splint into a tube of the gas.

At this stage replace the reaction mixture with fresh material, *if necessary*, i.e., if the supply of gas is dwindling. It is very important that sufficient gas is available to completely fill the apparatus used in the next test.

(f) Fit a small distillation flask with a short length of tubing drawn out to a fine tip, as shown in Fig. 13.3. Remove the tube and fill the flask with ammonia gas, *as completely as possible*. Dip the tip of the tube into some water, fit it quickly into the flask and *immediately* place the open end of the tube under the surface of some water in a beaker, to which has been added a few drops of Universal Indicator (pH) solution. If the experiment is going to work, it will do so without much delay. If it is unsuccessful, the flask was probably not sufficiently full of gas and a second attempt should be made in which more care is taken.

Try to explain what you have seen. What has happened to the Universal Indicator (pH) solution? What further properties of ammonia does this experiment illustrate?

This experiment is called the **fountain experiment.**

Experiment 13.3   *Investigating the properties of ammonia solution*

Carry out the following tests on a sample of ammonia solution:
(a) Test with Universal Indicator (pH) paper.
(b) Heat a small quantity of the liquid in a test-tube and identify any gases evolved.
(c) Test for conductance with some solution in a small beaker, using carbon electrodes connected into a circuit containing a bulb and using a 6 V d.c. supply.
(d) Add ammonia solution slowly, drop by drop, to about 2 cm^3 of each of the following aqueous solutions contained in test-tubes: iron(II) sulphate, iron(III) chloride, magnesium sulphate, copper(II) sulphate, and zinc sulphate.

When ammonia is dissolved in water, the following equilibrium is set up:

$$NH_3(aq) + H_2O(l) \rightleftharpoons NH_4^+(aq) + OH^-(aq)$$

Explain the properties of a solution of ammonia in terms of this equilibrium. Which metal ions dissolved in an excess of ammonia solution? Explain why they dissolved.

Experiment 13.4 *Breaking down ammonia*

Copper(II) oxide has been used in previous experiments to break down carbon compounds and you are now going to use it to try to prove that ammonia contains the elements hydrogen and nitrogen, as has been suggested.

Set up the apparatus as shown in Fig. 13.4. The reaction mixture is that used previously for generating ammonia (calcium hydroxide and ammonium

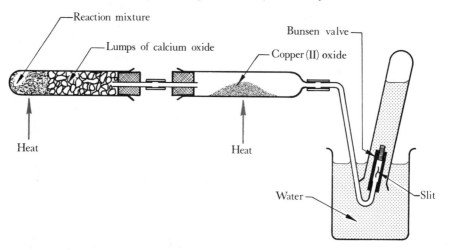

Figure 13.4 Breaking down ammonia

chloride). As water is one of the products of the reaction, the ammonia must be dried and this is conveniently done by filling up the remaining space in the tube with lumps of calcium oxide. This tube is connected to a combustion-tube in which is placed some dry copper(II) oxide (preferably wire-form; do *not* throw away at the end of the experiment as it can be recovered) and to this tube is connected a delivery-tube fitted with a bunsen valve to prevent water being sucked back into the hot combustion-tube. Any gas evolved is collected over water.

When everything is ready, heat the copper(II) oxide strongly and the ammonia mixture gently. Observe the combustion-tube carefully for the formation of any recognizable product and to see whether there is any change in the black copper(II) oxide. Test the gas evolved with moist Universal Indicator (pH) paper and with a lighted splint.

> If ammonia does contain hydrogen and nitrogen, what products would you expect if it reacts with copper(II) oxide? Did the experiment confirm your ideas? Write an equation for the reaction, by careful consideration of the products formed.

Experiment 13.5 *The composition of ammonia*

This experiment is best done by the teacher.

If we are now satisfied that ammonia does contain the elements hydrogen and nitrogen, the next step in our investigation is to find out the proportions of the two elements in the compound and see whether the results agree with the formula that we have been using for ammonia, i.e., NH_3.

Set up the apparatus as shown in Fig. 13.5. Three 100 cm^3 glass syringes (A, B, and C) are connected to two three-way taps (X and Y) and two silica tubes (P and Q). All connections are made with rubber sleeves which must be very tight-fitting and as short as possible. Silica tube P contains steel-wool, held in place by two pieces of glass rod which must be of slightly smaller diameter than that of the inside of the silica tube. In a similar way, silica tube Q contains wire-form copper(II) oxide. The apparatus is supported in clamps or on a special syringe bench. Gases are admitted or expelled through tap X, care being taken if gas cylinders are being used that the syringe plunger is not blown out by too great a pressure of gas.

All apparatus must be dry or satisfactory results will not be obtained.

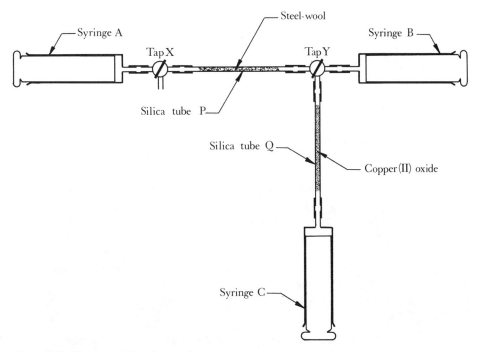

Figure 13.5   The composition of ammonia

To ensure that all oxide is removed from the surface of the steel-wool, it is heated in an atmosphere of hydrogen. This is done by flushing air out of the apparatus with nitrogen (from a cylinder) and then filling syringe A with about 50 cm^3 of hydrogen (also from a cylinder). Connect syringes A and B and pass hydrogen backwards and forwards across the steel-wool while it is being strongly heated. Cool the silica tube with a wet cloth and expel residual hydrogen.

Flush out the entire apparatus once more with nitrogen and fill syringe A with 40 cm^3 of dry ammonia obtained by warming some 0·880 ammonia solution in the apparatus shown in Fig. 13.6. Connect syringe A to syringe B,

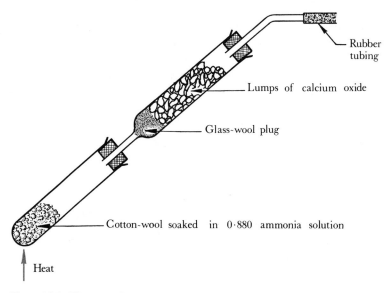

Figure 13.6   The ammonia generator

heat the steel-wool very strongly so that it is red-hot, and pass the ammonia backwards and forwards between syringe A and syringe B until no further increase in volume takes place. Cool the silica tube with a wet cloth, pass all the gases into syringe A and read the volume, which should have approximately doubled.

Pass the gases into syringe B, connect syringe B to syringe C and, while heating the copper(II) oxide, pass the gases backwards and forwards from syringe B to syringe C until there is no further decrease in volume. Cool the silica tube with a wet cloth and pass all the residual gases into syringe B to read the volume.

Ammonia was broken down by the red-hot iron into nitrogen and hydrogen.

Why did the volume of gases decrease when passed over hot copper(II) oxide? What was the gas remaining at the end of the experiment? Hence calculate the volumes of hydrogen and nitrogen produced during the experiment.

Your results should be as shown below, to the nearest 10 cm³. (This may seem very approximate, but it is only the relative number of moles taking part in the reaction that we are concerned with, as should become clear from what follows.)

	Ammonia	Nitrogen	Hydrogen
Volumes of gases	40 cm³	20 cm³	60 cm³
Relative volumes	2	1	3

The volume occupied by one mole of any gas under the same conditions of temperature and pressure is a constant (Avogadro's Law). Thus if the volume ratio is 2:1:3, the mole ratio must be the same. Hence:

Relative numbers of moles   2   1   3

If the formulae of nitrogen and hydrogen are assumed, the equation for the reaction can now be written:

$$2N_xH_y(g) \longrightarrow N_2(g) + 3H_2(g)$$

(where N_xH_y is the formula of ammonia). Hence:

$$x = 1 \quad \text{and} \quad y = 3$$

The formula of ammonia is thus NH_3.

In this experiment, ammonia was broken down into its elements. If it is possible to reverse the process we will then have a relatively simple and cheap method of preparing ammonia, since both hydrogen and nitrogen are readily available in large quantities.

Experiment 13.6 *To make ammonia from nitrogen and hydrogen*

This experiment is best done by the teacher.

Set up the apparatus as shown in Fig. 13.7. Two 100 cm³ glass syringes are connected by short lengths of rubber tubing through a three-way tap and a silica tube containing steel-wool held in place by two short pieces of glass rod (as in the previous experiment).

Flush out the apparatus with nitrogen and admit 20 cm³ of nitrogen and 60 cm³ of hydrogen into syringe A. Connect the two syringes and pass the gases backwards and forwards several times across the steel-wool while it is being very strongly heated. Cool the silica tube with a wet cloth, read the

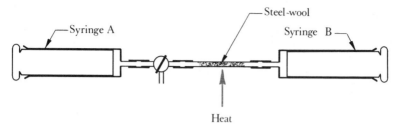

Figure 13.7   The synthesis of ammonia

final volume, and eject the gases onto (*a*) a piece of moist Universal Indicator (pH) paper and (*b*) the stopper of a concentrated hydrochloric acid bottle.

Was any ammonia detectable? If so, was it present in much quantity? Write an equation for the reaction. What part was played by the steel-wool? Why was the final volume not equal to half of the original?

The manufacture of ammonia

The method used in the last experiment for the preparation of ammonia, although successful, is obviously not very efficient as such a small quantity of ammonia gas was formed. The reason for this is that the reaction is reversible:

$$N_2(g) + 3H_2(g) \rightleftharpoons 2NH_3(g)$$

The forward reaction is exothermic.

As discussed in chapter 6, it can be seen that the forward reaction to produce ammonia will be favoured if the pressure is increased, as there is a reduction in volume in this direction. Although an increase in temperature will speed up both forward and reverse reactions and cause equilibrium to be attained more rapidly, it will also cause the proportion of ammonia produced to decrease since the forward reaction is exothermic. A catalyst will speed up both reactions and hence cause a more rapid attainment of equilibrium.

The problem of arriving at a suitable compromise between these conflicting factors was solved by Fritz Haber, who used a very high pressure (about 200 atmospheres) and a temperature high enough to achieve a reasonable rate of reaction but not so high that the yield of ammonia was too low (about 500°C). The catalyst was a mixture of iron with small quantities of oxides of other metals such as aluminium, potassium, and calcium.

The process was developed by Carl Bosch and the essential features are shown in the flow-diagram (Fig. 13.8).

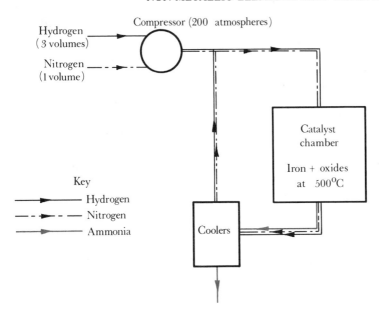

Figure 13.8 The Haber Process (simplified flow-diagram)

The nitrogen used is readily obtained from the air and the hydrogen, formerly made from steam, is now derived from petroleum products. The efficiency of conversion, which is approximately 15 per cent, is improved by re-cycling the unreacted gases once the ammonia has been removed by liquefaction, fresh feed-gases being added to make up for those that have reacted.

Vast quantities of ammonia are made by this process, which is the main source of artificial nitrogen compounds.

Nitrogen

The element nitrogen makes up about 80 per cent by volume of the atmosphere, but compounds of nitrogen do not occur in the earth's crust to any extent, the main source being the deposits of sodium nitrate that are found in Chile. However, as we have seen, nitrogen is contained in proteins, the complex compounds that are essential to life of all sorts as we know it.

Plants are able to synthesize proteins by absorbing the necessary elements (carbon, hydrogen, oxygen, nitrogen, phosphorus, potassium, calcium, etc.) through their leaves or roots.

Animals are unable to synthesize proteins directly and so must rely on the plant kingdom for their supply of these vital compounds. When an animal eats a plant, the **plant protein** is broken down in the digestive system to much

253

simpler substances, mostly **amino-acids**, which are then re-assembled into **animal protein**.

Plants must have a supply of soluble nitrogen compounds in order to synthesize proteins, as they are unable to do this directly from atmospheric nitrogen. When plants grow wild in nature, they are usually able to obtain all the nitrogen (and also other elements) needed because, when they die, they return their substance to the soil. In addition, they are likely to benefit at least locally from animal droppings and the decay of dead animals. Apart from death and decay, there are two other natural sources of nitrogen in a form that plants can use. During thunderstorms, the tremendous energy associated with a flash of lightning causes atmospheric nitrogen, oxygen, and water vapour to combine to give nitric acid, which falls to earth as a dilute solution in rain. This reacts with minerals in the soil to form soluble nitrates. Certain bacteria, notably in the roots of leguminous plants such as peas, beans, clover, and others, are able to convert atmospheric nitrogen to soluble nitrogen compounds.

However, when 'civilization' takes over with cultivation of the soil, sewage systems and burial or cremation of the dead, this natural balance is disturbed. There is a further loss of nitrogen as a result of the activity of another group of bacteria that converts soluble nitrogen compounds to atmospheric nitrogen. In addition, considerable quantities of soluble nitrogen compounds are washed out of the soil by rain-water.

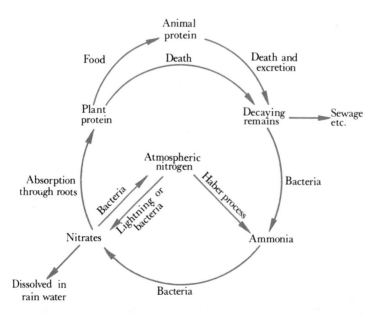

Figure 13.9   The nitrogen cycle

In order to return to the soil what has been taken from it, which is obviously essential if it is to remain fertile, the farmer must regularly treat his land with plant food or **fertilizer**.

Any process that brings about the conversion of atmospheric nitrogen to a form that plants can use is called **nitrogen fixation**. This may occur naturally by, for example, bacteria or artificially by the Haber Process, much of the ammonia made in this way being used to manufacture fertilizers, either directly or indirectly.

It can be seen that the use of nitrogen by living things is a continuous process and it can be summarized by the **nitrogen cycle** (Fig. 13.9).

Fertilizers

There are two main kinds of fertilizer, organic and inorganic. The organic fertilizer used most commonly is manure, which consists of the dung and urine of farm animals mixed with straw or whatever material was used for bedding. It is an excellent fertilizer, containing all the necessary elements, but there is not enough of it. Other organic fertilizers are dried blood and bone meal but these, and others like them, are available only on a limited scale and tend to be rather slow-acting. Thus inorganic fertilizers, which are simply compounds containing the necessary elements, must be used on a very large scale if intensive cultivation is to be possible, as it must be if the needs of the growing population of the world are to be met.

Nitrogenous fertilizers

Nitrogen compounds affect the yield of a crop more than any other plant food, particularly leafy crops such as grass and cereals. As we have seen, some nitrogen is returned to the soil by natural processes, such as the decay of previous crops and fixation from the air by bacteria and lightning, but much more is needed to maintain healthy plant growth and this can only be supplied by the application of nitrogenous fertilizers.

The first inorganic compound used for this purpose on a large scale was sodium nitrate from the deposits in Chile, but the supply was soon insufficient to meet the growing demand. The discovery of the Haber process provided the answer to the problem as this uses the limitless supplies of nitrogen from the air to produce ammonia, which can then be converted to compounds suitable for the farmer to use such as ammonium nitrate and sulphate, or, via nitric acid, sodium nitrate. The main bulk of nitrogenous fertilizers is now produced in this way. Where ammonium compounds are used, these are converted to nitrates by bacteria in the soil before absorption by the plants. This process obviously takes time and thus ammonium compounds act over a longer period than nitrates. Ammonium nitrate combines the short term benefit of a nitrate with the longer term benefit of an ammonium compound and is thus a particularly good fertilizer.

Phosphatic fertilizers

Phosphates stimulate root development and are usually applied at planting-time. The phosphatic fertilizer used most widely is calcium superphosphate (discussed later in this chapter), but others are basic slag from the iron and steel industry, and ammonium phosphate, the latter being particularly useful as it also supplies nitrogen.

Potassium fertilizers

These will generally improve the quality of crops and are necessary to ensure that plants use the available nitrogen as efficiently as possible. The most common potassium (or 'potash') fertilizers are the chloride and the sulphate.

Calcium fertilizers

Calcium is essential to plants in small quantities but the main use of calcium 'fertilizers', usually the carbonate (the so-called 'lime'), is in controlling the pH of the soil. The ideal pH for the growth of most plants is about 6·5, at which value most soil bacteria function satisfactorily. Some soils are naturally more acid than this and others can become so by the use of fertilizers with acid properties, such as ammonium sulphate. In these cases, the use of 'lime' to reduce the acidity is obviously essential.

The application of fertilizers

Most modern fertilizers are balanced to contain all the elements necessary for a particular purpose. This ensures that the material is of consistent composition and also saves considerable time for the farmer. Another comparatively recent development is the conversion of the powdered or crystalline material into granules, which not only store better but are easier to apply and are not so likely to blow away.

Experiment 13.7 *To prepare a fertilizer—ammonium sulphate*

Add 2 M ammonia solution, a few cm^3 at a time with stirring, to about 20 cm^3 of 1 M sulphuric acid contained in a beaker, until the solution has developed a distinct smell of ammonia.

Evaporate the solution slowly until it is saturated, which may be determined by dipping a glass rod into the liquid to see whether crystals form almost immediately on the rod when withdrawn from the liquid. When this stage has been reached, allow the solution to cool, when it should crystallize. Filter off the product and allow to dry.

Explain the reaction in terms of the ammonia/water equilibrium and write the appropriate equation.

Dissolve a little of your product in distilled water and test the solution with Universal Indicator (pH) paper.

What is the significance of the result of this test to the use of ammonium sulphate as a fertilizer? Calculate the percentage of nitrogen in the following: (a) ammonium sulphate, $(NH_4)_2SO_4$; (b) ammonium nitrate, NH_4NO_3; and (c) urea (a derivative of ammonia), $(NH_2)_2CO$. Comment on the usefulness of each of these compounds as a fertilizer.

Amino-acids

These compounds can be regarded as the 'building-bricks' that make up the much more complicated proteins. The simplest amino-acid is aminoethanoic acid (glycine), the structure of which is:

Other amino-acids have similar structures and all contain both the amino group, $-NH_2$, and the acid group, $-COOH$.

As we have seen, plants synthesize proteins by absorbing the necessary elements through their leaves and roots, amino-acids being formed as intermediates.

This process can be quite easily reversed and thus a study of amino-acids enables us to understand the structures of proteins. Such a study can be achieved by the use of chromatography.

Experiment 13.8 *To separate and detect amino-acids by chromatography*

Mark out a piece of chromatography paper and spot it with as many solutions of amino-acids as are available. **Take care to handle the paper as little as possible, as sweat on your hands contains amino-acids and you are likely to leave finger-prints on the paper!** Make sure that you have sufficient concentration of each spot (as described in earlier experiments).

Using a solvent of ethanol (45 volumes), 0·880 ammonia solution (2·5 volumes), and distilled water (2·5 volumes), develop the chromatogram for as long as possible.

Remove the chromatogram from the tank and dry fully. Locate the spots by spraying (or dipping) with a solution of ninhydrin in propanone and then placing the paper in an oven at 110°C for about fifteen minutes. Mark the positions of the spots with a pencil, as the colour tends to fade.

Experiment 13.9 *The amino-acids in orange juice*

This experiment can be used to make a survey of commercial 'orange' juices and squashes, with respect to their amino-acid content. If time is limited, it can be omitted or carried out as an alternative to Experiment 13.8.

Prepare the amino-acid samples from the orange juices or squashes by adding 3 cm^3 of ethanol to 1 cm^3 of the juice or squash to precipitate salts and proteins, followed by filtration or centrifuging. The filtrate is then ready for use.

Proceed exactly as described in Experiment 13.8 for spotting, development, and location of the amino-acids.

A particular brand of juice may be compared with standard spots of known amino-acids to see what it contains or, alternatively, a variety of brands can be compared with the juice from a fresh orange.

Experiment 13.10 *The reactions of ammonia with oxygen*

These experiments must be carried out by the teacher.

(*a*) Pass oxygen from a cylinder and ammonia obtained by warming some 0·880 ammonia solution into the apparatus shown in Fig. 13.10. The glass-wool serves to spread out the oxygen. Apply a light to the ammonia tube.

The ammonia burns in oxygen (but not in air at ordinary temperatures) to give nitrogen and water:

$$4NH_3(g) + 3O_2(g) \longrightarrow 2N_2(g) + 6H_2O(l)$$

(*b*) Put 25 cm^3 of 0·880 ammonia solution into a wide-necked flask. Wind a length of platinum wire into a spiral and attach it to a length of wooden or glass rod (see Fig. 13.11). Warm the 0·880 ammonia solution, heat the wire until it is red-hot and immediately place it so that the bottom is near (but not touching) the surface of the ammonia.

What evidence is there that a reaction is taking place? What role is the platinum playing? How does this relate to the theories of catalysis discussed in chapter 6?

The reaction in this case is as follows, the products being nitrogen monoxide and water:

$$4NH_3(g) + 5O_2(g) \longrightarrow 4NO(g) + 6H_2O(l)$$

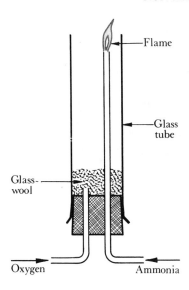

Figure 13.10 The burning of ammonia in oxygen

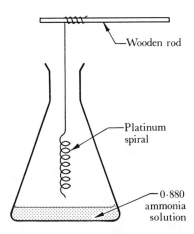

Figure 13.11 The catalytic oxidation of ammonia

If brown fumes were seen in the flask, this is due to the spontaneous reaction between nitrogen monoxide and oxygen in the air to form brown nitrogen dioxide:

$$2NO(g) + O_2(g) \longrightarrow 2NO_2(g)$$

259

The manufacture of nitric acid

Nitric acid is used mainly for the manufacture of fertilizers, such as ammonium nitrate, explosives such as nitroglycerine, nitrocellulose, and TNT, and in the production of organic chemicals such as adipic acid used in making Nylon 6.6.

The catalytic oxidation of ammonia by oxygen (as in the last-experiment) forms the basis of the manufacture of nitric acid by the **Ostwald process** (see Fig. 13.12).

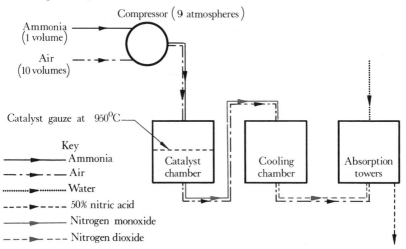

Figure 13.12 The Ostwald Process (simplified flow diagram)

Ammonia and an excess of air (about 10 volumes) at a pressure of about nine atmospheres are passed through a fine gauze made of platinum and rhodium (a metal similar to platinum). Initially, the catalyst is heated electrically but the reaction, which is exothermic, soon generates enough heat to maintain the gauze at the working temperature of about 950°C, with approximately 97 per cent conversion of ammonia:

$$4NH_3(g) + 5O_2(g) \longrightarrow 4NO(g) + 6H_2O(g)$$

On cooling, the nitrogen monoxide reacts with the excess air to give nitrogen dioxide:

$$2NO(g) + O_2(g) \longrightarrow 2NO_2(g)$$

The nitrogen dioxide then reacts with water in the presence of the remaining air, in absorption towers, to form nitric acid as a 50 per cent solution:

$$4NO_2(g) + 2H_2O(l) + O_2(g) \longrightarrow 4HNO_3(aq)$$

Experiment 13.11   *Some properties of nitric acid*

Carry out the following tests using dilute nitric acid:
 (*a*) Determine the pH of the solution.
 (*b*) Test the solution for conductance.
 (*c*) To a little of each of the following solids, contained in a test-tube, add about 2 cm^3 of dilute nitric acid: copper(II) oxide, magnesium oxide, calcium hydroxide, lead(II) carbonate, and sodium carbonate.

Name the products and write equations for each of the tests in (*c*) above. Are the results of all the above tests typical of those you would expect from an acid? Explain your answer.

 (*d*) Place some magnesium and some copper, preferably both as turnings, in separate test-tubes and add about 2 cm^3 of the dilute acid to each.

Are the reactions with metals typical of those you would expect from an acid? Explain your answer.

In the following tests, use the concentration of acid specified.

Test (*e*) should be performed by the teacher, in a fume-cupboard.

 (*e*) Place some copper turnings in a test-tube and add a few drops of con-centrated nitric acid.

Was the reaction with copper the same for both the dilute and the con-centrated acids?

 (*f*) To about 2 cm^3 of aqueous potassium iodide in a test-tube, add a few drops of dilute nitric acid. Repeat the experiment using a few drops of concentrated nitric acid.
 (*g*) Repeat test (*f*) with both concentrations of acid, using about 2 cm^3 of aqueous iron(II) sulphate in place of the potassium iodide. Test the solution remaining in each case for the presence of iron(III) ions.

In tests (*f*) and (*g*) were the same results obtained with both dilute and con-centrated nitric acid? Explain the chemistry of what has happened in these two tests, illustrating your answer with ionic equations.

Experiment 13.12   *Some properties of nitrates*

When nitric acid reacts with metals, or their oxides, hydroxides, and car-bonates, salts called **nitrates** are produced.

Carry out the following tests on the given nitrates:

(a) Solubility in water. Use approximately the same quantities of respectively the salt and the water in each case. Shake the solid with about 2 cm^3 of water in a test-tube.

(b) The effect of heat. Use an ignition-tube and a very small quantity of each solid. Heat gently at first and then strongly. Try to identify any gases evolved.

Summarize your results for tests (a) and (b) by grouping together those nitrates that appear to behave in a similar manner. How do these groupings compare with the positions of the appropriate metals in the activity series?

The following test is best carried out with sodium nitrate, although it is the general test and should therefore work for any nitrate.

(c) The 'Brown Ring Test'. To about 5 cm^3 of distilled water in a boiling-tube, add a small quantity of the solid nitrate and a small quantity of solid iron(II) sulphate. Shake or stir well and ensure that all the solids have dissolved. *Very carefully*, holding the tube on a slant, as in Fig. 13.13, add an

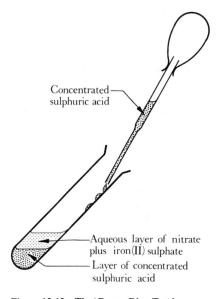

Concentrated sulphuric acid

Aqueous layer of nitrate plus iron(II) sulphate
Layer of concentrated sulphuric acid

Figure 13.13   The 'Brown Ring Test'

approximately equal volume of concentrated sulphuric acid, so that it forms a separate layer underneath the aqueous mixture. Look particularly at the junction of the two liquids.

Experiment 13.13   *The oxides of nitrogen*

The three most important oxides of nitrogen are:
(*a*) Dinitrogen monoxide (nitrous oxide), N_2O.
(*b*) Nitrogen monoxide (nitric oxide), NO.
(*c*) Nitrogen dioxide, NO_2.

(*a*) Dinitrogen monoxide is prepared by the action of heat on ammonium nitrate:

$$NH_4NO_3(s) \longrightarrow N_2O(g) + 2H_2O(l)$$

However, the commercial grade of ammonium nitrate is liable to explode when heated and so it is not advisable to attempt this preparation. Dinitrogen monoxide is known as 'laughing-gas' and is used as an anaesthetic, particularly by dentists.

(*b*) Nitrogen monoxide. In a test-tube place some copper turnings and about 2 cm^3 of water. Add an approximately equal quantity of concentrated nitric acid, quickly fit the delivery-tube as in Fig. 13.14 and collect the gas

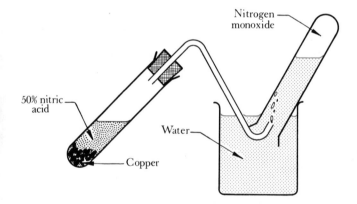

Figure 13.14   The preparation of nitrogen monoxide

evolved over water. You will need two tubes of gas in order to carry out the following tests:
(*i*) Expose a tube of the gas to the air.
(*ii*) Cork the second tube (or put your thumb over the end) to prevent the air getting into it. Remove the cork just long enough to add a few cm^3 of iron(II) sulphate solution and then replace it and shake the tube.

Name the product in test (*i*) and explain the reaction.

The product in test (*ii*) contains the complex ion $[Fe(NO)]^{2+}$ and because of its characteristic appearance, its formation can be used as a test for nitrogen monoxide.

| In which previous reaction have you seen the formation of this compound?

The chemistry of the reaction between copper and nitric acid is complex, but may be represented as follows:

With dilute nitric acid, nitrogen monoxide is the main product, as shown in the equation:

$$3Cu(s) + 8H^+(aq) + 2NO_3^-(aq) \longrightarrow 3Cu^{2+}(aq) + 4H_2O(l) + 2NO(g)$$

With concentrated nitric acid, nitrogen dioxide is the main product:

$$Cu(s) + 4H^+(aq) + 2NO_3^-(aq) \longrightarrow Cu^{2+}(aq) + 2H_2O(l) + 2NO_2(g)$$

However, it should be clear that in practice, both reactions will proceed at the same time, with one or other predominating, depending on the conditions.

(*c*) Nitrogen dioxide.

This gas is very poisonous and the face should be kept well away from it at all times.

The gas is more conveniently prepared by the action of heat on the appropriate nitrate, for example lead nitrate, than by the reaction between copper and concentrated nitric acid, as it is not then contaminated with nitrogen monoxide.

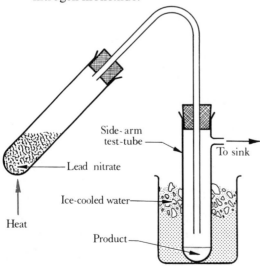

Side-arm test-tube

To sink

Lead nitrate

Ice-cooled water

Heat

Product

Figure 13.15   The preparation of nitrogen dioxide

Set up the apparatus as shown in Fig. 13.15. Lead nitrate is placed in a test-tube, which is connected to the side-arm test-tube, in turn surrounded by ice-cooled water. Any excess gas is led by a length of rubber tubing down the nearest sink. Heat the tube containing the lead nitrate until no more gas is evolved. Examine the product in the side-arm test-tube and then allow it to warm up to room temperature. Replace the tube in the ice-cooled water and then re-examine it. Pour some of the liquid into a beaker of water and determine the pH of the resulting solution.

Write an equation for the reaction. Why was it possible to collect the nitrogen dioxide by the method used? What was the product of the reaction between nitrogen dioxide and water? Write an equation for the reaction.

As discussed in chapter 6, nitrogen dioxide is in equilibrium with dinitrogen tetroxide:

$$N_2O_4(g) \overset{\text{heat}}{\underset{\text{cool}}{\rightleftharpoons}} 2NO_2(g)$$

Dinitrogen	Nitrogen
tetroxide	dioxide
(colourless)	(brown)

In terms of this equilibrium, explain the changes that you observed in the product of the reaction, when you treated it as instructed.

Phosphorus

The element is not found in the free state, occurring usually as deposits of phosphates, such as phosphorite or rock phosphate, $Ca_3(PO_4)_2$, and apatite, $CaF_2.3Ca_3(PO_4)_2$. Phosphorus is an essential element to life of all sorts, and bones and teeth consist largely of calcium phosphate.

Phosphorus is extracted from calcium phosphate by reaction with sand and coke at high temperature and is used for making a wide range of phosphorus compounds, these in turn finding such diverse uses as detergent and oil additives and insecticides. The quantity of the element used in the match industry is relatively small (approximately 1 per cent in the UK).

Phosphatic fertilizers have already been discussed earlier in this chapter, but the manufacture of the most common, calcium superphosphate, requires explanation. Calcium phosphate is too insoluble to be of much use as a fertilizer and would merely lie in the ground, giving up very little of its vital phosphorus to plant life. For this reason, it is converted to a more soluble form by treatment with moderately concentrated sulphuric acid:

$$Ca_3(PO_4)_2(s) + 2H_2SO_4(aq) \longrightarrow Ca(H_2PO_4)_2(s) + 2CaSO_4(s)$$

The product is a mixture of calcium dihydrogen phosphate and calcium sulphate and is used in this form as 'calcium superphosphate'.

Phosphorus vapour consists of free, tetrahedral molecules, P_4. In the solid state, there are several allotropes in each of which such tetrahedral molecules are arranged in different patterns. The most important of these are the white (or yellow) and the red varieties.

Experiment 13.14   *To investigate some of the properties of white and red phosphorus*

This experiment must be carried out by the teacher, as white phosphorus in particular is very poisonous and dangerous to handle.

(*a*) Dissolve a small piece of white phosphorus in a little carbon disulphide in a test-tube and pour some of the solution over a piece of filter-paper, **which must be placed on an asbestos mat.** Leave for a few minutes and describe what happens.

(*b*) Place a small piece, no bigger than a match-head, of white phosphorus at one end of a strip of steel, approximately 30 cm long and about 2 cm wide, which is being supported on a tripod (see Fig. 13.16). At the other end of the strip put a small pile of red phosphorus. Heat the strip in the middle and await developments.

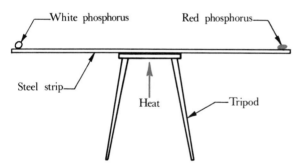

Figure 13.16   The effect of heat on white and red phosphorus

Table 13.1 is partly completed. From your observations in Experiment 13.14, complete the table. Which of the two allotropes is the more reactive? Explain your answer.

A comparison of nitrogen and phosphorus

These two elements, which occur in Group V of the Periodic Table, show very few of the group similarities that we have seen with other groups studied so far. Some of their properties are shown in Table 13.2.

Table 13.1   The allotropes of phosphorus

Property	White phosphorus	Red phosphorus
Appearance		
Melting point	44°C	About 600°C
Density	1·83 g cm^{-3}	2·2 g cm^{-3}
Solubility in water		Insoluble
Solubility in carbon disulphide		Insoluble
In air		Stable
Ignition temperature	35°C	260°C
Toxicity	Very poisonous	Non-poisonous

Table 13.2   A comparison of nitrogen and phosphorus

Property	Nitrogen	Phosphorus
Physical form at room temperature	Colourless gas (b.p. −196°C)	White or red solid
Character	Non-metal	Non-metal
Electrical conductance	Non-conductor	Non-conductor
Solubility in water	Slightly soluble	Insoluble
Combustibility in air	Does not burn	Burns readily
Oxides and their character	N_2O(g), neutral NO(g), neutral NO_2(g), strongly acidic	P_4O_6(s), acidic P_4O_{10}(s), acidic
Principal hydride	Ammonia, NH_3(g)	Phosphine, PH_3(g)
Chlorides	NCl_3(l), very unstable and explosive	PCl_3(l), PCl_5(s)

Summary

Complex compounds of nitrogen called **proteins**, are essential to both plant and animal life. When they are decomposed by heating with soda lime, they give off ammonia, a gas that can be detected by its alkaline character and the white fumes of ammonium chloride formed with hydrogen chloride. Ammonia is so soluble in water that the 'Fountain Experiment' works and the solution produced is a weak alkali, in which ammonia and water molecules are in equilibrium with ammonium and hydroxide ions. This solution precipitates the insoluble hydroxides of metals from their aqueous solutions and forms complex ions, called ammines, with certain transition metal ions. Ammonia reduces some metal oxides to the metal, being itself oxidized to water and nitrogen, thus proving that it contains the elements nitrogen and hydrogen. The formula for ammonia can be proved to be NH_3 by decomposing the compound to its elements with hot iron wire. This reaction is reversible and the synthesis of ammonia from its elements is carried out by the **Haber Process**.

The **nitrogen cycle** describes how the element is used in natural processes and how it is lost and gained. Civilization and intensive cultivation result in a deficiency of nitrogen in the soil and the balance must be restored by the use of **nitrogenous fertilizers**. Fixation of atmospheric nitrogen occurs naturally but not in sufficient quantity and so vast quantities of the element are 'fixed' by the Haber Process to give ammonia which, in turn, is converted to ammonium compounds or, via nitric acid, to nitrates. Apart from nitrogen, the elements essential for healthy plant growth are phosphorus, potassium, and calcium, together with traces of other elements. If these are lacking in the soil, they must be added in the form of an appropriate fertilizer.

The 'building-bricks' for proteins are called **amino-acids**. These compounds can be readily separated and detected by chromatography.

Ammonia burns in oxygen to give nitrogen but, in the presence of a suitable catalyst, nitrogen monoxide is formed. The latter reaction is the basis of the **Ostwald Process** for the manufacture of nitric acid. This acid is strong and, in addition, is a powerful oxidizing agent. Because of this, when it reacts with metals, oxides of nitrogen are usually produced, rather than the hydrogen that might be expected. The salts of nitric acid, called **nitrates**, are all water-soluble compounds which break down on heating to give a variety of products, the details of which depend on the position of the metal in the activity series.

The three most important oxides of nitrogen are dinitrogen monoxide, nitrogen monoxide, and nitrogen dioxide. Nitrogen monoxide is unstable in the presence of air, reacting spontaneously to give the dioxide. Nitrogen dioxide exists as the dimer N_2O_4 at low temperatures, but this dissociates at higher temperatures to give the monomer NO_2.

Phosphorus, which is also vital to life, has very different properties to nitrogen, despite the two elements being in the same group of the Periodic Table. Phosphorus shows allotropy, the two main varieties being the white and the red forms.

Questions

1. Describe an experiment to demonstrate that ammonia is a compound of hydrogen and nitrogen. What further information is required to establish that the formula of ammonia is NH_3? Show how this information can be used to deduce the formula.

Calculate the maximum mass of ammonium sulphate obtainable from $5 \cdot 6$ dm^3 of ammonia gas at stp. (Atomic masses: $N = 14$, $H = 1$, $S = 32$, $O = 16$.)   (C)

2. State the conditions under which ammonia is manufactured from nitrogen and hydrogen. Calculate the mass of ammonia that can be made from 1 kg of nitrogen. (Atomic masses: $N = 14$, $H = 1$.)

Outline, briefly, the method by which ammonia is converted into nitric acid. State why it is important to manufacture large quantities of ammonia and nitric acid.

(O & C)

3. Write down one possible structural formula for glycine. How does this compound react with (a) sodium hydroxide solution, (b) hydrochloric acid?

Describe what happens when a protein, such as egg-white, is boiled for a long time with dilute hydrochloric acid. What class of product is obtained?   (O & C)

4. The protein in a high protein breakfast cereal A contained amino-acids which may be referred to as X, Y, and Z. When another manufacturer marketed B, a similar cereal, the first manufacturer analysed this new product to find out whether it contained the same protein as their own cereal A. They found amino-acids X and Y but *not* Z.

Describe carefully how you would have attempted this analysis.

If X is NH_2CH_2COOH (or $NH_3^+CH_2COO^-$) and Y is $NH_2CH(CH_3)COOH$ (or $NH_3^+CH(CH_3)COO^-$) give one kind of structure which is possible for the protein in the new cereal B.   (LN)

5. (a) Describe in outline the manufacture of nitric acid from ammonia. Give **two** large-scale uses of nitric acid.

(b) Making use of concentrated nitric acid, magnesium, copper, and a supply of water, but no other chemicals, describe briefly experiments by which you could show the formation of **three** different gases.   (C)

6. A gaseous oxide of nitrogen is completely reduced by passing it over heated copper powder. It is found that the volume of nitrogen formed is equal to the original volume of gaseous oxide, both volumes being measured at the same temperature and pressure. The density of the oxide is $1 \cdot 964$ g dm^{-3} at stp. Deduce the formula of the oxide, explaining the reasoning used in your deduction.

Give the names and formulae of **two** other oxides of nitrogen. State briefly how these two oxides can be formed from nitric acid and give **two** chemical differences between them.   (C)

7. The two gases, nitrogen monoxide and oxygen, react immediately at room temperature to form another gas, nitrogen dioxide. The two reactants are said to react in the ratio 2 moles of nitrogen monoxide to 1 mole of oxygen. Nitrogen dioxide dissolves readily in 2 M sodium hydroxide, but pure nitrogen monoxide and oxygen do not.

Devise an apparatus and procedure by which you could check whether nitrogen monoxide and oxygen react in the given ratio. Indicate what results you would expect and how these results lead to your conclusions.   (LN)

8. When lead nitrate crystals are heated, a gas is evolved which, when cooled to 0°C in dry apparatus, gives a yellow liquid, dinitrogen tetroxide. On heating this liquid, a gas is formed which quickly becomes a dark brown gas A. When A is strongly heated, the colour disappears leaving a colourless mixture B.

Identify A and B and write equations for **two** of the reactions.   (JMB)

14

Non-metallic elements and their compounds—III

Group VI—oxygen and sulphur

Oxygen

This is by far the most abundant element in the earth's crust which contains about 50 per cent of it by mass, largely because it is a constituent of most rocks and clays, and of many minerals. In addition, the seas are composed of about 86 per cent of oxygen by mass and the atmosphere of about 21 per cent of the molecular element by volume. This latter proportion remains approximately constant because the oxygen used during respiration and combustion is replaced by that liberated as the result of photosynthesis.

Oxygen is essential to all animal life and over 70 per cent by mass of the human body consists of the element in a combined state as water, sugars, fats, and other compounds.

Oxygen is found in Group VI of the Periodic Table and can thus form O^{2-} ions as in some oxides, but it also readily forms covalent bonds (two) with many elements. It exists most commonly as the diatomic molecule O_2, but there is also another allotrope O_3, called **ozone**.

The largest single use of the gas is in the steel industry (see chapter 11) but, being essential to respiration it is also used extensively in breathing apparatus of all descriptions. Other industrial uses include metal-cutting and welding with oxy-hydrogen and oxy-acetylene equipment, and the production of a number of other chemicals.

The liquefaction of air

This is the process by which oxygen and nitrogen are obtained on a large scale. Purified air is compressed to 150 to 200 atmospheres and then cooled (Fig. 14.1). Cold air passes to the liquefier where the gas is allowed to

271

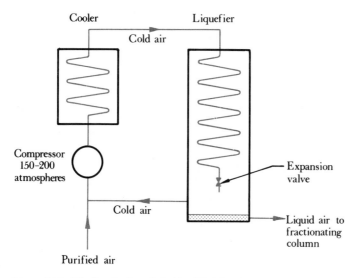

Figure 14.1   The liquefaction of air (simplified flow diagram)

expand through a small valve, which causes it to cool very suddenly (cf., the air let out of a bicycle tyre). Some of the air will liquefy and the remainder helps to cool further the gas entering the liquefier. It then passes out to re-mix with incoming air and go through the cycle again. The liquid air is admitted to a fractionating column where the more volatile nitrogen (b.p. $-196°C$) boils off leaving the oxygen (b.p. $-183°C$), which can be obtained with a purity of over 98 per cent, if required, the main impurity being argon. The oxygen is stored as a liquid in special containers or as a gas in cylinders under pressure. Where required on a very large scale, such as in the steel industry, a medium-purity grade is often used (85 to 95 per cent gaseous oxygen). This 'tonnage oxygen' is obviously much cheaper than the high-quality grade and is perfectly adequate for many purposes.

The nitrogen obtained in the liquefaction process exceeds demand but large quantities are used in the Haber Process (chapter 13), apart from being used as the coolant in the liquefaction itself.

Oxides

Most elements will form the corresponding oxide when heated in oxygen and many will burn vigorously in doing so. Some of these oxides are gaseous, but most are solid.

Describe, with equations, the burning of six different elements in oxygen, using as your examples reactions that you have seen in previous work. How may elements be classified according to the type of oxide produced?

272

Experiment 14.1 *To prepare some oxides of elements within a*
period (sodium to chlorine)

This experiment must be performed by the teacher.

It uses the same method as was used in Experiment 8.1, but a wider range
of oxides is prepared.

Place a little of each solid element in turn in the tube shown in Fig. 14.2,
pass in a slow stream of oxygen from a cylinder and heat gently with a small
burner. (This experiment obviously cannot be carried out with chlorine as
it is a gas.)

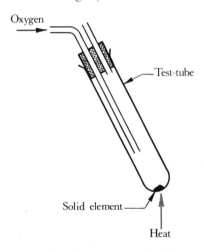

Oxygen

Test-tube

Solid element

Heat

Figure 14.2   The preparation of oxides

In each case, observe what happens and note the appearance of any
residue.

NB: Some elements form more than one oxide, e.g., sodium (sodium peroxide), phosphorus (phosphorus(III) oxide), sulphur (sulphur trioxide),
chlorine (chlorine monoxide).

Experiment 14.2 *Investigating the properties of the*
oxides of the elements in the sodium period

**The experiments with the oxides of sodium and phosphorus must be carried
out by the teacher. Those with dichlorine heptoxide are too difficult to perform.**

(*a*) Appearance and physical state. Use your observations from Experiment 14.1 to fill in the appropriate spaces in Table 14.1.

(b) Add a little water to a sample of the oxide in a test-tube and test with Universal Indicator (pH) paper.

Tests (c) and (d) are only to be carried out if the oxide did not react with water.

(c) Add a little dilute hydrochloric acid to the sample in a test-tube and warm if there is no apparent reaction.

(d) Add a little sodium hydroxide solution to the sample in a test-tube and warm if there is no apparent reaction.

Table 14.1   The properties of some oxides

	Oxides of						
	Sodium	Mag-nesium	Alu-minium	Silicon	Phos-phorus	Sulphur	Chlorine
Name	Sodium mon-oxide	Mag-nesium oxide	Alu-minium oxide	Silicon oxide	Phos-phorus (V) oxide	Sulphur dioxide	Dichlorine heptoxide
Formula	Na_2O	MgO	Al_2O_3	SiO_2	P_4O_{10}	SO_2	Cl_2O_7
Appearance							Colourless, oily, liquid
m.p. (in °C)	920	2800	2047	1610	Sublimes (b.p. 359°C)	−75 (b.p. −10°C)	−91·5 (b.p. 80°C)
ΔH_f (in kJ per mole oxygen atoms)	−416	−602	−556	−455	−291	−148	−38
Solubility in water							Slightly soluble
pH of solution							Acid
Solubility in HCl							Slightly soluble
Solubility in NaOH							Soluble

Using your results, complete Table 14.1 as far as is possible. Comment on any trends in properties that are apparent. On the same side of a piece of graph-paper (using appropriate scales), plot graphs of (a) melting point and (b) enthalpy of formation (ΔH_f) per mole of oxygen atoms, for each oxide against the atomic number of the *element* concerned. Comment on the shapes of the graphs.

Water

Water, an oxide of hydrogen, covers about three-quarters of the earth's surface and is, of course, vital to life. The melting and boiling points are taken as fixed points in thermometry for the Celsius scale ($0°$ and $100°$ respectively).

Water is an excellent solvent because of its special structure and consequent polarity. (Frequent references have been made to this property earlier in the book.)

Other properties of water (also dealt with earlier) are:

(*a*) Its reactions with metals.

(*b*) Its reactions with oxides and hydroxides and the consequent effect on acidity and alkalinity.

(*c*) The formation of hydrates.

Sulphur

Sulphur occurs in the free state, dispersed in limestone, as deposits in the American States of Texas and Louisiana. These provide about 80 per cent of the world's supply of sulphur. There are also small deposits of free sulphur in volcanic regions such as Sicily. In addition, the element is found widely distributed in the combined state, usually as sulphides but also as sulphates. Another important source of the element is as a by-product from petroleum refining.

Most of the sulphur produced is converted to sulphur dioxide and hence to sulphuric acid (as described later in this chapter). Smaller quantities of the element are used for vulcanizing (i.e., hardening) rubber, as a fungicide, and in the manufacture of other chemicals, such as carbon disulphide.

The extraction of sulphur

The American deposits of sulphur would be very difficult to mine by conventional methods as they are more than 200 m below the surface, underneath layers of quicksand. This is overcome by the **Frasch Process**, in which three concentric pipes are sunk into the sulphur-bearing layer by conventional drilling, the largest pipe being approximately 15 cm in diameter (see Fig. 14.3).

Superheated water, at $170°C$ and under pressure, is pumped down the outer tube to melt the sulphur. Hot compressed air is passed down the innermost tube to force the molten sulphur up the middle tube as a light froth. When it reaches the surface, it is allowed to solidify in large tanks before being

Hot compressed air

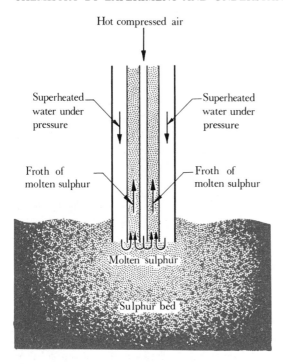

Superheated water under pressure

Superheated water under pressure

Froth of molten sulphur

Froth of molten sulphur

Molten sulphur

Sulphur bed

Figure 14.3   The Frasch Process

broken up to be removed. The sulphur is approximately 99·8 per cent pure and normally needs no further purification.

Experiment 14.3   *To prepare some different varieties of sulphur and examine the effect of heat on the element*

(*a*) To about 2 cm depth of carbon disulphide in a test-tube, add a spatula-measure of powdered roll-sulphur. Shake the tube, but do not warm it, until most of the sulphur has dissolved and then decant the solution onto a watch-glass in a fume-cupboard. Cover with a piece of filter-paper and leave for about thirty minutes. Examine the product, leave overnight and re-examine it.

NB: **Carbon disulphide is very volatile, inflammable and toxic, and must be handled with extreme care.**

(*b*) To about 2 cm depth of xylene in a test-tube, add a spatula-measure of roll-sulphur. Warm the tube, but do not boil the contents, until the sulphur has all dissolved (if necessary, add a little more xylene). If the sulphur dissolves easily, add a little more until a saturated solution is obtained (i.e., a little solid sulphur remains). Leave the solution to cool and examine the product. Leave overnight and then re-examine the sample.

NB: Xylene is inflammable but not very volatile and there is thus little danger if it is not boiled.

(*c*) Heat about 3 cm depth of powdered roll-sulphur very slowly in a test-tube until it boils, observing all changes very carefully but in particular, changes in viscosity. When boiling, pour the molten sulphur into cold water contained in a beaker. When the sulphur has cooled, remove it from the water and examine it. Leave overnight and then re-examine the sample.

The three varieties of sulphur are allotropes and are called respectively (in the order that you prepared them) **rhombic, monoclinic,** and **plastic sulphur.** (See Fig. 14.4.)

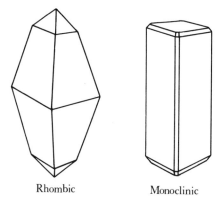

Rhombic   Monoclinic

Figure 14.4 Sulphur crystals

Describe the differences in the three allotropes. Do they all appear to be crystalline? Is there any evidence to suggest which of the allotropes is the most stable?

There is a definite temperature (95·6°C) at which rhombic sulphur changes into monoclinic sulphur and vice versa, this being called the **transition temperature**. The one allotrope is stable above this temperature (up to the melting point) and the other is stable below it.

Which allotrope do you think is stable at room temperature?

X-ray diffraction (chapter 4) has shown that in the solid state, sulphur forms molecules consisting of rings of eight atoms, i.e., S_8, as shown in Fig. 14.5. The different allotropes occur because these rings can be packed together in different ways to give different structures. When sulphur is molten, the rings tend to break open and form long chains, which, at higher temperatures, split up into shorter chains.

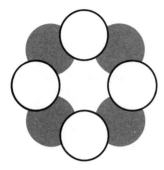

Plan View

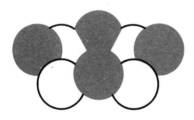

Side View

Figure 14.5   The S₈ molecule

Try to explain the changes that you observed when solid sulphur was gently heated.

Experiment 14.4   *To make a model of the S₈ molecule*

On the equator of one of the polystyrene spheres provided and using a jig or a protractor, put two marks 105° apart. Repeat this procedure with another seven spheres. Using short lengths of pipe-cleaner, assemble the eight-membered ring so that four atoms are below, in the form of a square, with the other four in a square above them, at 45° to the first square, as shown in Fig. 14.5.

By using the model, check the answer you gave to the question on the changing structure of sulphur when it is being heated.

Experiment 14.5   *To prepare sulphur dioxide and investigate its properties*

Place some crystals of sodium sulphite in the test-tube (Fig. 14.6) together with some dilute hydrochloric acid. Fit the delivery-tube and gently warm the contents of the tube. Carry out tests (*a*), (*b*), and (*c*) on the gas emerging from the delivery-tube and then collect two test-tubes of the gas.

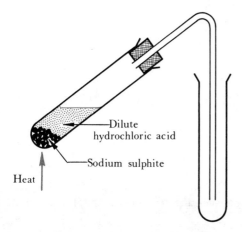

Heat

Dilute hydrochloric acid

Sodium sulphite

Figure 14.6   The preparation of sulphur dioxide

Care should be taken not to inhale the gas.

(*a*) Appearance.
(*b*) Test with moist Universal Indicator (pH) paper.
(*c*) On a piece of filter-paper place a spot of each of the following solutions (as shown in Fig. 14.7) and then expose each in turn to the gas:
   (*i*) Potassium permanganate acidified with dilute sulphuric acid.
   (*ii*) Potassium dichromate acidified with dilute sulphuric acid.
   (*iii*) Iodine.

Write an equation for the reaction between sodium sulphite and hydrochloric acid. From the method of collection used, what can you deduce about the density of the gas? When collecting tubes of the gas, how can you tell when the tube is full? What do the reactions of the three substances in test (*c*) with sulphur dioxide have in common? What part is the sulphur dioxide playing in these reactions? Write ionic equations to represent each of the reactions.

279

(*d*) Plunge a lighted splint into the gas.

(*e*) Plunge a piece of burning magnesium attached to the end of a spatula into the gas.

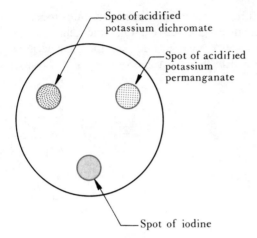

Figure 14.7   **Testing for sulphur dioxide**

What essential difference is there between the reactions of sulphur dioxide in (*c*) and (*e*) respectively?

Sulphur dioxide, in the presence of water, ionizes *slightly* to form hydrogen sulphite ions (HSO_3^-) and also some sulphite ions (SO_3^{2-}):

$$SO_2(aq) + H_2O(l) \rightleftharpoons HSO_3^-(aq) + H^+(aq) \rightleftharpoons SO_3^{2-}(aq) + 2H^+(aq)$$

There are thus two series of salts, the **sulphites** and the very unstable **hydrogen sulphites**.

Discuss any similarities that you know between carbon dioxide and sulphur dioxide.

Experiment 14.6   *The oxidation of sulphur dioxide*

This experiment must be carried out by the teacher.

Set up the apparatus **in a fume-cupboard**, as shown in Fig. 14.8. Oxygen and sulphur dioxide (best obtained from cylinders) are dried by bubbling through the concentrated sulphuric acid. Excess sulphur dioxide is absorbed in sodium hydroxide solution.

Adjust the flow of gases to a steady stream (judged by the bubbles of gas) and then heat the platinized asbestos. After a while, turn off the gas supplies

280

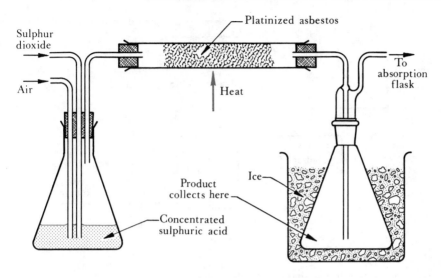

Figure 14.8   The oxidation of sulphur dioxide

and observe the appearance of the product. Finally, add a little water, shake and test the pH of the solution.

The product of the reaction is **sulphur trioxide** (SO_3).

| Write an equation for the reaction. What part was played by the platinum?

When sulphur trioxide dissolves in water, it produces sulphuric acid.

| Write an equation for this reaction.

The manufacture of sulphuric acid

Sulphuric acid is manufactured on a vast scale and used chiefly for making the fertilizers calcium superphosphate and ammonium sulphate. Other large-scale uses are in the manufacture of pigments, viscose rayon (artificial silk), detergents, dyes, drugs, explosives, and many others.

The chemistry of the manufacture of the acid by the **Contact Process** is that observed in Experiment 14.6. Sulphur dioxide obtained from various sources, such as burning sulphur, heating sulphide ores such as zinc blende, heating calcium sulphate (anhydrite) with coke, sand, and aluminium oxide, and burning hydrogen sulphide associated with natural gas, is mixed with air and then the mixture is carefully purified and dried (see Fig. 14.9). The gases pass into the catalyst chamber containing vanadium(V) oxide (which is much cheaper than platinum) in a finely divided condition, at about 450°C, where

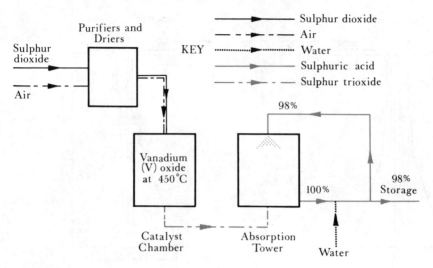

Figure 14.9   **The Contact Process (simplified flow diagram)**

the sulphur dioxide and oxygen combine with approximately 98 per cent efficiency to give sulphur trioxide:

$$2SO_2(g) + O_2(g) \rightleftharpoons 2SO_3(g)$$

The equilibrium lies well to the right and thus high pressure is unnecessary. The reaction is highly exothermic and some of the heat produced is used to heat the incoming gases via a heat-exchanger. The cooled sulphur trioxide then passes to the absorption tower where it is dissolved in 98 per cent sulphuric acid. (The reaction with water is so vigorous that a mist of acid droplets forms which is very difficult to condense.) The 100 per cent acid normally produced is diluted back to 98 per cent by adding water and so the effective reaction is:

$$SO_3(g) + H_2O(l) \longrightarrow H_2SO_4(l)$$

Some of the acid produced is used for absorbing more sulphur trioxide and the remainder passes to storage tanks.

Experiment 14.7   *Investigating the properties of sulphuric acid*

Carry out tests (*a*) and (*b*) using dilute sulphuric acid.
(*a*) Determine the pH of the solution.
(*b*) Test the solution for conductance.
(*c*) To a little of each of the following solids contained in a test-tube, add about 2 cm³ of dilute sulphuric acid: copper(II) oxide, magnesium oxide, zinc hydroxide, and sodium carbonate.

Name the products and write equations for each of the tests in (c) above. Are the results of all the above tests typical of those you would expect from an acid? Explain your answer.

In the following tests, use the concentration of acid specified.

Great care must be taken when handling concentrated sulphuric acid. When a test is completed, carefully add water to the products and then pour down a sink. NEVER treat hot sulphuric acid in this way; allow it to cool before disposal.

(d) Place some magnesium and copper turnings in separate test-tubes and add about 2 cm³ of the dilute acid to each. If either metal does not react, take a fresh sample and to it add a few drops of the concentrated acid and then warm gently. In each case, identify any gas evolved.

Are the reactions of dilute sulphuric acid with metals typical of those you would expect from an acid? How does the reaction of concentrated sulphuric acid with a metal differ from that of the dilute acid? What type of reaction is occurring when the concentrated acid reacts with a metal?

(e) Add a few drops of concentrated sulphuric acid to a small quantity of sodium chloride in a test-tube.

(f) Add a few drops of concentrated sulphuric acid to a small quantity of sodium nitrate in a test-tube. Then add a little copper turnings and warm gently.

In this test, which gas was evolved? As copper was used in order to obtain this gas, what substance must have been present in the test-tube as the result of the reaction between the concentrated sulphuric acid and the sodium nitrate? What is there in common between the reactions in tests (e) and (f)?

NB: Nitric acid may be prepared by heating together concentrated sulphuric acid and sodium nitrate.

(g) Add a few drops of concentrated sulphuric acid to a small quantity of hydrated (i.e., blue) copper(II) sulphate on a watch-glass.

From earlier work, remind yourself of the reaction between concentrated sulphuric acid and water. How is this reaction related to what you have observed in test (g)?

(h) Using a glass rod or a teat-pipette, write your name on a piece of paper with dilute sulphuric acid. *Warm* the paper over a bunsen flame, taking care not to set it alight!

The next test should be carried out by the teacher, using a fume-cupboard.

(*i*) Make a concentrated solution of cane sugar and pour about 10 cm^3 into a boiling-tube. Add some concentrated sulphuric acid and leave for a short time.

| Try to explain what has happened in these two tests.

Experiment 14.8   *Investigating the properties of sulphates*

Sulphuric acid gives rise to two series of salts, the **sulphates** ($SO_4{}^{2-}$) and the **hydrogen sulphates** ($HSO_4{}^-$).

Carry out the following tests:
(*a*) Solubility in water. Shake some of each of the given sulphates, in turn, with about 2 cm^3 of water in a test-tube. Try to use approximately the same quantity of solid in each case.

To approximately 2 cm^3 of lead(II) nitrate solution in a test-tube, add about the same volume of dilute sulphuric acid. Repeat this test using calcium chloride solution instead of lead(II) nitrate.

| Are all sulphates soluble in water? If not, name those that are insoluble. Write equations to represent the reactions between dilute sulphuric acid and the two aqueous solutions used in the last test.

(*b*) The effect of heat. Use an ignition-tube and a small quantity of each of the given solids in turn. Heat gently at first and then strongly. Try to identify any gases evolved.

| Arranging the metals in their order in the activity series, compare the stability to heat of nitrates and sulphates.

Experiment 14.9   *Distinguishing between sulphites and sulphates*

Use aqueous solutions of sodium sulphite and sodium sulphate for the following tests.
(*a*) Add a few drops of aqueous barium nitrate to each solution in turn.
(*b*) Add a few drops of dilute nitric acid followed by some aqueous barium nitrate to each solution in turn.
(*c*) Add a few drops of aqueous potassium permanganate acidified with dilute sulphuric acid to each solution in turn.
Carry out the following test on solid samples of sodium sulphite and sodium sulphate, contained in separate test-tubes:
(*d*) Add some dilute hydrochloric acid and warm gently. Identify any gas evolved.

| Make a table to summarize the differences between sulphites and sulphates.

A comparison of oxygen and sulphur

There are marked differences between these two Group VI elements, just as there are between nitrogen and phosphorus in Group V. Some of their properties are shown in Table 14.2.

Table 14.2   A comparison of oxygen and sulphur

Property	Oxygen	Sulphur
Physical form at room temperature	Colourless gas (b.p. −183°C)	Yellow solid (m.p. 114–120°C)
Formula of molecule at room temperature	$O_2(g)$	$S_8(s)$
Allotropy	Oxygen O_2 Ozone O_3	Rhombic (up to 95·6°C) Monoclinic (95·6–120°C) Various allotropes in liquid state
Character	Non-metal	Non-metal
Electrical conductance	Non-conductor	Non-conductor
Solubility in water	Slightly soluble	Insoluble
Combustibility in air	—	Burns readily
Oxides and their character	—	$SO_2(g)$, acidic $SO_3(s)$, acidic
Principal hydride	$H_2O(l)$	$H_2S(g)$
Monatomic ions formed	Oxide O^{2-}	Sulphide S^{2-}

Summary

Oxygen is a very abundant element that is essential to life and is readily obtained by the liquefaction of air. Most elements form oxides when heated in oxygen, the properties of which change in a periodic way with increasing atomic number of the element. In general, metallic elements form basic oxides and non-metallic elements form acidic oxides. Probably the most important oxide is water, which has many unique properties, the most significant being its solvent action.

Sulphur, the second element in Group VI, is found in the free state principally in America, and is extracted from these deposits by the **Frasch Process**.

285

It exhibits allotropy, **rhombic** sulphur being stable up to 95·6°C and **monoclinic** sulphur being stable from this **transition temperature** up to the melting point (about 120°C). Both these allotropes consist of eight-membered rings arranged in different ways. When sulphur melts, these rings break open and then join into long chains which cause the liquid to become very viscous. At higher temperatures, these break up into smaller chains and the liquid becomes more mobile once more. Thus there are several allotropes in liquid sulphur, one of which is **plastic** sulphur. All other allotropes revert to the rhombic variety if kept at room temperature.

Sulphur dioxide, a pungent-smelling gas obtained by burning sulphur in air or oxygen, is acidic in the presence of water due to the reaction that liberates some hydronium ions and forms **hydrogen sulphite** ions and **sulphite** ions, both of which can exist in the form of salts. It is also a powerful reducing agent which itself can only be reduced with difficulty, as for example by burning magnesium. On catalytic oxidation, sulphur dioxide will form **sulphur trioxide** which, in the presence of water, gives **sulphuric acid**. This sequence of reactions is used in the **Contact Process** for the manufacture of sulphuric acid. When dilute, sulphuric acid behaves like a normal acid, but when concentrated it is an oxidizing agent (when hot) and also a powerful dehydrating agent, being able to remove not only moisture but also the elements of water from a compound. This acid also gives rise to two series of salts, the **sulphates** and **hydrogen sulphates**. Nearly all sulphates are soluble in water and, in general, these compounds are more stable to heat than are nitrates. They can be distinguished from sulphites by their lack of reducing properties and their stability to dilute acids.

In general, oxygen and sulphur show marked differences in their properties, as do carbon and silicon, and nitrogen and phosphorus, the first two elements in respectively Groups IV and V. The most likely explanation of these differences can be found when the electronic structures (see chapters 1 and 9) of the elements are compared, as shown in Table 14.3.

Table 14.3 The electronic structures of some elements in Periods 2 and 3

Period 2	Element	Carbon	Nitrogen	Oxygen
	Electronic structure	$1s^2\, 2s^2\, 2p^2$	$1s^2\, 2s^2\, 2p^3$	$1s^2\, 2s^2\, 2p^4$
Period 3	Element	Silicon	Phosphorus	Sulphur
	Electronic structure	$1s^2\, 2s^2\, 2p^6\, 3s^2\, 3p^2$	$1s^2\, 2s^2\, 2p^6\, 3s^2\, 3p^3$	$1s^2\, 2s^2\, 2p^6\, 3s^2\, 3p^4$

It can be seen that the Period 2 elements have only one completed orbital ($1s$) between the nucleus and the electrons used for bonding ($2s$ and $2p$), whereas the Period 3 elements have three such orbitals ($1s$, $2s$, and $2p$). It follows that the nucleus must have a much greater effect on the outer electrons of the Period 2 elements than it does with Period 3 elements, thus accounting for the observed differences in properties.

Questions

1. (*a*) Describe in outline the commercial preparation of oxygen from the air. Mention **three** large-scale uses of oxygen.

(*b*) How do the processes of respiration and the burning of fuels (*i*) resemble one another, (*ii*) differ from one another?

(*c*) 'When we burn coal, we are making use of stored energy that came originally from the sun.' Explain this statement. (C)

2. Name **three** different chemical sources of sulphur. Give **two** reasons for regarding sulphur as a non-metal. Describe how you could obtain a sample of pure sulphur from a mixture of sulphur and sand. Calculate the mass of sulphuric acid that could be made from one kilogramme of sulphur. (Atomic masses: S = 32, H = 1, O = 16.)
(O & C)

3. Explain the statement that sulphur has two crystalline allotropes.

Describe **one** process for the manufacture of sulphuric acid.

Given dilute aqueous solutions of sodium hydroxide and sulphuric acid, describe how you would obtain crystalline sodium sulphate. (O & C)

4. You are provided with dilute sulphuric acid and are required to prepare samples of (*a*) lead sulphate, (*b*) magnesium sulphate crystals, (*c*) sulphur dioxide, (*d*) sodium hydrogen sulphate solution. Name the other substances you would require and write equations for **each** preparation.

Describe in detail how you would carry out **two** of these preparations. (C)

15

Non-metallic elements and their compounds—IV

Group VII—the halogens

The halogens are all too reactive to occur naturally in the free state. Fluorine is found in the mineral fluorspar, CaF_2; chlorine most commonly as chlorides, notably sodium chloride in the form of rock salt and in sea-water; bromine as bromides again in sea-water; and iodine as iodates present in the Chile nitrate deposits and iodides found in sea-weed.

Many of the properties of the elements have already been studied in chapter 9, when it was found that there were very marked similarities between them but that the general reactivity decreased with increasing atomic number, so that fluorine is the most reactive and iodine is the least reactive. They all form ions of the type X^-, but also readily form covalent bonds, usually with non-metallic elements.

Chlorine is the most widely used halogen. The element itself is used for killing bacteria, particularly in drinking water and swimming pools, and in the manufacture of a large number of other chemicals such as hydrochloric acid, PVC (polyvinyl chloride—the plastic), drugs, dyes, and solvents. Fluorine has only recently become available in large quantities but is of increasing importance for the manufacture of a wide range of fluorides and fluorocarbons (fluorinated hydrocarbons) such as PTFE (polytetrafluoroethene) which is remarkably inert chemically and is used as an electrical insulator and a 'non-stick' surface (e.g., in cooking utensils). Bromine is mainly used for making dibromoethane for the petroleum industry but is also important as bromides, notably for photography. Iodine is a powerful germicide and is used as a 2 per cent solution in alcohol ('tincture of iodine'). It is also used in photography as iodides and for making other iodine compounds.

Chlorine

On an industrial scale, nearly all the chlorine used is manufactured by electrolysis, notably in the production of sodium hydroxide from brine (see chapter 10). This involves the loss of an electron from the chloride ion (i.e., oxidation of the chloride ion) to form the atom, two of which then combine to form the molecule:

$$Cl^-(aq) + e^- \longrightarrow Cl$$
$$Cl + Cl \longrightarrow Cl_2(g)$$

Oxidation of chloride ions is also the principle used in the laboratory preparations of the gas.

Experiment 15.1 *To prepare chlorine from hydrochloric acid*

Add a few drops of concentrated hydrochloric acid, in turn, to each of the following substances contained in test-tubes: potassium dichromate, $K_2Cr_2O_7$; lead(IV) oxide, PbO_2; potassium permanganate, $KMnO_4$; manganese(IV) oxide, MnO_2. If no gas is evolved, warm the contents of the tube gently. In each case, test for the evolution of chlorine.

What is the simplest test to use to detect chlorine? What type of reaction has occurred in each case? Write ionic equations to represent each reaction. Which of these methods would be the most convenient to use for the preparation of several gas-jars of chlorine?

Experiment 15.2 *To prepare the chlorides of elements*
  within the sodium period

This experiment must be performed by the teacher.

It uses the same technique as was used in Experiment 9.4, but with a wider range of elements.

Place a little of each solid element in turn in the tube shown in Fig. 15.1, pass in a slow stream of chlorine from a cylinder or generator and heat gently with a small bunsen flame. In each case, observe what happens and note the appearance of any product.

Using your observations, complete Table 15.1. For each chloride, by consideration of its physical properties, comment on the probable bonding.

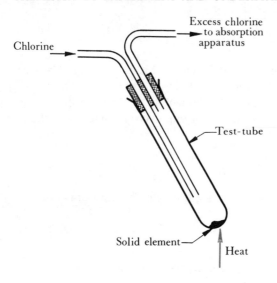

Figure 15.1 **The preparation of chlorides**

Table 15.1 **The properties of some chlorides**

	Chlorides of					
	Sodium	Magnesium	Aluminium	Silicon	Phosphorus	Sulphur
Name	Sodium chloride	Magnesium chloride	Aluminium chloride	Silicon tetra-chloride	Phosphorus (III) chloride*	Disulphur dichloride
Formula	NaCl	$MgCl_2$	$AlCl_3$	$SiCl_4$	PCl_3	S_2Cl_2
Appearance						
m.p. (in °C)	808	714	193	−70	−92	−80
b.p. (in °C)	1517	1416	423	57	76	137

* Phosphorus(V) chloride, PCl_5, may also be formed.

Experiment 15.3 *The reaction between chlorine and hydrogen*

These experiments must be performed by the teacher.

Experiment I

Fill the plastic bottle shown in Fig. 15.2(*a*) with water. Displace half of the water by bubbling in chlorine (see Fig. 15.2(*b*)) from a cylinder or generator, and then the remaining half with hydrogen from a cylinder. Stopper the bottle and stand it on the bench. Ignite a length of magnesium ribbon held in tongs, and bring the burning magnesium close to the 'window' in the bottle.

What part do you think was played by the burning magnesium in this experiment?

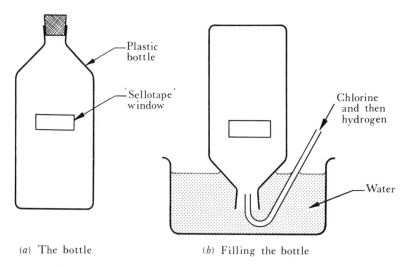

(a) The bottle　　　　　　　(b) Filling the bottle

Figure 15.2　The hydrogen/chlorine reaction

Experiment II

(a) Fill the flask (see Fig. 15.3) with chlorine from a cylinder or generator. Connect the glass jet to a cylinder of hydrogen, turn on the gas, light it at the jet and adjust the flow to give a flame about 2 cm long. Insert the jet into the flask and observe the flame.

What do you think is left in the flask?

(b) When the flame goes out, remove the jet and immediately stopper the flask. Turn off the hydrogen and disconnect the jet from the cylinder. Dip the tip of the jet into water and replace it in the flask, having removed the stopper. Immediately invert the flask so that the end of the protruding glass tube is below the surface of some water coloured with Universal Indicator (pH) solution in a large beaker.

You have seen a similar experiment to part (b) before; what was it called? Why does it work?

The final product of this reaction is called **hydrochloric acid**.

Is this an appropriate name? Explain your answer.

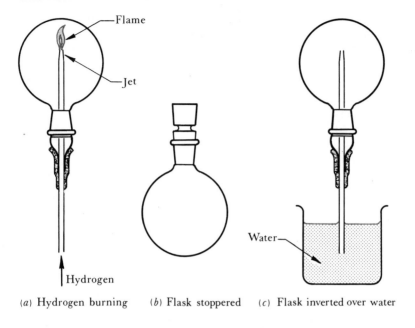

(a) Hydrogen burning   (b) Flask stoppered   (c) Flask inverted over water

Figure 15.3   Burning hydrogen in chlorine

Hydrogen chloride

You have met the gas hydrogen chloride several times earlier in this book. As you have just seen, it can be made by burning hydrogen in chlorine and this is one method used for the manufacture of the gas.

Starting with sodium chloride, by what other method could you prepare hydrogen chloride in the laboratory? Summarize the properties of hydrogen chloride. How does the structure of hydrogen chloride differ when it is respectively dry and wet?

Most of the hydrogen chloride prepared is dissolved in water to make hydrochloric acid.

Hydrochloric acid

The acid is used to 'pickle' metals (i.e., remove oxide from the surface before galvanizing, tinning, or plating), and in the preparation of chlorides.

Experiment 15.4 *Investigating the properties of hydrochloric acid*

Carry out test (*a*) and (*b*) using dilute hydrochloric acid:
(*a*) Determine the pH of the solution.
(*b*) Test the solution for conductance.
(*c*) To a little of each of the following solids, contained in a test-tube, add about 2 cm^3 of dilute hydrochloric acid: copper(II) oxide, magnesium oxide, zinc hydroxide, and sodium carbonate.

Name the products and write equations for each of the tests in (*c*) above. Are the results of all the above tests typical of those you would expect from an acid? Explain your answer.

(*d*) Place some magnesium and copper turnings in separate test-tubes and add about 2 cm^3 of dilute hydrochloric acid to each.
(*e*) Repeat test (*d*) using concentrated hydrochloric acid.

Are there any differences obtained with the respective metals in the results of tests (*d*) and (*e*)? In what respects does hydrochloric acid differ from nitric and sulphuric acids?

Experiment 15.5 *Investigating the properties of chlorides*

Carry out the following tests:
(*a*) Solubility in water. Shake some of each of the given chlorides, in turn, with about 2 cm^3 of water in a test-tube. Try to use approximately the same quantity of solid in each case.
To approximately 2 cm^3 of lead(II) nitrate solution, add about the same volume of dilute hydrochloric acid. Warm the mixture, allow it to cool, and observe carefully for any changes. Repeat this test using silver nitrate solution instead of lead(II) nitrate.

Are all chlorides soluble in water? If not, name those that are insoluble and comment on the effect of temperature on their solubility. Write equations to represent the reactions between dilute hydrochloric acid and the two aqueous solutions used in the last test.

(*b*) The effect of heat. Use an ignition-tube and a small quantity of each of the given solids in turn. Heat gently at first and then strongly.

Comment on the stability to heat of chlorides.

Experiment 15.6 *To distinguish between chlorides, bromides, and iodides*

Carry out the following tests on each of the samples of sodium chloride, sodium bromide, and sodium iodide:

(*a*) To the solid, add a few drops of concentrated sulphuric acid and test any gas evolved.

(*b*) To the solid add a little manganese(IV) oxide, followed by a few drops of concentrated sulphuric acid.

(*c*) To an aqueous solution, add a few drops of aqueous silver nitrate solution. (*NB:* It is normal practice, when conducting this test, to add a little dilute nitric acid to the solution before adding the silver nitrate. This is to prevent interference by any other ions that might be present. It does *not* help to distinguish the three halides.)

(*d*) To an aqueous solution add a few drops of chlorine water and shake.

Explain the chemistry of the above tests. Summarize the differences between the three halides.

Experiment 15.7 *To investigate the reactions between the halogens and aqueous iron(II) ions*

Put about 2 cm^3 of aqueous iron(II) sulphate into each of three test-tubes. To the first add a few drops of chlorine water, to the second some bromine water and to the third some iodine solution. Then add a few drops of potassium thiocyanate to each tube.

What do you deduce from your observations? What has happened to the iron(II) ions? Explain the reactions by means of ionic equations.

Experiment 15.8 *A survey of liquid bleaches*

Carry out this experiment on as many liquid domestic bleaches as possible (e.g., Domestos, Brobat, etc.). In each case, the price should be noted at the time of purchase. Carefully measure the volume of each bleach supplied.

Take 25 cm^3 of the concentrated bleach (i.e., out of the bottle as purchased) and dilute it to 250 cm^3 with distilled water. Measure 25 cm^3 of the diluted bleach into a conical flask containing 10 cm^3 of 10 per cent potassium iodide solution together with 10 cm^3 of 2 M sulphuric acid.

These liquid bleaches are made by dissolving chlorine in sodium hydroxide solution to form sodium hypochlorite solution. If acid is added to this solution free chlorine is formed, which liberates iodine from the potassium iodide.

Using a burette, add 5 per cent sodium thiosulphate solution to the contents of the flask, with shaking, until the iodine colouration has just disappeared.

The volume of sodium thiosulphate used effectively measures the quantity of chlorine present and may be called the 'bleaching power' of the sample. The 'bleaching value' can be calculated from the following expression:

$$\text{Bleaching value} = \frac{\text{'bleaching power'} \times \text{volume supplied}}{\text{cost in new pence}}$$

Calculate the 'bleaching value' for each available bleach and plot the results in the form of a histogram, as shown in Fig. 15.4.

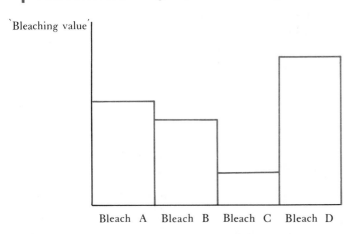

Figure 15.4 'Bleaching Value'

Summary

In contrast to the non-metals studied in previous chapters, the Group VII elements (the halogens) show remarkable similarities in their properties, within the group. All are very reactive, fluorine being so much so that it cannot be safely handled in a school laboratory, but the reactivity decreases down the group from fluorine to iodine.

Chlorine can readily be prepared by oxidation of hydrochloric acid but on an industrial scale it is normally obtained by electrolysis of brine (see chapter 10). Most chlorides can be prepared by the direct action of chlorine on the element. The chlorides of metals are generally ionic solids but those of non-metals are covalent and often liquid. Hydrogen will burn in chlorine but a mixture of the two gases will explode if initiated by intense ultra-violet light (as for example provided by burning magnesium). In both cases, the product is hydrogen chloride, a gas that has a polar covalent structure (see chapter 4) when dry but which reacts readily with water to form ions (see chapter 8). It is thus very soluble in water, the solution being called **hydrochloric acid**. This acid behaves in a typical manner at all concentrations, unlike nitric acid (chapter 13) and sulphuric acid (chapter 14), and gives rise to just one series of salts, the **chlorides**. Most of these are soluble in water and are very stable to heat. Lead chloride is insoluble in cold water but much more soluble in hot water, from which it may be crystallized.

Chlorides, bromides, and iodides can be distinguished by their reactions with an oxidizing agent in the presence of concentrated sulphuric acid, and with silver nitrate in dilute nitric acid.

The free halogens are oxidizing agents, chlorine being stronger than in turn bromine and iodine, as shown by their reactions with iron(II) ions and by the fact that they can displace each other in this order from their compounds (see also chapter 9). The oxidizing power of chlorine can be used to test the relative merits of liquid bleaches.

Questions

1. Give an account of the experimental evidence which might be collected in a school laboratory which indicates that the halogens (chlorine, bromine, and iodine) belong to the same group in the Periodic Table of the elements and that each of these halogens has a particular position in the group. (LN)

2. The second short period is Na Mg Al Si P S Cl Ar. Describe simple experiments you have done with (a) the hydroxides and (b) the chlorides of sodium, magnesium, and aluminium which illustrate a gradual change in chemical behaviour across a period. Use these trends to predict some of the properties of the chloride and hydroxide of phosphorus. (LN)

3. You have been provided with a mixture of copper(II) oxide and common salt (sodium chloride). How would you obtain from this (a) pure dry sodium chloride, (b) pure copper, and (c) chlorine gas? (L)

Table of atomic masses

Element	Symbol	Atomic Number	Atomic Mass	Element	Symbol	Atomic Number	Atomic Mass
Actinium	Ac	89	227	Mercury	Hg	80	200·6
Aluminium	Al	13	27	Molybdenum	Mo	42	96
Americium	Am	95	243	Neodymium	Nd	60	144·2
Antimony	Sb	51	121·7	Neon	Ne	10	20·2
Argon	Ar	18	40	Neptunium	Np	93	237
Arsenic	As	33	75	Nickel	Ni	28	58·7
Astatine	At	85	210	Niobium	Nb	41	93
Barium	Ba	56	137·3	Nitrogen	N	7	14
Berkelium	Bk	97	249	Nobelium	No	102	254
Beryllium	Be	4	9	Osmium	Os	76	190·2
Bismuth	Bi	83	209	Oxygen	O	8	16
Boron	B	5	10·8	Palladium	Pd	46	106·4
Bromine	Br	35	80	Phosphorus	P	15	31
Cadmium	Cd	48	112·4	Platinum	Pt	78	195
Caesium	Cs	55	133	Plutonium	Pu	94	242
Calcium	Ca	20	40	Polonium	Po	84	210
Californium	Cf	98	251	Potassium	K	19	39
Carbon	C	6	12	Praseodymium	Pr	59	141
Cerium	Ce	58	140	Promethium	Pm	61	145
Chlorine	Cl	17	35·5	Protactinium	Pa	91	231
Chromium	Cr	24	52	Radium	Ra	88	226
Cobalt	Co	27	59	Radon	Rn	86	222
Copper	Cu	29	63·5	Rhenium	Re	75	186·2
Curium	Cm	96	247	Rhodium	Rh	45	103
Dysprosium	Dy	66	162·5	Rubidium	Rb	37	85·5
Einsteinium	Es	99	254	Ruthenium	Ru	44	101
Erbium	Er	68	167·3	Samarium	Sm	62	150·3
Europium	Eu	63	152	Scandium	Sc	21	45
Fermium	Fm	100	253	Selenium	Se	34	79
Fluorine	F	9	19	Silicon	Si	14	28
Francium	Fr	87	223	Silver	Ag	47	108
Gadolinium	Gd	64	157·2	Sodium	Na	11	23
Gallium	Ga	31	69·7	Strontium	Sr	38	87·6
Germanium	Ge	32	72·6	Sulphur	S	16	32
Gold	Au	79	197	Tantalum	Ta	73	181
Hafnium	Hf	72	178·5	Technetium	Tc	43	99
Helium	He	2	4	Tellurium	Te	52	127·6
Holmium	Ho	67	165	Terbium	Tb	65	159
Hydrogen	H	1	1	Thallium	Tl	81	204·4
Indium	In	49	115	Thorium	Th	90	232
Iodine	I	53	127	Thulium	Tm	69	169
Iridium	Ir	77	192·2	Tin	Sn	50	118·7
Iron	Fe	26	56	Titanium	Ti	22	48
Krypton	Kr	36	83·8	Tungsten	W	74	183·8
Lanthanum	La	57	139	Uranium	U	92	238
Lawrencium	Lw	103	257	Vanadium	V	23	51
Lead	Pb	82	207·2	Xenon	Xe	54	131·3
Lithium	Li	3	7	Ytterbium	Yb	70	173
Lutetium	Lu	71	175	Yttrium	Y	39	89
Magnesium	Mg	12	24·3	Zinc	Zn	30	65·4
Manganese	Mn	25	55	Zirconium	Zr	40	91·2
Mendelevium	Md	101	256				

Index

THIS BOOK HAS BEEN SET IN MONOPHOTO TIMES NEW ROMAN
AND PRINTED AND BOUND IN GREAT BRITAIN BY
WILLIAM CLOWES & SONS, LIMITED, LONDON, BECCLES AND COLCHESTER

Teacher's notes

Contents

Introduction

Every care has been taken by the authors in writing this text to ensure accuracy and relevancy. If, however, any teacher has constructive comments to make on improving the contents, these would be greatly welcomed.

Using the book with some examination syllabuses

It is not essential that the contents of the book be used in sequence. Nor will any particular course necessarily use all the material it contains. The sample schemes given below are intended to show how the requirements of six O-level syllabuses could be covered but similar schemes can easily be devised for all the other Examination Boards. In their construction it has been assumed that the pupils are of average or above average O-level standard. With less able classes, the teacher would have to 'prune' some of the more difficult parts of the work. Portions of any section that could be omitted if time is limited are shown in square brackets, thus: [   ].

In all the suggested schemes the material has been arranged so that theoretical principles are introduced early enough to be used in understanding the factual part of the course.

All of these schemes are based on the relevant syllabus for 1971.

A *Nuffield*

		Reference to Nuffield Sample Scheme Stage II
Chapter 1:	Atoms [Mass spectrometer]	11: Atoms in Chemistry 24: Radiochemistry
Chapter 2:	Molecules	11: Atoms in Chemistry 15: Solids, Liquids, and Gases
Chapter 3:	Chemistry and Electricity	16: Explaining the Behaviour of Electrolytes
Chapter 4:	The Structure of Substances [Experiment 4.5]	14: Finding out how Atoms are arranged in Elements 15: Solids, Liquids, and Gases
Chapter 5:	Formulae, Equations, and Molecular Masses (Omit Experiment 5.11 and all that follows) [Experiments 5.5, 5.9, and 5.10]	11: Atoms in Chemistry 17: Finding the Relative Numbers of Particles involved in Reactions
Chapter 6:	Rates of Reaction and Equilibrium	18: How Fast? Rates and Catalysts 19: How Far? The Idea of Dynamic Equilibrium

Chapter 7: Energy Changes Accompanying Chemical Changes	23: Chemicals and Energy
Chapter 8: Two Patterns of Chemical Change [Ion-electron method for balancing redox equations; Experiment 8.7]	20: Investigating the Substances called Acids
Chapter 9: Elements and the Periodic Table (Omit 'The Periodic Table and Electronic Structure')	13: Looking at Elements in the Light of the Periodic Table
Chapter 10: Omit	—
Chapter 11: Omit	—
Chapter 12: Carbon and Silicon (Omit Experiments 12.4, 12.5, 12.12(a) to (d), Terylene, Experiment 12.20 and remainder of chapter, except Experiment 12.23) [Experiments 12.14, 12.16, 12.18(c))]	21: Breaking Down and Building Up Large Molecules
Chapter 13: Nitrogen and Phosphorus (Omit Experiment 13.10 and remainder of chapter)	22: Chemistry and the World Food Problem
Chapter 14: Oxygen and Sulphur (Experiment 14.3 and 14.4 only)	14: Finding out how Atoms are arranged in Elements
Chapter 15: The Halogens (Experiment 15.3 only) [Experiment 15.8]	12: Investigation of Salt and 'Salt Gas'.
	13: Looking at Elements in the Light of the Periodic Table

It will be observed that this scheme considerably alters the suggested teaching order from that published in the Nuffield Sample Scheme Stage II. These changes reflect the teaching experience of the authors. In particular the Periodic Table is considered very much later in the course so that ideas concerning energy, rates and equilibrium, and oxidation states, can be used to bring deeper understanding of such work. A few additional ideas, such as the oxidation state concept, have been introduced because it has been found essential for a proper understanding of the chemistry of the elements.

Options: If the scheme outlined above is undertaken in its entirety, there is excellent coverage of Option 10 (Acidity and Alkalinity) and Option 12 (Atoms into Ions). With a little additional material Option 5 (Chemical Changes and the Production of Electrical Energy) is readily covered. Some other options are considered below:

Option 4 (Metals and Alloys): Chapter 10 (Experiment 10.1 and Extraction of Metals). Background reading on occurrence and uses of metals from chapters 10 and

3

11. Additional material on physical properties of metals from the Nuffield Stage III book must be included.

Option 1 (Water): This could be based on Experiments 12.19, 12.20, 12.21, and 12.22. A discussion of hydrogen-bonding in water follows well from the consideration of the polar nature of water molecules in chapter 4.

Option 7 (Giant Molecules): Additional material selected from chapter 12, with some work on thermosetting plastics and the distinction between these and thermoplastics, would ensure adequate coverage.

Option 8 (The Chemical Industry): Many industrial processes that could be considered here are discussed in the pupils' text, largely in terms of energetics, rates of reaction, and equilibrium. These include the manufacture of sodium hydroxide and sodium carbonate (chapter 10), ammonia and nitric acid (chapter 13), and sulphuric acid (chapter 14).

Option 13 (Periodicity and Atomic Structure): Section on the Periodic Table and electronic structure from chapter 9. Calcium and magnesium from chapter 10, in particular Experiments 10.5, 10.6, and 10.7 compared with Experiment 10.2. Halogens from chapter 15, in particular Experiments 15.5 and 15.6. Additional theoretical material from the end of the published material for this option.

B *London*

		Syllabus Reference
Chapter 1:	Atoms (Omit all sections on radioactivity and stability of the nucleus) [Mass spectrometer]	3.1, 3.8
Chapter 2:	Molecules	3.9
Chapter 3:	Chemistry and Electricity	1.3, 3.5
Chapter 4:	The Structure of Substances	3.7
Chapter 5:	Formulae, Equations, and Molecular Masses [Experiments 5.11, 5.12]	3.2, 3.3, 3.4, 3.9
Chapter 6:	Rates of Reaction and Equilibrium	3.11, 3.12
Chapter 7:	Energy Changes Accompanying Chemical Change [Tabulation of Energy Data and all that follows]	3.10
Chapter 8:	Two Patterns of Chemical Change [Ion-electron method of balancing redox equations]	2.2, 2.7, 1.6, 2.15, 3.5
Chapter 9:	Elements and the Periodic Table [Experiments 9.7 and 9.8]	2.8, 2.1, 3.6, 3.8
Chapter 10:	Metallic Elements and their Compounds—I	2.6, 4.2, 2.8, 4.6, 2.9, 2.10, 2.11, 2.16
Chapter 11:	Metallic Elements and their Compounds—II (Omit Experiments 11.1, 11.2, 11.3 and sections on tin, zinc, and nickel) [Steel]	4.2, 2.12, 2.13, 2.14

Chapter 12: Carbon and Silicon (Omit all work on silicon)	2.6, 2.17, 4.3, 4.4, 4.5, 4.6
Chapter 13: Nitrogen and Phosphorus (Omit Experiments 13.8 and 13.9)	2.4, 4.5, 4.6, 4.7, 2.5
Chapter 14: Oxygen and Sulphur [Experiment 14.1]	2.2, 2.3, 4.6
Chapter 15: The Halogens [Experiment 15.8]	2.1, 4.6

Only the major syllabus references are given above, some syllabus sections being spread over several chapters of the book, e.g., most of Section 1, 2.12, 4.1.

C Oxford and Cambridge

	Syllabus Reference
Chapter 1: Atoms (Omit all sections on radioactivity and stability of the nucleus) [Mass spectrometer]	6, 3, 18
Chapter 2: Molecules	6, 3
Chapter 3: Chemistry and Electricity	5, 18
Chapter 4: The Structure of Substances	6, 7
Chapter 5: Formulae, Equations, and Molecular Masses (Omit sections on Boyle's and Charles' Laws)	11
Chapter 6: Rates of Reaction and Equilibrium [Complete section on equilibrium]	15
Chapter 7: Energy Changes Accompanying Chemical Change [Tabulation of Energy Data; Using ΔG to Predict the Feasibility of Reaction]	4, 16, 13
Chapter 8: Two Patterns of Chemical Change [Ion-electron method of balancing redox equations]	7, 14, 8
Chapter 9: Elements and the Periodic Table [Experiments 9.7, 9.8]	10
Chapter 10: Metallic Elements and their Compounds—I	8, 16
Chapter 11: Metallic Elements and their Compounds—II [Steel; modern coinage metals]	8, 16
Chapter 12: Carbon and Silicon (Omit all work on silicon)	6, 9, 12, 13, 17
Chapter 13: Nitrogen and Phosphorus [Experiments 13.8 and 13.9]	9, 15

Only the major syllabus references are given above, some syllabus sections being spread over several chapters of the book, in particular Sections 1, 2, 3, 4, and 7. Some points in the syllabus would need expanding, in particular the laws of chemical combination and the determination of equivalent weights.

D *Cambridge 'T'*

	Syllabus Reference
Chapter 1: Atoms (Omit all sections here, and in later chapters, on orbital distribution of electrons) [Mass spectrometer]	8, 12(c)
Chapter 2: Molecules	8
Chapter 3: Chemistry and Electricity	10
Chapter 4: The Structure of Substances	12(a), 12(b), 7
Chapter 5: Formulae, Equations, and Molecular Masses	8, 9(a)
Chapter 6: Rates of Reaction and Equilibrium [Complete section on equilibrium]	9(b)
Chapter 7: Energy Changes Accompanying Chemical Change [Tabulation of Energy Data; Using ΔG to Predict the Feasibility of Reaction]	9(b)
Chapter 8: Two Patterns of Chemical Change (Omit Experiment 8.11 and all that follows) [Experiment 8.12; oxidation states]	2, 4, 6(b), 10, 3
Chapter 9: Elements and the Periodic Table (Omit Classification of the Elements and all that follows.)	6(b)
Chapter 10: Metallic Elements and their Compounds—I [The theory of extraction of metals]	2, 3, 4, 7, 6(b), 5, 13
Chapter 11: Metallic Elements and their Compounds—II [The Modern Coinage Metals]	2, 3, 4, 7, 13
Chapter 12: Carbon and Silicon (Omit all work on silicon)	6(a), 5, 11
Chapter 13: Nitrogen and Phosphorus (Omit all work on phosphorus) [Section on amino-acids]	6(d), 13

| Chapter 14: Oxygen and Sulphur | 2, 3, 6(*c*), 13 |
| Chapter 15: The Halogens [Experiment 15.8] | 6(*b*) |

Only the major syllabus references are given above, some syllabus sections being spread over several chapters of the book, notably Sections 1, 2, and 3.

E *Joint Matriculation Board*

	Syllabus Reference
Chapter 1: Atoms (Omit all sections on radioactivity and stability of the nucleus) [Mass spectrometer]	2.1, 2.2
Chapter 2: Molecules	2.1, 2.2, 1.1
Chapter 3: Chemistry and Electricity	5.1, 5.2
Chapter 4: The Structure of Substances	2.3, 2.9
Chapter 5: Formulae, Equations, and Molecular Masses [Experiments 5.11, 5.12]	2.4, 1.3, 1.1
Chapter 6: Rates of Reaction and Equilibrium	7, 10.2.5, 8
Chapter 7: Energy Changes Accompanying Chemical Change [Tabulation of Energy Data and all that follows]	6
Chapter 8: Two Patterns of Chemical Change [Ion-electron method of balancing redox equations]	10.2.5, 3, 6, 4, 5.3
Chapter 9: Elements and the Periodic Table [Experiments 9.7, 9.8]	2.5, 10.1, 10.2.7
Chapter 10: Metallic Elements and their Compounds—I [Theory of extraction of metals]	5.3, 10.1, 11
Chapter 11: Metallic Elements and their Compounds—II [Sections on tin and nickel]	5.3, 10.1, 11
Chapter 12: Carbon and Silicon	9, 10.2.2, 11, 1.3, 10.2.3
Chapter 13: Nitrogen and Phosphorus (Omit sections on amino-acids) [Phosphorus]	10.2.4, 11, 10.1
Chapter 14: Oxygen and Sulphur	1.3, 10.2.5, 10.2.6, 11, 10.1
Chapter 15: The Halogens [Experiment 15.8]	2.5, 10.2.7, 10.1

Only the major syllabus references are given above, some syllabus sections being spread over several chapters, in particular Sections 1.2, 1.4, and 1.5.

CHEMISTRY BY EXPERIMENT AND UNDERSTANDING

F   *Scottish Certificate—Ordinary Grade*

	Syllabus Reference
Chapter 1: Atoms (Omit all sections on radioactivity and stability of the nucleus)	G1, G2, G3, G4, G5, G6, G7
Chapter 2: Molecules	G1
Chapter 3: Chemistry and Electricity	H1, H2, H3, I5, H5, H6, I7, J9
Chapter 4: The Structure of Substances (Include only those sections on ionic and covalent bonds)	H2
Chapter 5: Formulae, Equations, and Molecular Masses (Omit sections on Boyle's and Charles' Laws)	H7, H8, H9
Chapter 6: Rates of Reaction and Equilibrium (Omit)	—
Chapter 7: Energy Changes Accompanying Chemical Change (Omit)	—
Chapter 8: Two Patterns of Chemical Change	J1, J2, J3, J4, J5, J6, I2, I4, I6
Chapter 9: Elements and the Periodic Table (Omit Experiment 9.2 and all that follows)	I1
Chapter 10: Metallic Elements and their Compounds—I (Omit the theory of extraction of metals and all that follows *except* Experiment 10.5)	I1, I2, I3
Chapter 11: Metallic Elements and their Compounds—II (Include only Experiment 11.1 and the principles of the extraction of aluminium)	I1, I2, I6
Chapter 12: Carbon and Silicon (Omit Experiment 11.1)	L1, L2, L3, L4, L5, L6, N1, N2, O1, N3, O2
Chapter 13: Nitrogen and Phosphorus (Omit all sections on phosphorus) [Manufacture of nitric acid]	M2, M3, M7, M6, N4, M4, M5
Chapter 14: Oxygen and Sulphur (Omit Experiments 14.1, 14.2, and the extraction of sulphur)	K1, K2, K3, K4, K5, K6, J3, K7
Chapter 15: The Halogens (Include only those sections on hydrochloric acid)	J3

The contents of the book also provide adequate coverage of the Higher Grade syllabus, as outlined below:

Syllabus Section P	Chapters 1 and 2
Syllabus Section Q	Chapters 7, 8, and 9
Syllabus Section R	Chapter 6
Syllabus Section S*	Chapter 12

* Some extra material would be required here.

Basic apparatus

Whenever the pupils' text refers to 'test-tubes', it should be taken to infer a hard-glass (borosilicate) tube of a size approximating to 100 × 16 mm. The terms 'boiling-tube' and 'ignition-tube' should be taken to specify hard-glass tubes approximating to 150 × 25 mm and 75 × 12 mm respectively. It will be assumed that a rack containing sufficient of such tubes, in a clean and dry condition, will be available to each working group. Other apparatus regarded as basic and therefore not specifically mentioned for each experiment will be:

(*a*) A bunsen burner.

(*b*) A tripod with wire gauze.

(*c*) An asbestos mat to protect the working surface.

(*d*) A test-tube holder of the appropriate size.

(*e*) A metal spatula; the Nuffield type is particularly suitable.

Some of the apparatus shown in the diagrams in the pupils' book is ground-glass jointed, but equivalent conventional apparatus would be equally suitable in the majority of experiments. In general, B.14 ground-glass joints are suitable for class apparatus but for demonstrations B.19 or B.24 joints are preferable.

When the text refers to a 'high-resistance voltmeter', several suitable instruments are available:

(*a*) A valve voltmeter; these have an input resistance of the order of 10^{14} ohm and are thus extremely effective. They are, however, expensive. A good instrument, in terms of both value and efficiency, which operates both as a valve voltmeter and as a pH meter is the 501 A pH/mV meter from Carwyn Instruments, Carwyn, Pentraeth Road, Menai Bridge, Anglesey.

(*b*) A multimeter, of the AVO type. The more modern of these have input resistances of the order 10^4 ohm which is adequate for the experiments described.

(*c*)

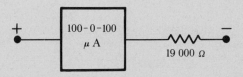

A 100–0–100 μA meter of the type available from Barnet Factors Ltd., 4 Lisle Street, London WC2, may be modified as shown above to provide an instrument with an input resistance of about 2×10^4 ohm. The meter is in the distributor's '**sew panel**' range and they will provide a free leaflet giving details of price, sizes available, and quantity discount offered.

Throughout the course more electrical measurements are taken than has been customary in chemistry at this stage and you may feel that the purchase of some meters specifically for use in chemistry would be desirable. Details will be found, in the leaflet referred to above, of meters very suitable for this purpose at most advantageous prices.

If a low-voltage d.c. supply is not already available, appropriate batteries can be used. If a more permanent solution is required, a cheap method is to use a battery charger, which, with various distribution points can supply adequate current for a whole class at either 6 V or 12 V.

9

Laboratory reagents

It is assumed that pupils will have access to supplies of concentrated hydrochloric, nitric, and sulphuric acids and 0·880 ammonia solution. The teacher may prefer to keep the supplies of such materials in a reserved place for work in junior laboratories. When dilute acids and alkalis are specified in the pupils' text, these should be taken to mean solutions of the following concentrations:

Solution	Nominal concentration	Method of preparation
Dilute hydrochloric acid	2 M	400 cm^3 of concentrated acid made up to 2 dm^3 of solution
Dilute nitric acid	2 M	250 cm^3 of concentrated acid made up to 2 dm^3 of solution
Dilute sulphuric acid	1 M	120 cm^3 of concentrated acid made up to 2 dm^3 of solution*
Dilute ammonia solution	2 M	215 cm^3 of 0·880 ammonia solution made up to 2 dm^3
Sodium hydroxide solution	2 M	160 g of solid sodium hydroxide made up to 2 dm^3 of solution

* The dilution of concentrated sulphuric acid is a highly exothermic process and should be carried out as follows to avoid any risk of hot acid spray being formed. Place 1·5 dm^3 of distilled water in a 2 dm^3 plastic measuring cylinder. Surround this with a large reservoir of cold water and add 120 cm^3 of concentrated acid in portions, stir constantly and ensure that the temperature is kept below 50°C throughout. Make up the volume to 2 dm^3 with distilled water.

It will be assumed that supplies of these solutions will be available to the pupils and they will not be referred to in the lists of requirements for specific experiments.

Similarly, Universal Indicator (pH) paper (preferably in dispensers) and solution (in dropping bottles) should be available at all times and so will not be mentioned in the lists of requirements.

When other reagents are specified for particular experiments, 0·1 M solutions (the exact concentration is not critical) should be used unless otherwise stated.

Teachers may prefer to use deionized water as a substitute for distilled water; this would, of course, be satisfactory. Details of suitable equipment may be obtained from The Permutit Company Limited, Pemberton House, 632/652 London Road, Isleworth, Middlesex.

For all experiments in which ethanol is required, Industrial Methylated Spirits may be used.

Gases

Cylinders

Supply from a cylinder is the most convenient source of any gas, since it is readily available, the flow can be easily controlled and is continuous, and the gas needs no drying. It is useful to have plentiful supplies of oxygen, hydrogen, and nitrogen, and these are available in large cylinders, together with the appropriate regulators, from BOC Ltd. (Regional depots).

A large range of gases in small cylinders can be obtained from BDH Chemicals Ltd., Poole, Dorset. Probably the most useful of these is sulphur dioxide.

Generators

These can be used when relatively small quantities of gas are required. All the gases in the following table can be simply prepared with the generator (or its equivalent) shown in Fig. TN1. Also given in the table are the most suitable reagents and drying agents, since a dry gas is often necessary. Concentrated sulphuric acid is best contained in a Dreschel bottle (or its equivalent) and phosphorus pentoxide in a U-tube.

Gas	Reagents	Drying Agent
Carbon dioxide	Marble/50% hydrochloric acid	Conc. sulphuric acid
Hydrogen chloride	Rock salt/conc. sulphuric acid	Conc. sulphuric acid
Nitrogen dioxide	Copper/conc. nitric acid	Conc. sulphuric acid
Hydrogen sulphide	Iron(II) sulphide/50% hydrochloric acid	Phosphorus(V) oxide
Chlorine	Potassium permanganate/conc. hydrochloric acid	Conc. sulphuric acid

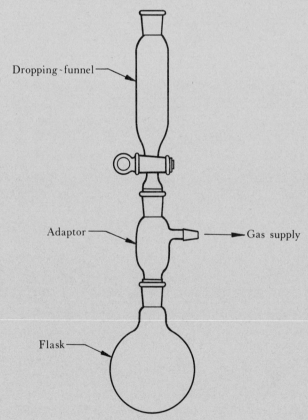

Dropping-funnel

Adaptor — Gas supply

Flask

Figure TN1 A gas generator

11

NB: Hydrogen can also be generated in this way but this is not advisable, unless absolutely necessary, because of the risk of explosion. If the method is to be used, great care must be taken to flush out all the air in the apparatus to avoid the formation of an explosive air/hydrogen mixture.

Kipp's apparatus can be used, if available, for certain gases and is particularly suitable for carbon dioxide and hydrogen sulphide.

Ammonia is best prepared, as shown in Fig. 13.5 of the pupils' text, by warming 0·880 ammonia solution and drying with calcium oxide.

Safety

The strongly acidic gases, hydrogen chloride, sulphur dioxide, and nitrogen dioxide can cause chest illness and must normally be handled in a fume-cupboard unless the quantities concerned are very small or adequate disposal arrangements are made. In addition, nitrogen dioxide is also extremely poisonous, as is chlorine, and particular care must be taken when using these gases.

It is of great importance that the pupils are taught how to test correctly for the odour of a gas, by wafting it towards them and **not** sticking the source of the gas under their noses!

Reading material for teachers

1. The enormous debt owed by the authors to the Nuffield sponsored O-level teaching project in Chemistry will be readily apparent to those using this book. The following publications of that body can be highly recommended:

> The Sample Scheme Stages I and II $\left.\right\}$
> The Sample Scheme Stage III   All published by
> Collected Experiments   Penguin
> Handbook for Teachers

2. An excellent and readable discussion of many of the newer chemical concepts introduced in this book will be found in 'An Introduction to Modern Chemistry' by M. J. S. Dewar, published by the Athlone Press of the University of London.

3. Several interesting social applications of the chemistry found in this book are discussed in 'Modern Chemistry—Applied and Social Aspects' by J. Gordon Raitt, published by Edward Arnold Ltd.

4. A considerable amount of additional experimental material may be found in the 'Chemical Education Materials Study' publications, details of which may be obtained from W. H. Freeman and Co. Ltd.

5. 'New Trends in Chemistry Teaching' published by UNESCO, in two volumes, contains essays by a series of authoritative writers on a wide range of topics currently finding their way into school chemistry syllabuses.

6. Further ideas for experiments using gas syringes can be found in 'Gas Syringe Experiments' by Martin Rogers, published by Heinemann Educational Books Ltd.

7. Much information can be found in 'Useful Addresses for Science Teachers' by R. W. Wilson, published by Edward Arnold Ltd.

Supplementary reading material for pupils

Some parts of the pupils' text direct them to simple literature searches for information. It is important, therefore, they have access to suitable material either in the school or in the science library. Many books suitable for this purpose will be found in the publishers' catalogues—many older textbooks are useful in this connection. The following Nuffield background readers are suitable to supplement the work in this book:

Chapter 1: Dalton and the Atomic Theory (M. J. W. Rogers)
Inside the Atom (H. P. H. Oliver)
Radioactive Chemicals (R. A. Faires)
Chapter 3: The Discovery of the Electric Current (G. Van Praagh)
Michael Faraday (H. G. Andrew)
Chapter 4: The Structure of Substances (C. V. Platts)
The Start of X-ray Analysis (Sir Lawrence Bragg)
Growing Crystals (G. Van Praagh)
Chapter 6: Catalysis (D. Waddington)
Chapter 7: Energy and Chemicals (W. Hughes)
Chemistry and Electricity (Iolo Wyn Williams)
Chapter 8: What is an Acid? (H. P. H. Oliver)
Atoms into Ions (T. Healey)
Corrosion of Metals (H. P. H. Oliver)
Chapter 9: Periodicity and Atomic Structure (Prof. N. N. Greenwood)
The Periodic Table (N. Coats)
The Chemical Elements (H. P. H. Oliver)
Chemicals from Nature (Miss E. W. Howard)
The Discovery of the Inert Gases (W. S. Richardson and J. Hall)
Chapter 10: Metals and Alloys (H. Moore)
Chapter 12: Making Diamonds (H. Judith Milledge)
Coal (H. Donaldson and H. B. Locke)
Petroleum (H. P. H. Oliver)
Plastics (O. J. Walker)
Detergents (R. J. Taylor)
Man-made Fibres (H. P. H. Oliver)
Chapter 13: The Nitrogen Problem (L. F. Haber)
Fertilizers and Farm Chemicals (J. L. Hunt)
Chapter 14: Burning (William Anderson)
Water (R. W. Thomas)
Sulphuric Acid (T. Ashman and G. G. Cremonesi)

A catalogue giving details of all the Nuffield O-level Chemistry Publications, including some special package offers for teachers, can be obtained from: Educational Dept., Penguin Books Ltd., Harmondsworth, West Drayton, Middlesex.

Catalogues, or lists, of booklets, wall-charts, and other visual aid material—much of it free—may be obtained from, for example:
(a) Shell International Petroleum Co., Ltd., Shell Centre, London SE1
(b) Unilever Education Section, Unilever House, Blackfriars, London EC4
(c) Copper Development Association, 55 South Audley Street, London W1
(d) Education Section, BP Chemical (UK) Ltd., West Halkin House, West Halkin Street, London SW1

Chapter 1   Atoms

Experiment 1.1   *The effect of certain chemicals on photographic film*

Each group of pupils will require:

Polythene bag containing a suitable radioactive compound such as thorium nitrate or uranyl nitrate (no special authorization is required for their purchase). The bag should be carefully sealed; with practice this can be accomplished with a not too hot soldering iron.

Key, coin, or other suitable metallic object to cast 'shadow'.

3·25 × 4·25 in. envelope wrapped X-ray film. Kodak 'Crystallex' EP25 box contains 25 individually wrapped pieces of film.

Access to photographic darkroom illuminated by safelight with 6B brown wratten filter. This should also contain: Dish of Kodak DX-80 developer, diluted as directed in the manufacturer's instructions.

Dish of Kodak X-ray Rapid Acid Fixer Powder, prepared as directed in the manufacturer's instructions.

An 'Industrial X-ray Catalogue' containing full details of all the photographic items required can be obtained from: Industrial Sales Division, Kodak Limited, Kodak House, Kingsway, London WC2.

An excellent account of Becquerel's work and its influence on the discovery of atomic structure can be found in 'The Restless Atom' (Romer), which is no. 10 in Heinemann's Science Study Series.

Experiment 1.2   *To investigate the rate of a radioactive decay*

The teacher will require:

35 per cent aqueous solution of uranyl nitrate.

4-methylpentan-2-one.

Separating funnel (about 100 cm^3 capacity).

Scaler with liquid counter, lead and holder.

Stop-clock.

Two 10 cm^3 measuring cylinders.

100 cm^3 beaker (to hold waste).

Winchester quart bottle for 'Liquid Radioactive Waste', which is so labelled.

Plastic waste-bin with Polythene liner, labelled 'Solid Radioactive Waste'.

Non-porous tray, such as a 20 × 16 in. photographic tray.

Tray-liners; Whatmans 'Benchkote' or disposable paper tissues.

Pair of disposable Polythene gloves.

All the operations described should be carried out over the tray, lined with 'Bench-kote' or paper tissues. The teacher should wear gloves and laboratory coat. The liquid radioactive waste bottle should be emptied, when half full, directly into a drain with at least ten times its own volume of water. The Polythene bin-liner should be sealed when full and disposed of with a large quantity of normal waste.

The accepted value for the half-life of protactinium-234 is 72 s. This isotope is preferentially dissolved in the ketone because in concentrated hydrochloric acid un-ionized H_2PaCl_6 is formed.

The Nuffield Science Teaching Project Chemistry Film Loop 'Radioactive Materials—Uses' is useful when teaching this chapter. Several suitable films showing the uses of radioactive isotopes are obtainable on free loan from UKAEA Film Library, 11 Charles II Street, London SW1.

Chapter 2   Molecules

Experiment 2.1   *To measure the approximate size of a molecule of oil*

Each group of pupils will require:

> Bowl or tray at least 50×50 cm.
> Olive oil.
> Ruler.
> Short length of wire approximately 0·2 mm in diameter.
> Baby powder in sprinkling container (or Lycopodium powder).

As the experiment provides an approximate answer only, little is lost by taking the drop as a cube and the area of oil-patch as a square. Typical results are:

$$\text{Volume of oil drop} = (0·1 \text{ cm})^3 = 10^{-3} \text{ cm}^3$$
$$\text{Area of oil-patch} = 45 \times 45 \text{ cm} \simeq 2000 \text{ cm}^2$$

Let thickness be t cm, then:

$$\text{Volume of oil drop} = \text{volume of oil-patch}$$
$$10^{-3} \text{ cm}^3 = 2000 \text{ cm}^2 \times t \text{ cm}$$

Thus:
$$t = \frac{10^{-3}}{2 \times 10^3} \text{ cm}$$
$$= 5 \times 10^{-7} \text{ cm} = 5 \text{ nm}$$

Calculation of L: The given volume of 1 mole (316 cm^3) is in fact that for oleic acid. Calculation:

$$\text{Number of molecules in 1 cm}^3 = \frac{1}{(5 \times 10^{-7})^3} = 8 \times 10^{18}$$
$$\text{Number of molecules in 1 mole} = 316 \times 8 \times 10^{18}$$
$$= 2·5 \times 10^{21}$$

(which is approaching the correct order of magnitude).

Experiment 2.2   *To investigate some properties of molecules*

Each group of pupils will require:

> Two gas jars (approximately 20×5 cm).
> Access to tin of Vaseline.
> Access to bottle of bromine with teat-pipette in a fume cupboard.
> 50 cm^3 and 600 cm^3 beaker.
> Approximately 0·02 M solution of potassium permanganate (50 cm^3).
> Glass tube approximately 1 m long by 0·5 cm internal diameter, fitted with a cork at each end.
> Small quantity of cotton wool.

Solid ammonium dichromate.

250 cm^3 beaker.

Supply of nitrogen dioxide, prepared as described on page 11 of the Teacher's Notes.

The pupils should realize that these experiments suggest that matter is composed of small particles that are in motion.

Experiment 2.3 *The 'smoke-cell' experiment*

Each group of pupils will require a smoke-cell, as supplied by the laboratory apparatus manufacturers, e.g., MLI, and a suitable microscope.

They should conclude that the relatively large smoke particles are being jostled by constantly moving air molecules.

A useful aid to teaching the distribution of molecular energies is the film-loop 'Boltzmann-Maxwell Distribution of Energies' produced by Macmillan. This is well within the capabilities of most 13 year olds.

Most modern mathematics courses contain sections on frequency distribution curves that the pupils may have encountered to assist them in understanding this concept. A useful supplementary exercise to help those who have not been taught this is described below.

Two dice are thrown 180 times and the total score obtained with each throw is recorded in a table as shown:

Score	2	3	4	5	6	7	8	9	10	11	12
Frequency score is made											

The results are then plotted graphically. It can be pointed out that with sufficient mathematical skill, the outcome of the experiment could be predicted in advance:

Score with second dice	Score with first dice 1	2	3	4	5	6
1	2	3	4	5	6	7
2	3	4	5	6	7	8
3	4	5	6	7	8	9
4	5	6	7	8	9	10
5	6	7	8	9	10	11
6	7	8	9	10	11	12

Thus in 36 throws, a combined score of 2 or 12 would only be expected once, whereas a score of 7 would be expected six times. The expected frequency of obtaining each score can thus be calculated, multiplied by five so that the total number of throws considered is once more 180 and the result plotted on the same graph axis as before.

The pupils will be impressed by the close agreement between the 'experimental' and the 'theoretical' result. If the film loop referred to above is employed, the direct determination of molecular energy distribution by the Zartmann experiment will have been considered. The pupils could then be told that using purely statistical methods, Boltzmann and Maxwell were able to arrive at a confirmation of this, independent of an experiment.

Another useful film-loop, when teaching this chapter, is 'Movement of Molecules' produced by Nuffield.

Chapter 3 Chemistry and electricity

Experiment 3.1 *Investigating the electrical conduction of various substances*

Each group of pupils will require:

6 V bulb in holder.
6 V d.c. source.
Two carbon electrodes (these may be placed through the holes of a rubber bung to hold them conveniently and prevent shorting).
Connecting leads.
Solid samples of carbon, iron, perspex, sulphur, copper, and Polythene.
Access to bottles of distilled water, ethanol, lime-water, dilute sulphuric acid, copper sulphate solution (about 1 M), zinc sulphate solution (about 1 M), sugar solution (about 1 M), mercury. (Precautions should be taken to prevent spillage of mercury and pupils warned not to handle it. Accidental spillage of mercury should be sprinkled with powdered sulphur and disposed of with care.)
100 cm^3 beaker.

The pupils should appreciate that conducting materials complete the circuit and light the bulb. The distinction between those electrical conductors that are changed by the current and those that are not should be observed.

Experiment 3.2 *Do metals always conduct electricity?*

Each group of pupils will require:

Apparatus as listed for Experiment 3.1.
'Pepper-pots' containing (a) iron filings and (b) copper powder.

It will be seen that electrical conduction only takes place when there is continuity of contact throughout the circuit.

Experiment 3.3 *Do crystals conduct electricity?*

Each group of pupils will require:

Electrical apparatus as listed for Experiment 3.1.
100 cm^3 beaker.
Access to solid samples of lithium chloride, potassium iodide, lead chloride, and lead bromide.

These substances will be found to be non-conductors in the solid state.

17

Experiment 3.4 *Investigating the effect of heat on solid non-conductors*

Each group of pupils will require:

Electrical apparatus as listed for Experiment 3.1, with 12 V supply if available. Electrode assembly as shown in Fig. TN2 or its equivalent.

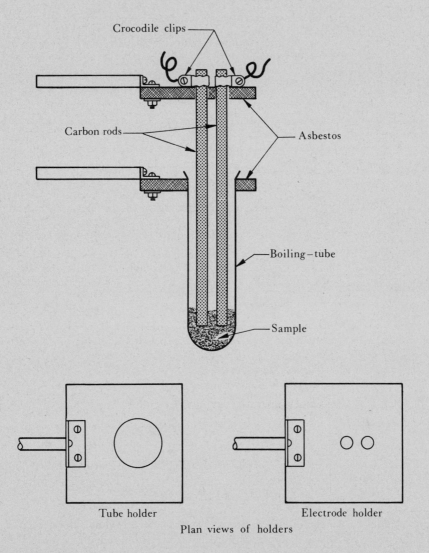

Crocodile clips

Carbon rods

Asbestos

Boiling–tube

Sample

Tube holder   Electrode holder

Plan views of holders

Figure TN2

Four boiling-tubes cut to about half their length. This can be done by making a groove round the total circumference of the tube at the appropriate place and placing a red-hot glass rod on the groove. The cut end of the tube should be held in a flame to smooth it and while it is pliable a new rim made with a suitable metal tool.

Access to the solid samples listed for Experiment 3.3.

The pupils will observe that the molten salts conduct electricity with the formation of the metal at the cathode and non-metal at the anode. The Nuffield film-loop 'Electrolysis of Lead Bromide' is relevant at this point.

Experiment 3.5 *To determine the quantity of electricity needed to deposit one mole of lead atoms*

The teacher will require:

Electrode assembly as listed for Experiment 3.4.
6 or 12 V d.c. supply.
Connecting leads.
Ammeter reading up to at least 4 A.
Rheostat (approx. 20 ohm).
Access to top pan balance.
Stop-clock or sight of clock with seconds hand.
Two small dishes or beakers (50 cm³).
Unused sample of lead bromide.
Spatula.

Specimen results and calculation:

Current: 4 A   Time: 12 minutes = 720 s   Mass of lead: 2·97 g
Quantity of electricity = 4 × 720 coulombs = 2880 coulombs
Quantity of electricity to liberate 1 mole of lead atoms (207 g)

$$= 2880 \times \frac{207}{2·97} = 201\ 000 \text{ coulombs}$$

Slightly higher values than expected are generally obtained from this experiment because a little of the lead liberated dissolves in the molten lead bromide. It is for this reason that unused lead bromide is essential for this experiment.

Experiment 3.6 *Does the presence of water affect the products of electrolysis?*

Each group of pupils will require:

Electrical apparatus as listed for Experiment 3.1.
Electrolysis cell shown in Fig. 3.4 of pupils' text; the two collection tubes should be of *10 mm* diameter as they may then be inverted, when full of water, without emptying (due to the surface tension effect). (*NB:* The normal ignition-tube is 12 mm in diameter.)
Bottle containing freshly cut pieces of sodium (size of rice grains) stored under naphtha oil; 1 bottle per bench will suffice.
Pair of balance forceps for handling the sodium.

Experiment 3.7 *The electrolysis of aqueous solutions*

Each group of pupils will require:

Electrical apparatus as for Experiment 3.1 with electrolysis cell as for Experiment 3.6.

Solutions of copper(II) chloride, zinc bromide, potassium iodide, and hydrochloric acid. (Salts should be about 1 M.)

Expected products are:

Electrolyte	Anode product	Cathode product
Copper(II) chloride	chlorine	copper
Zinc bromide	bromine	zinc
Potassium iodide	iodine	hydrogen
Dilute hydrochloric acid	chlorine (with some oxygen)	hydrogen

It should be realized that metals that react vigorously with water, such as potassium, are not likely products of electrolysis in aqueous solution. The discharge of ions in such experiments is further discussed in the next section of the pupils' text.

Experiment 3.8 *To measure the quantity of electricity required to liberate one mole of hydrogen atoms*

Each group of pupils will require:

U-tube fitted with carbon rod electrodes and gas syringe as shown in Fig. 2.5 of pupil's text.
Rheostat (about 20 ohm).
Stop-clock.
12 V d.c. supply.
Connecting leads.
Ammeter reading to about 1 A.

The straight line graph, passing through the origin, shows that volume (and hence mass) of hydrogen liberated is proportional to the time for which the current is passed. As each group find that slightly less than 100 000 coulombs are required to liberate 1 mole of hydrogen atoms, these results also constitute a confirmation of Faraday's First Law of Electrolysis.

Experiment 3.9 *To measure the quantity of electricity required to deposit one mole of copper atoms*

Each group of pupils will require:

50 cm^3 beaker.
Milliammeter reading to at least 200 mA.
Leads and crocodile clips.
Rheostat (about 20 ohm).
12 V d.c. supply.

0·2 M solution of copper sulphate made up in dilute sulphuric acid.
Two pieces of copper foil as electrodes.
Access to a cleaning set for electrodes consisting of beakers of propanone and
water, steel-wool on tile, and box of paper tissues.
Stop-clock.

Specimen results and calculation:

Current: 0·15 A   Time: 30 min = 1800 s   No. of coulombs: 270
Gain in cathode mass: 0·092 g   Loss in anode mass: 0·094 g
Hence quantity of electricity to deposit 1 mole of copper atoms (64 g) at cathode

$$= \frac{270 \times 64}{0·092} = 190\,000 \text{ coulombs}$$

The calculation based on anode loss is similarly made. The slight mass discrepancy is due to a small proportion of copper failing to adhere to the cathode. The accuracy of the experiment is limited principally by the accuracy of the meters.

The pupils should now be in a position to state Faraday's First Law in a form such as 'the mass of product liberated during electrolysis is proportional to the number of coulombs passed'.

Experiment 3.10   *To measure the quantity of electricity required to liberate one mole of copper atoms under differing conditions*

Each group of pupils will require:

Two 50 cm^3 beakers.
Milliammeter reading to at least 200 mA.
Leads and crocodile clips.
Rheostat (about 20 ohm).
12 V d.c. supply.
Four pieces of copper foil as electrodes.
Solution of copper(II) sulphate (0·2 M in dilute sulphuric acid).
Solution containing 100 g sodium chloride and 1 g sodium hydroxide in 1 dm^3 of
solution.
Thermometer.
Access to electrode cleaning apparatus as for previous experiment.
Stop-clock.

The pupils find that for the loss of one mole of copper from the anode in copper(II) sulphate solution, nearly 200 000 coulombs are required as before. For the loss of one mole of copper from the anode in the other electrolyte, only half that number of coulombs are required. This suggests that in the former case Cu^{2+}(aq) ions form and in the latter, the ions forming are Cu^+(aq). From this and from completing the Table 3.3, it becomes clear that (a) charges on simple ions can be obtained from quantitative electrolysis experiments and (b) some elements can form more than one type of ion. The faraday is thus identified as a mole of electrons. Faraday's Second Law can then be developed in the form 'the quantity of electricity to liberate one mole of atoms of any element during electrolysis is 'n' faradays, where 'n' is the charge on the ion.

21

CHEMISTRY BY EXPERIMENT AND UNDERSTANDING

Experiment 3.11   *Observing the movement of ions*

Each group of pupils will require:

Piece of filter paper.
Microscope slide.
Leads and crocodile clips.
6 or 12 V supply.
Access to bottle of potassium permanganate and bottle of copper(II) sulphate crystals.
Source of hydrogen sulphide fumes (a bottle of ammonium polysulphide is suitable).

The pupils will observe that, as expected, the negative permanganate ion migrates to the anode and the positive copper ion to the cathode.

NB: In very soft water districts it may be necessary to use water containing a little dissolved electrolyte such as sodium sulphate.

Experiment 3.12   *Electroplating with various metals*

Each group of pupils will require:
6 V d.c. supply.
6 V lamp and holder.
Leads and crocodile clips.
50 cm^3 beaker.
1 M solution of zinc sulphate made up in dilute sulphuric acid, with about 1 g dm^{-3} of orthoboric acid.
Ammonium nickel sulphate solution containing 50 g dm^{-3}.
Strip of zinc and strip of nickel foil.
Suitable objects for plating.

Experiment 3.13   *Anodizing and dyeing aluminium*

Each group of pupils will require:

6 V d.c. supply.
Leads and crocodile clips.
Three 150 cm^3 beakers.
Cylinder of thin aluminium sheet to fit into the beaker (as the cathode).
Strip of aluminium sheet (as the anode).
Forceps.
Access to beaker of propanone.
Dilute aqueous solutions of various dyes, e.g., various coloured inks, alizarin, eosin, etc.

22

Chapter 4   The structure of substances

Experiment 4.1   *To determine the molar latent heats of vaporization of liquids*

Each group of pupils will require:

The distillation apparatus shown, fitted with an electrical heating element (consisting of 35 cm of 28 swg Nichrome wire covered with 0·5 mm bore silicone sleeving available from Radiospares, P.O. Box 427, 13/17 Epworth Street, London EC2) soldered to substantial copper leads leading outside the flask.
Rheostat (approx. 20 ohm).
12 V d.c. supply.
Ammeter reading to at least 3 A.
Voltmeter reading to at least 12 V.
Connecting leads.
Conical flask.
Bottle containing cyclohexane.
Lagging (this can be of felt, cotton wool, or shaped expanded polystyrene).

Specimen results and calculation:

Liquid: Cyclohexane   Formula-mass: 84   Current: 2·8 A
Voltage: 9·5 V   Time of operation: 300 s
Mass of liquid distilled: 21·8 g

$$\text{Energy supplied} = \frac{9 \cdot 5 \times 2 \cdot 8 \times 300}{1000} = 7 \cdot 98 \text{ kJ}$$

21·8 g of cyclohexane required 7·98 kJ for vaporization, thus 84 g (1 mole) of cyclohexane require

$$\frac{7 \cdot 98 \times 84}{21 \cdot 8} = 30 \cdot 7 \text{ kJ}$$

The latent heat of vaporization of cyclohexane is thus $30 \cdot 7$ kJ mol^{-1}. The pupils should conclude that as the energy to separate a mole of water molecules is greater than that to separate a mole of cyclohexane molecules even though the latter are heavier, the forces *between* the water molecules must be greater.

Experiment 4.2   *Finding out more about the nature of the forces between the molecules in a liquid*

Each group of pupils will require:

A Polythene rod.
Piece of cat's fur.
Two burettes capable of delivering a slow, steady stream of liquid.
Bottle of cyclohexane.

The pupils should conclude that forces between the water molecules are electrostatic in nature. A more detailed consideration of the experiment will be found later in the chapter.

Boiling point and structure

The graph takes the form of a straight line which on extrapolation cuts the temperature axis at absolute zero ($-273°C$). The slope of the graph, the teacher may wish to know, is the molar entropy of vaporization and the graph shows this to be constant for all those liquids having negligible intermolecular forces whilst for those with such forces, there is slight deviation from the line.

Melting points and latent heats of fusion

That there is no simple relationship here is due to the fact that when considering the fusion of solids the arrangement of the particles affects the energy that is required. In liquids, which have no definite structure, this effect is not shown.

Compound formation

To illustrate this topic, the teacher may like to carry out the sodium/chlorine reaction, as described in Experiment 9.4, and then investigate the product.

Experiment 4.3 *A light analogue of the X-ray diffraction method of investigating the arrangement of the particles in crystalline structures*

Requirements:

A bulb holder with a 6 V bulb with suitable power supply and leads.
Set of 'Nuffield' diffraction cards.

A useful hint on the organization of this lesson is to make up sets containing the three standard cards plus three unknowns and place each set in a separate envelope. The pupils can exchange unknowns between groups but are made to understand that each envelope is to be returned with its original complement of cards. Class sets of the X-ray diffraction patterns of aluminium and diamond are supplied with the cards but these are best reserved for distribution at the end of the experiment.

Supplementary equipment is available for use with ripple tanks that provides a further analogue of X-ray diffraction and the pupils are likely to have met this in their physics lessons. Several pieces of apparatus that allow a von Laue pattern with X-rays to be obtained are available and physics departments teaching to A-level may have one of these.

Experiment 4.4 *Is there any evidence that metals are crystalline?*

Each group of pupils will require:

Access to approx. 0·05 M solutions of silver nitrate and lead(II) nitrate.
Piece of zinc foil.
Piece of copper wire (about 2 mm in diameter).

Test tube containing a drop of mercury.
Access to a hand-lens or low-powered microscope (if possible).
Piece of iron rod about 30 × 0·25 cm that has been annealed by raising to red heat, maintained for several minutes at this temperature, and allowed to cool slowly.
Set of mechanics weights.
Stick of tin about 10 × 0·5 cm (this can be cast in a mould of aluminium foil from other tin samples).

The pupils will see the crystallinity of the metals displaced in (*a*), and hear the crystal lattice cracking in (*c*). The results from (*b*) can be explained in terms of the breaking up of the crystal lattice on bending resulting in 'jamming' and the friction between these layers producing heat.

Experiment 4.5   *Comparing the hardness of metals*

Each group of pupils will require:

Ball-bearing about 1·5 cm in diameter.
Sellotape.
1 kg weight.
Metre or half-metre rule.
Samples of copper, brass, bronze, aluminium, and duralumin.

It will be seen that the harder the metal, the smaller the diameter of the indentation. Alloying, in general, increases the hardness of metals because 'foreign' atoms distort the regular crystal lattice making movement of the layers (indentation) more difficult.

Experiment 4.6   *Investigating the structure of metals using models*

Each group of pupils will require three rafts of polystyrene spheres, of any convenient diameter, constructed as shown in Fig. 4.14.
    The properties of metals (thermal conductivity, malleability, and ductility) the pupils are asked to consider are discussed at the end of the summary.

Chapter 5   Formulae, equations, and molecular masses

Experiment 5.1   *To determine the formula of black copper oxide*

Each group of pupils will require:

Hard-glass test-tube, with cork and glass and rubber connectors, with hole blown in end as illustrated in Fig. 5.2.
Access to bottle of copper(II) oxide (this must be a good grade reagent dried by strong heating prior to the experiment).
If town gas is not available, a cylinder of hydrogen will be required. In this case a teacher demonstration will probably be more convenient.

The class should generally obtain results that suggest 80 per cent of copper oxide is copper. This leads to a value of CuO for the formula.

Experiment 5.2 *To determine the formula of magnesium oxide*

Each group of pupils will require:

Porcelain crucible and lid.
Pair of crucible tongs.
A pipe-clay triangle.
Piece of magnesium ribbon weighing 0·24 g (best obtained by weighing a long piece of ribbon and dividing the length by proportion).

It is advisable to collect the class results. Many groups will obtain a mass of 0·40 g for magnesium oxide which leads to the formula MgO.

Experiment 5.3 *To determine the formula of a chloride of mercury*

The teacher will require:

100 cm^3 beaker.
Sample of mercury(II) chloride.
Bottle of hypophosphorous acid solution.
Bottle of propanone.
Metal water-bath.

Specimen results and calculation:

Mass of mercury chloride: 5·13 g
Mass of mercury obtained: 3·78 g; thus mass of chlorine: 1·35 g
Atomic masses: Hg = 200; Cl = 35·5

$$\text{Moles of mercury atoms} = \frac{3·78}{200} = 0·0189$$

$$\text{Moles of chlorine atoms} = \frac{1·35}{35·5} = 0·0380$$

Thus one mole of mercury atoms combines with two moles of chlorine atoms. Thus formula of mercury chloride is $HgCl_2$.

The following is an interesting alternative to Experiment 5.3, which should be carried out by the teacher as a demonstration. An excess of bromine is added to a known mass of mercury in a boiling-tube. The two liquids are stirred together while cooling the tube in a beaker of cold water. When the reaction is complete, excess bromine is removed by using a water pump, leaving mercury(II) bromide as a white solid. The mass of this is determined and the results calculated in a similar manner to Experiment 5.3.

Experiment 5.4 *Investigating a reaction involving the formation of a precipitate*

Each group of pupils will require:

Two burettes (graduated pipettes, with fillers, could be used).
Access to bottle of 1 M lead nitrate and 1 M potassium iodide.

Access to centrifuge, with tubes.
Metric ruler.

The height of precipitate ceases to increase after the addition of 2·5 cm^3 of lead nitrate solution. This suggests that the reaction involves one mole of lead nitrate to two moles of potassium iodide. This is consistent with the equation:

$$Pb^{2+}(aq) + 2I^-(aq) \longrightarrow PbI_2(s)$$

Experiment 5.5 *Investigating the reaction between mercury(II) ions and iodide ions*

Each group of pupils will require:

Two burettes, or graduated pipettes with fillers.
0·2 M mercury(II) chloride solution (not to be pipetted by mouth).
1 M potassium iodide solution.
Conical flask.

Specimen results and calculation:

A typical volume of potassium iodide solution to just redissolve the precipitate that forms is 20 cm^3.

$$\text{Moles of iodide ions:} \quad \frac{20}{1000} \times 1 \;\; = 0 \cdot 02$$

$$\text{Moles of mercury(II) ions:} \quad \frac{25}{1000} \times 0 \cdot 2 = 0 \cdot 005$$

Thus in the complex ion there are four moles of iodine to one of mercury (formula is therefore $HgI_4{}^{2-}$) and 'n' = 2.

Experiment 5.6 *Investigating the reaction between iron and a solution of copper(II) sulphate*

Each group of pupils will require:

Access to bottle of finely divided iron filings.
1 M solution of copper(II) sulphate.
Measuring cylinder (10 cm^3).
Water-bath or beaker.
Access to bottle of propanone.

The pupils should find that approximately 0·64 g of copper is precipitated which indicates that the first equation represents the reaction that takes place.

Experiment 5.7 *A reaction in which a gas is evolved*

Each group of pupils will require:

A boiling tube fitted with a stopper and bent glass and rubber tubing as illustrated in Fig. 5.5, containing an ignition-tube as a 'trigger'.

Gas syringe with holder.
Piece of magnesium ribbon weighing 0·024 g (best obtained by weighing a long length of ribbon and cutting into calculated lengths).

Specimen results and calculation:

Moles of magnesium that react: $\dfrac{0·024}{24} = 0·001$

Volume of hydrogen evolved: 24 cm^3.
Volume of 1 mole: 24 dm^3; thus mole of hydrogen evolved: 0·001.
The equation for the reaction is thus:

$$Mg(s) + 2H^+(aq) \longrightarrow Mg^{2+}(aq) + H_2(g)$$

Experiment 5.8 *To find the volume percentage of oxygen in the air and the molecular mass of oxygen*

Each group of pupils will require:

Two gas syringes, with rubber tubing connectors.
Silica tube (about 10 cm by 0·25 cm inside diameter) containing wire-form copper-(II) oxide previously reduced in town gas.
Syringe bench or equivalent stands and holders.

The pupils will find that 80 cm^3 of 'inactive air' (largely nitrogen) remain and the mass of the copper containing tube increases by about 0·026 g.
    Mass of 20 cm^3 of oxygen = 0·027 g

Thus mass of 24 dm^3 of oxygen = $\dfrac{0·027 \times 24 \times 1000}{20} = 32$ g

Experiment 5.9 *To determine the molecular mass of sulphur dioxide*

Each group of pupils will require:

Flask (nominally of 250 cm^3 capacity) fitted with tubes and taps or clips as illustrated.
Access to sulphur dioxide cylinder in fume cupboard.

Warning: This experiment should only be carried out if efficient fume-cupboards are available. Carbon dioxide, conveniently generated in a Kipp's apparatus, can be substituted if you do not have such facilities.

Specimen results and calculations:

Mass of flask, fittings and air: 86·786 g.
Volume of water flask will hold: 270 cm^3 = 0·270 dm^3.
Thus mass of air in flask = 1·2 × 0·270 = 0·324 g.
Thus mass of evacuated flask and fittings: 86·786 − 0·324 = 86·462 g.
Mass of flask, fittings and sulphur dioxide: 87·182 g.
Thus mass of sulphur dioxide = 0·720 g.

Thus 0·270 dm^3 of sulphur dioxide weigh 0·720 g.

24 dm^3 of sulphur dioxide weigh $\dfrac{0·720 \times 24}{0·270} = 64$ g.

Hence the molecular mass of sulphur dioxide is 64 g.

Experiment 5.10 *Investigating the reaction that occurs when sulphur burns in oxygen*

Each group of pupils will require:

> Gas syringe, and holder.
> Access to oxygen cylinder.
> Boiling tube fitted with stopper, glass and rubber tubing as shown in diagram.
> Roll sulphur.
> 2 cm^3 hypodermic syringe with needle (small size).
> Access to bottle of approx. 5 M potassium hydroxide.

The pupils will find that there is no volume change when the sulphur burns in oxygen, hence $y = 1$. On absorption of the sulphur dioxide with potassium hydroxide solution a volume diminution of about 24 cm^3 will be observed. This means that 0·001 mole of sulphur have reacted to form 0·001 mole of sulphur dioxide and hence the value of x is 1.

Experiment 5.11 *To investigate the effect of pressure changes on the volume of a fixed mass of gas at constant temperature*

Each group of pupils will require:

> Glass tube (approximately 30 cm by 0·2 cm internal diameter), sealed at one end. This contains a thread of mercury about 15 cm^3 long trapping an air sample about 10 cm^3 long between it and the sealed end.
> Metric ruler.
> Access to a barometer reading to 1 mm of mercury.

Experiment 5.12 *To investigate the effect of temperature on the volume of a fixed mass of gas at constant pressure*

Each group of pupils will require:

> Piece of thin-walled glass tubing (approximately 20 cm by 0·2 cm internal diameter) sealed at one end and containing a bubble of concentrated sulphuric acid about 3 cm long which ends about 12 cm from the sealed end of the tube.
> Metric ruler.
> Thermometer reading to 100°C.
> Two rubber bands (for holding assembly together).
> Tall-form 1 dm^3 beaker.

The sulphuric acid should be carefully placed in the glass tubing using a teat-pipette drawn out to fit inside it. This method can also be used for inserting the mercury in the tube for Experiment 5.11.

Chapter 6   Rates of reaction and equilibrium

Experiment 6.1   *To investigate the effect of particle size on the rate of a reaction*

Each group of pupils will require:

Marble chips (of various particle sizes).
100 cm^3 conical flask.
50 cm^3 measuring cylinder.
Watch-glass.
Stop-clock.
Cotton wool.

It may be necessary for this to be conducted as a pupil assisted demonstration if sufficient semi-automatic balances are not available. The most suitable type of balance for this experiment (and 6.2(*a*)) is the top pan variety. A piece of filter paper may be substituted for the watch-glass if the total mass to be weighed exceeds the balance capacity.

The same final loss in mass is observed in all cases because the same quantity of hydrochloric acid is used up each time.

Experiment 6.2   *The effect of concentration on the rate of reaction*

(*a*) Each group of pupils will require:

Apparatus specified for Experiment 6.1.
Apparatus suitable for diluting bench (2 M) hydrochloric acid to 1·0 M and 0·5 M.

The same final loss in mass is not observed here because the quantity of hydrochloric acid differs in each case.

(*b*) Each group of pupils will require:

250 cm^3 conical flask.
4 per cent solution of sodium thiosulphate.
Stop-clock.
50 cm^3 measuring cylinder.

Experiment 6.3   *The effect of temperature on the rate of reaction*

Each group of pupils will require:

Apparatus and reagents specified for experiment 6.2(*b*).
−10/110°C thermometer (short-form is suitable and most robust).

Catalysts

The teacher may like to introduce this topic by demonstrating the following experiments:

(a) Immediately prior to the lesson, warm a piece of platinized asbestos in a bunsen flame until it is thoroughly dry. Allow to cool and place in an air-tight container. Show the class that if the hydrogen is allowed to escape from a gas-jar and mix with the air, there is no evidence of it reacting with the oxygen in the air in accordance with the equation:

$$2H_2(g) + O_2(g) \longrightarrow 2H_2O(l).$$

Open a second gas-jar of hydrogen and hold in the mouth the previously dried platinized asbestos gripped in a pair of tongs. The gas will now ignite spontaneously due to the catalytic activity of the platinum.

(b) Prepare prior to the lesson (i) a '10 volume' solution of hydrogen peroxide and (ii) a 10 per cent solution of hydrazinium sulphate. Mix equal volumes of the two solutions in front of the class. There is no evidence of the expected reactions:

$$2H_2O_2(aq) + N_2H_5{}^+(aq) \longrightarrow H^+(aq) + N_2(g) + 4H_2O(l)$$

Lower into the mixture a muslin bag containing coarse copper powder; there is a rapid evolution of nitrogen. If the bag is removed before the temperature of the mixture has risen very much the reaction slows almost to a halt again. The colour of the solution does not change to blue which suggests that the action of the copper is catalytic. It is not necessary for the pupils to remember the chemistry of the reaction.

Experiment 6.4 *An investigation of a catalysed chemical reaction*

Each group of pupils will require:

Gas syringe, with holder.
Divided flask with stopper, rubber and glass tubing as illustrated; if divided flasks are not available, a conical flask with an ignition-tube suspended inside may be substituted.
'20-volume' hydrogen peroxide solution.
Manganese(IV) oxide.

Access to a variety of measuring cylinders for making dilutions. The open ended nature of this experiment means that additional apparatus and materials may be requested. The Nuffield film-loop 'Catalysis in Industry' could be shown at this point.

The extent of reaction

If the teacher wishes to demonstrate the iodine monochloride/trichloride equilibrium described in the text he will require a U-tube with taps fitted as illustrated in Fig. 6.9 of the pupils' text, connected to a chlorine generator as described on page 11 of the Teacher's Notes. The experiment must be carried out in a fume-cupboard. Prior to the lesson pass chlorine over a small sample of iodine in the U-tube and then allow the excess chlorine to escape and leave iodine monochloride in the U-tube. At the end of the experiment the iodine monochloride can be stored in a glass-stoppered bottle for future use.

Experiment 6.5 *Investigating an equilibrium system using a radioisotope labelling method*

This experiment must, by law, be performed by the teacher. The protective clothing and disposal arrangements specified for Experiment 1.2 should be employed. In addition the teacher should prepare shortly beforehand the following materials:

(*a*) A saturated solution of lead chloride. This is the filtrate obtained when equal volumes of 2 M hydrochloric acid and 1 M lead nitrate solution are mixed and the mixture centrifuged.

(*b*) Sample of solid lead chloride containing a proportion of lead-212. This is made by mixing together 5 cm^3 each of 1 M lead nitrate and thorium(IV) nitrate and 2 M hydrochloric acid. Centrifuge and wash the residue.

Apparatus required:

Scaler with liquid counter, holder and lead.
Stop-clock.
Centrifuge and tubes.

NB: Lead-212 has a half-life of just over 10 hours and the solid sample should, therefore, not be prepared too long before the lesson.

Teachers who have attended courses approved by the Department of Education and Science to allow them to handle open sources of artificial isotopes may prefer to use a modification of this method using a sample of silver chloride containing a proportion of silver-111. This, being a considerably stronger source, gives an even more convincing result.

Experiment 6.6 *An investigation of the effect of changing concentrations on some equilibrium systems in aqueous solution*

Each group of pupils will require:

Access to bottle of bismuth carbonate.
Small dropper bottle of concentrated hydrochloric acid.
Teat-pipette.
0·1 M (approx.) solution of iodine in 1 M potassium iodide.
1 M and 0·1 M solutions of iron(III) chloride.
1 M and 0·1 M solutions of potassium thiocyanate.

Experiment 6.7 *To investigate the effect of temperature on a gaseous equilibrium*

The teacher will require:

Apparatus for preparation and collection of nitrogen dioxide as described on page 11.

Each group of pupils will require:

Teat-pipette.
One-holed bung to fit boiling-tube.
250 cm^3 beaker.
Ice and salt to make freezing mixture.

Experiment 6.8   *To investigate the effect of pressure on a gaseous equilibrium*

Each group of pupils will require:

Sample of equilibrium mixture prepared by the teacher as in Experiment 6.7.
Teat-pipette.
Side-arm boiling-tube.
Glass taps fitted with rubber tubing and bungs as illustrated in Fig. 6.11 of pupils' text.
Access to tap-pump (or electrical pump if water-pressure is low).

Chapter 7   Energy changes accompanying chemical changes

If the teacher intends to demonstrate the introductory experiments on energy changes he will require:

Two 2 dm^3 beakers each containing 1 dm^3 of water.
Watch-glass on which is weighed out 80 g ammonium nitrate (1 mole).
Measuring cylinder containing 53·5 cm^3 conc. sulphuric acid (1 mole).
$-10/110°C$ thermometer; a demonstration type showing the temperature change on an electrical meter is ideal. Details of suitable instruments will be found in laboratory suppliers' catalogues.

It is essential that in the introductory lesson for this section the calculation of energy changes is thoroughly explained to the class, particularly if their background in physics is not strong.

Experiment 7.1   *To determine ΔH for some chemical reactions*

Each group of pupils will require:

(*a*) Spirit lamp, as shown in Fig. 7.3 of the pupils' text.
   Measuring cylinder (100 cm^3).
   Metal can (old copper calorimeters are suitable).
   $-10/110°C$ thermometer, preferably short-form.
(*b*) 2 M solutions of calcium chloride and potassium carbonate.
   Heat-insulating plastic cup (as used by mass caterers).
   Measuring cylinder (50 cm^3).
   0/50°C thermometer measuring to 0·1°, as temperature change is small.
(*c*) 0·2 M copper(II) sulphate solution.
   Finely divided zinc filings (reasonably new sample free from oxide coating).
   Transparent plastic bottle fitted with stopper and thermometer as shown in Fig. 7.4 of the pupils' text.

It is advisable that the class carry out each part of the experiment and then have a discussion about the interpretation of the results with the teacher before proceeding to the next part.

In part (b) it must be carefully explained to the pupils that the temperature change that occurs when 50 cm³ of 2 M calcium chloride is added to 50 cm³ of 2 M potassium carbonate (i.e., 0·1 mole of each in a total volume of 100 cm³) is the same as that produced when 1 mole of each reacts in a total volume of 1000 cm³ (i.e., 1 dm³). A similar argument applies in other experiments of this type.

Experiment 7.2 *Constructing and investigating a Daniell cell*

Each group of pupils will require:

> Empty Daniell cell as supplied by manufacturers.
> 1 M solutions of copper(II) sulphate and zinc sulphate.
> High resistance voltmeter.
> 1·5 V electric motor.
> Connecting leads.
> Ammeter (reading to 0·1 mA).
> Rheostat (50 kΩ) (suitably mounted Radiospares potentiometer).

The Daniell cell may have too low an internal resistance to show a marked falling off of voltage with high current demand. If this is so, a second cell with construction as for Experiment 7.3(b) will be required for part (c) of this investigation. The pupils will observe from the second graph that there is a voltage at which the maximum power can be obtained.

Experiment 7.3 *To measure ΔH and ΔG for the displacement of silver by copper*

Each group of pupils will require:

> 0·2 M silver nitrate solution.
> Electrolytic grade copper powder.
> 25 cm³ measuring cylinder.
> Transparent plastic bottle fitted with stopper and thermometer as shown in Fig. 7.4 of the pupils' text.
> Short specimen tube fitted with cork and inner glass tube.
> Slender strips of copper and silver foil.
> Approximately 1 M solutions of silver nitrate and copper(II) sulphate.
> High-resistance voltmeter.
> Leads and crocodile clips.
> 'Polyfilla'.
> Saturated potassium nitrate solution.

Experiment 7.4   *Using ΔG to predict the feasibility of some reactions*

(*a*) Pupils will probably suggest mixing solutions of lead nitrate and dilute sulphuric acid and seeing if a precipitate forms.

(*b*) Pupils will probably suggest putting pieces of lead into a solution of a magnesium salt.

(*c*) Pupils will probably suggest passing chlorine into a solution of a soluble iron(II) salt. The teacher may prefer to guide them into substituting chlorine water for chlorine; ΔG for the dissolution of chlorine in water is small enough to be ignored. The reaction with potassium thiocyanate as a test for Fe^{3+}(aq) ions may have to be suggested; the reaction has been encountered in the previous chapter.

Experiment 7.5   *To make a simple fuel cell*

Each group of pupils will require:

Electrolysis cell as shown in Fig. 7.15 of the pupils' text.
High resistance voltmeter.
6 V d.c. supply.
Connecting leads.

The cell will operate a high input impedance transistor radio if one is available.

The Heinemann film loop HC3 is useful in giving a dynamic picture of the dissolution of an ionic crystal by polar water molecules and the Nuffield film-loop 'Energy Changes in HCl' could also be shown at the appropriate time.

Chapter 8   Two patterns of chemical change

Experiment 8.1   *Is there a pattern in the acidity or alkalinity of oxides in aqueous solution?*

The teacher will require:

Six test-tubes with bung and glass tubing as illustrated in Fig. 8.1.
Oxygen cylinder with two-stage control valve and gauges.
Samples of magnesium, calcium, graphite (lumps).
Sulphur (fragments of roll), sodium, and phosphorus (red).

The pupils should conclude that the oxides of non-metallic elements dissolve in water to give acids while those of metallic elements dissolve to give alkalis.

Experiment 8.2   *Reactions of acids and alkalis on some oxides that are insoluble in water*

Each group of pupils will require:

Samples of copper(II) oxide, zinc oxide, lead(II) oxide, silicon oxide, and aluminium oxide (the latter must be freshly prepared by the thermal decomposition of aluminium nitrate).

Experiment 8.3 *Do acids having the same concentration have the same pH?*

Each group of pupils will require:

0·01 M solutions of hydrochloric, ethanoic, and nitric acids.
Access to pH meter correctly adjusted. (If this is not available, Universal Indicator (pH) solution or paper may be used.)

The pupils should conclude that while hydrochloric and nitric acids appear to be completely dissociated into ions at this concentration, ethanoic acid is only partially dissociated.

Experiment 8.4 *Comparing the properties of solutions of hydrogen chloride in water and toluene*

Each group of pupils will require:

(*a*) − 10/110°C thermometer (short-form preferable).
Toluene.
Two gas-jars of hydrogen chloride (dry) in fume-cupboard, prepared as described on page 11 of the Teacher's Notes.

The teacher may prefer to demonstrate the first part of the experiment. An electrical thermometer is very suitable if this is done.

(*b*) Solutions of hydrogen chloride in water and in dry toluene (the toluene should be stood overnight over anhydrous calcium chloride, decanted into a dreschel bottle and dried hydrogen chloride passed into it).
Universal Indicator (pH) paper stored in dessicator.
Anhydrous sodium carbonate (well heated prior to experiment).
Magnesium ribbon.
Apparatus for conductivity testing (as for Experiment 3.1).

Experiment 8.5 *Comparing the reaction of glacial ethanoic acid with those of an aqueous solution of ethanoic acid*

Each group of pupils will require:

Glacial ethanoic acid (sufficient ethanoic anhydride should be added to the sample a few hours prior to experiment to ensure it is anhydrous).
Universal Indicator (pH) paper stored in a dessicator.
Anhydrous sodium carbonate (well heated prior to experiment).
Magnesium ribbon.
Apparatus for conductivity testing (as for Experiment 3.1).

The pupils should suggest that ethanoic acid is partially dissociated on addition of water according to the equilibrium:

$$HAc(aq) + H_2O(l) \rightleftharpoons Ac^-(aq) + H_3O^+(aq)$$

Experiment 8.6 *To find the enthalpies of neutralization of some acids and alkalis*

Each group of pupils will require:

Heat-insulating plastic cup (as used in Experiment 7.1).
Two 50 cm^3 measuring cylinders.
$-10/110°C$ thermometer.
2 M solutions of hydrochloric, nitric, and ethanoic acids.
2 M solutions of sodium hydroxide and potassium hydroxide (these should be free from carbonate formed by absorption of atmospheric carbon dioxide).

The pupils should appreciate that the hydrochloric and nitric acids react with each of the alkalis according to the equation:

$$H_3O^+(aq) + OH^-(aq) \longrightarrow 2H_2O(l)$$

Ethanoic acid, being largely un-ionized, reacts according to the equation:

$$HAc(aq) + OH^-(aq) \longrightarrow Ac^-(aq) + H_2O(l)$$

and thus has a different value for ΔH.

Experiment 8.7 *To test our prediction about the relative strengths of chloride ions and ethanoate ions as bases*

The pupils should have predicted that the ethanoate ion will be a stronger base than the chloride ion. They will require access to:

1 M solutions of sodium chloride and sodium ethanoate.

From their previous work the pupils should conclude that the ethanoate ion is a more powerful base than the chloride ion and the experimental result should confirm this.

Experiment 8.8 *Examining the relative oxidizing and reducing powers of some metals*

Each group of pupils will require:

A small tile with at least six indentations.

Solutions that are approximately 1 M of copper(II) nitrate, lead(II) nitrate, iron(II) sulphate, magnesium nitrate, zinc nitrate, and tin(II) chloride. The latter is best made by reacting granulated tin with dilute hydrochloric acid until there is no further reaction and filtering to remove excess tin and impurities. The iron(II) sulphate must be freshly prepared with distilled water that has been boiled free from dissolved carbon dioxide and allowed to cool in a stoppered bottle.
Small pieces of magnesium ribbon, copper, lead, zinc and tin foil, small pieces of iron nail cleaned with emery cloth.

The correct order of activity is magnesium, zinc, iron, tin, lead, and copper.

Experiment 8.9 *An electrical method of comparing the reducing power of some metals*

Each group of pupils will require:

Strips of copper, lead, iron, magnesium, zinc, and tin.
High-resistance voltmeter (reading to 2 V) and leads.
100 cm^3 beaker.
10 per cent solution of sodium chloride.

The metals should take the same place in the list as they did in the previous experiment.

Experiment 8.10 *Some reactions of iron considered on an oxidation-reduction basis*

Each group of pupils will require:

Two 100 cm^3 beakers.
Two 50 cm^3 measuring cylinders.
Fine iron filings.
'20-volume' solution of hydrogen peroxide.
Filter funnel and papers.
Two evaporating basins.
Approximately 0·1 M solution of iron(III) chloride.
Copper powder, electrolytic grade.
Approximately 0·1 M solutions of copper(II) sulphate and iron(II) sulphate.
Chromatography paper and suitable tank.
Chromatography solvent of propanone, distilled water and concentrated hydro-chloric acid in volume proportions 85:5:10.
Hair-dryer (if available).
Dip-tray (a large flat dish would be suitable) **or** chromatographic spray.
Glass-tubing drawn out to capillary.
0·1 per cent solution of dithio-oxamide (rubeanic acid) in ethanol.

The results should show the reaction taking place to be:

$$2Fe^{3+}(aq) + Cu(s) \longrightarrow 2Fe^{2+}(aq) + Cu^{2+}(aq)$$

Experiment 8.11 *Investigating the reaction between iron(II) ions and permanganate ions in acidic conditions*

Each group of pupils will require:

U-tube with plug of cotton wool soaked in dilute sulphuric acid.
Approx. 0·1 M solutions of iron(II) sulphate and potassium permanganate.
Milliammeter (reading to 1 mA) with leads and crocodile clips.
Two Nichrome electrodes.
Accurately 0·1 M solution of iron(II) ammonium sulphate and 0·025 M potassium permanganate.

25 cm³ pipette ⎱ (or two graduated pipettes with fillers; in this case the volumes
50 cm³ burette ⎰ of solutions used could be appropriately modified).
Two 250 cm³ conical flasks.

The pupils should find that five moles of iron(II) ions react with one mole of permanganate ion. The oxidation state of the manganese thus becomes $+2$ and the
equation for the reaction:

$$5Fe^{2+}(aq) + MnO_4^-(aq) + 8H^+(aq) \longrightarrow 5Fe^{3+}(aq) + Mn^{2+}(aq) + 4H_2O(l)$$

Chapter 9   Elements and the periodic table

Experiment 9.1   *To investigate some reactions of the elements
lithium, sodium, and potassium*

Each group of pupils will require:

Three squares of asbestos paper (about 2×2 cm).
Pair of tongs.
Small beaker or crystallizing dish.

The teacher will require bottles of sodium, potassium, and lithium stored under
naphtha oil, a small tile, knife, and forceps to dispense them.

The teacher may prefer to carry out this complete experiment as a demonstration.

Experiment 9.2   *To investigate some reactions of the elements
chlorine, bromine, and iodine*

The teacher will require:

Chlorine generator as described on page 11 of the Teacher's Notes.
Hard-glass tube (about 15×2 cm internal diameter) with tubing fitted as shown in
    Fig. 9.2.
Iron-wool.
Bromine, with leak-proof teat-pipette to dispense it.

Each group of pupils will require:

Iron-wool.
Iodine.

The product formed in the reaction between iron and chlorine is $FeCl_3$ and between
iron and bromine is $FeBr_3$, but between iron and iodine is FeI_2. Iron(III) iodide does
not exist.

Experiment 9.3   *Further evidence of the relative
reactivity of the halogens*

Each group of pupils will require:

Approximately 1 M solutions of potassium chloride, potassium bromide, and
    potassium iodide.

Chlorine water (made by bubbling chlorine through water until the solution is saturated).

Bromine water (made by adding about five drops of bromine to 250 cm^3 of water).

From this and the previous experiment, the pupils should conclude that the reactivity of the halogens *decreases* with increasing atomic number while that of the alkali metals *increases* with increasing atomic number. Taking the elements overall, the most reactive pair should be fluorine and francium.

Experiment 9.4 *To investigate the reactions between chlorine and the alkali metals*

The teacher will require:

Test-tubes fitted with bungs and glass tubing as illustrated in Fig. 9.3.

Chlorine generator as described on page 11 of the Teacher's Notes.

Samples of sodium, lithium, and potassium with tile, knife, and forceps for handling.

Experiment 9.5 *To compare the properties of some transition metals with those of the alkali metals*

Each group of pupils will require:

Samples in foil form of several first-row transition metals such as copper, nickel, iron, and zinc.

Tongs.

Experiment 9.6 *To compare some properties of transition element and alkali metal compounds*

Each group of pupils will require:

Samples of a wide range of transition metal and alkali metal compounds in clear glass containers, with IUPAC names.

Experiment 9.7 *To prepare a sample of a compound containing a complex ion—tetrammine copper(II) sulphate*

Each group of pupils will require:

Approximately 1 M solution of copper(II) sulphate.

Ethanol.

50 cm^3 measuring cylinder.

100 cm^3 conical flask (or beaker).

250 cm^3 beaker (to contain ice/water mixture).

Ice (optional).

Apparatus for filtration or centrifuging.

Copper(II) sulphate crystals contain five moles of water in every mole of solid, four moles being complexed with the copper(II) ion and the fifth associated with the sulphate ion. Strictly considered, the hydrated copper(II) ion is a complex ion.

Experiment 9.8 *To investigate some reactions of chromium compounds*

Each group of pupils will require:

250 cm³ conical flask, which can be fitted with a bunsen valve as shown in Fig. 9.7.
Approximately 1 M solution of potassium dichromate.
Granulated zinc.
'20-volume' hydrogen peroxide.
4 M potassium hydroxide.

The blue chromium(II) ions are unstable in the presence of air (or oxygen), but if all air is boiled out of the solution as described in the pupils' text, it is possible to get a clear, pale blue solution on reduction which immediately reverts to the green chromium(III) on admission of air. Complete oxidation of chromium(III) to dichromate takes a long time, but the filtrate obtained is a clear orange within a few minutes.

Chapter 10 Metallic elements and their compounds—I

Experiment 10.1 *To investigate the ease of reduction of certain metal oxides*

Each group of pupils will require:

Charcoal block and blow-pipe.
Magnesium, aluminium, iron(III), lead(II), and copper(II) oxides.
Test-tube with hole blown in end fitted with bung and glass-tubing as illustrated in Fig. 10.2.

If town gas is not available, a cylinder of hydrogen will be required. In this case, a teacher demonstration will probably be more convenient.

Experiment 10.2 *To test for alkali metal compounds; the flame test*

Each group of pupils will require:

Watch-glass.
Platinum or Nichrome wire sealed in glass rod (for method II).
Samples for test (the chlorides of lithium, sodium, and potassium are suitable).

The teacher may care to extend the scope of this test by showing that the potassium flame colour can be detected even in the presence of the more powerful sodium colour by using a suitable filter. In this case the pupils will also require small squares of cobalt glass.

Experiment 10.3 *To investigate the properties of sodium hydroxide (caustic soda)*

Each group of pupils will require:

Pellet or flake samples of sodium hydroxide.
Watch-glass.
Solutions of copper(II) sulphate, iron(II) sulphate, iron(III) chloride, zinc sulphate, lead(II) nitrate, and calcium chloride.
Solid ammonium chloride.

Deliquescence should be recognized as the tendency to absorb water from the moist atmosphere.

The pupils should learn that the hydroxides of many metals are insoluble and, in the case of transition metals, often have distinctive colours suitable for identification purposes. Some metal hydroxides, those described as amphoteric, will dissolve in excess of sodium hydroxide. Pupils should be encouraged to write ionic equations for these reactions.

Chapter 8 contains more about the chemistry of such reactions and that between the ammonium and hydroxide ions.

Experiment 10.4 *To investigate the properties of sodium carbonate*

Each group of pupils will require:

Samples of anhydrous sodium carbonate and hydrated sodium carbonate (these should be stored in air-tight containers).
Watch-glass.
Solutions of copper(II) sulphate, iron(II) sulphate, iron(III) chloride, zinc sulphate, lead(II) nitrate, and calcium chloride.

Efflorescence should be recognized as the tendency to give up water to the atmosphere.

Experiment 10.5 *To investigate some properties of calcium and magnesium*

Each group of pupils will require:

Calcium turnings.
Small lengths of magnesium ribbon.
Tongs.

The teacher will require:

Test-tube with cotton wool and tube and cork as illustrated in Fig. 10.8.
Small length of magnesium ribbon.

Experiment 10.6 *To test for compounds of calcium and magnesium*

Each group of pupils will require:

Platinum or Nichrome wire (if flame test method II is used).
Approximately 2 M solutions of calcium and magnesium chlorides.

0·1 per cent aqueous solution of Titan Yellow.
Calcichrome reagent.
Samples for test such as the chlorides of calcium and magnesium.

Experiment 10.7 *To investigate the properties of some compounds of calcium and magnesium*

Each group of pupils will require:

Marble chips.
Length of thick iron wire (about 15 cm × 2 mm).
Powdered magnesium and calcium carbonates.
Lime-water.
Watch-glass.
100 cm³ beaker.
Carbon dioxide generator (as described on page 11 of the Teacher's Notes **or** a Kipp's apparatus).

The reaction taking place when calcium carbonate is heated is:

$$CaCO_3(s) \longrightarrow CaO(s) + CO_2(g)$$

The calcium oxide reacts with a *small* quantity of water thus:

$$CaO(s) + H_2O(l) \longrightarrow Ca(OH)_2(s)$$

With more water the slaked lime dissolves to give a solution of free calcium and hydroxide ions.

With carbon dioxide, the lime-water so formed first reacts to precipitate calcium carbonate:

$$Ca^{2+}(aq) + 2OH^-(aq) + CO_2(g) \longrightarrow CaCO_3(s) + H_2O(l)$$

With excess carbon dioxide this redissolves with the formation of calcium hydrogen carbonate:

$$CaCO_3(s) + H_2O(l) + CO_2(g) \longrightarrow Ca^{2+}(aq) + 2HCO_3^-(aq)$$

This reaction is reversed when any attempt is made to heat or otherwise concentrate the solution and so calcium hydrogen carbonate only exists in solution.

Magnesium carbonate is less thermally stable than calcium carbonate.
The Nuffield Chemistry film-loop 'Limestone' could be shown when appropriate.

Chapter 11 Metallic elements and their compounds—II

Experiment 11.1 *To investigate some properties of aluminium and lead*

Each group of pupils will require:

Pieces of lead and aluminium foil.
Powdered samples of lead and aluminium.
Squares of asbestos paper.
Tongs.
Apparatus illustrated in Fig. 10.8.

Solution of mercury(II) chloride.
Approximately 5 M solution of sodium hydroxide.

Experiment 11.2 *Tests for aluminium and lead compounds*

Each group of pupils will require:

Powdered samples of lead(II) nitrate and aluminium sulphate.
Platinum or Nichrome wire (if flame test method II is used).
Potassium iodide solution.
0·1 per cent solution of Alizarin Red S.

Experiment 11.3 *The amphoteric nature of the hydroxides of aluminium and lead*

Each group of pupils will require:

Solutions of aluminium sulphate and lead(II) nitrate.

The chemistry of these reactions is discussed in chapter 8.

Experiment 11.4 *Tests for iron compounds*

Each group of pupils will require:

Solution of iron(III) chloride.
Solution of ammonium iron(II) sulphate (freshly prepared).
Solution of potassium hexacyanoferrate(III).
Solution of ammonium thiocyanate.

The pupils should recall the reaction of iron(II) and iron(III) with sodium hydroxide giving precipitates with distinctive colours. The chemistry of the reaction with thiocyanate ions has been encountered in chapter 6.

Experiment 11.5 *To detect the metals present in a coin by chromatography*

Each group of pupils will require:

Chromatography paper and suitable chromatography tank.
Glass-tubing drawn out to a capillary.
1 per cent solutions of silver, nickel, and copper(II) nitrates.
Running solvent of propanone, distilled water, and concentrated hydrochloric acid in volume proportions 85:5:10.
Hair-dryer (if available).
Dip-tray **or** chromatographic spray.
Either saturated solution of hydrogen sulphide **or** 0·1 per cent solution of dithio-oxamide (rubeanic acid) in ethanol.

Experiment 11.6 *To test for compounds of copper, tin, zinc, and nickel*

Each group of pupils will require:

Platinum or Nichrome wire (if flame test method II is used).

Solutions of the chlorides of copper(II), zinc, nickel, and tin(II). The latter is best prepared by reacting tin with dilute hydrochloric acid until reaction ceases, and filtering the product.
Mercury(II) chloride solution.
1 per cent solution of dimethylglyoxime in ethanol.

The following Nuffield Chemistry film-loops could be shown during the teaching of this chapter:

'Iron Extraction'
'Copper Refining'
'Gold Mining'

The main basis for classification of the metals studied in chapters 10 and 11 has been the Activity Series. The teacher may think it appropriate, if time allows, to discuss the properties of the metals and their compounds in terms of the Periodic Table and to construct corresponding charts and tables.

Chapter 12   Non-metallic elements and their compounds—I Group IV—carbon and silicon

Experiment 12.1 *The action of heat on substances of plant and animal origin*

Each group of pupils will require:

Squares of asbestos paper.
Access to samples of starch, sucrose, rice, cheese, wood, meat, etc. (The pupils could be asked the previous period to bring their own samples.)
Scissors.

Experiment 12.2 *The effect of heating some substances of plant and animal origin with dry copper(II) oxide*

Each group of pupils will require:

Copper(II) oxide dried prior to use by strong heating.
Substances listed for Experiment 12.1.
Teat-pipette.

These experiments should establish the carbon content of such materials.

Experiment 12.3   *Making models of the crystal structures of graphite and diamond*

Each group of pupils will require:

27 expanded polystyrene spheres of identical diameter.
Moderately stiff cardboard   {(A very satisfactory alternative is the template
Compasses and ruler.   supplied with polystyrene spheres by Griffin and George Ltd., Ealing Road, Alperton, Wembley, Middlesex.)
Scissors.
Lengths of pipe-cleaner about 2 cm in length.

The suggested work with a data book will reveal that diamond is, predictably, more dense than graphite.

The pupils should be able to correlate the 'softness' of graphite with the ease the planes of atoms can slip over each other and the 'hardness' of diamond with the rigidity of the tetrahedral structure. The hardest substance known is boron nitride (BN)—boron occurs in Group III of the periodic table and nitrogen in Group V. Its structure is tetrahedral like that of diamond.

Experiment 12.4   *The laboratory preparation of carbon dioxide*

Each group of pupils will require:

Test-tube fitted with bung and delivery tube as shown in Fig. 12.3.
Shallow beaker, or dish, for collection of the gas over water.
Wooden splints.
Length of magnesium ribbon.
Lime-water.

Experiment 12.5   *The preparation and properties of carbon monoxide*

The teacher will require:

Carbon dioxide generator as illustrated in Fig. 12.4 **or** a Kipp's apparatus.
Silica or hard-glass tube packed with lumps of charcoal and fitted with bungs and glass tubes as illustrated.
Dreschel bottle containing sodium hydroxide solution.
Trough or suitable substitute.

It is advisable to prepare beforehand enough corked tubes of the gas for the class practical. The teacher may prefer the preparation from sodium formate and concentrated sulphuric acid for this purpose, details of which are to be found in most advanced inorganic texts.

Each group of pupils will require:

Wooden splints.
Length of magnesium ribbon.
Lime-water.

Experiment 12.6 *The destructive distillation of coal*

Each group of pupils will require:

Test-tube fitted with bung and delivery tube as illustrated in Fig. 12.5.
Side-arm test-tube fitted with bung.
Small pieces of coal.

Teachers who would like to know more about the chemical nature of coal should consult the article by J. Dryden in the Journal of the Institute of Fuel, April 1957.

The use of models, preferably by the class, when studying the structures of carbon compounds and in particular isomerism, is highly recommended. There are a number of very suitable kits in the catalogues of laboratory equipment suppliers. These may be the 'ball and spring' type or the 'space-filling' variety.

Experiment 12.7 *The fractionation of crude oil*

Each group of pupils will require:

Side-arm test-tube fitted with delivery tube as shown in Fig. 12.6.
0/360°C thermometer (short-form preferable).
Sample of crude oil.
Crystallizing dish.

As the first fraction tends to be lost from crude oil without condensing, it may be advisable to surround the collecting tube with a beaker of cold water when collecting this fraction.

Experiment 12.8 *Comparing the reactions of glucose, fructose, maltose, sucrose, and starch*

Each group of pupils will require:

Glucose, fructose, maltose, sucrose, and starch.
Fehling's solution I: Dissolve 18 g of copper(II) sulphate pentahydrate in 250 cm^3 of distilled water and add two drops of concentrated sulphuric acid.
Fehling's solution II: Dissolve 88 g of potassium sodium tartrate and 25 g of sodium hydroxide in 250 cm^3 of distilled water.
Approx. 0·1 M solution of iodine made up in 0·5 M potassium iodide solution.
Anhydrous sodium carbonate.

The Venn diagram is correctly completed as below.

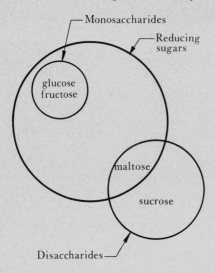

Experiment 12.9   *Can starch be broken down into anything simpler?*

Each group of pupils will require:

Starch solution: Make 0·5 g of starch into a paste with cold water and boil with 250 cm³ of distilled water.
Fehling's solutions I and II.
50 cm³ beaker.
Anhydrous sodium carbonate.
Chromatography tank and paper.
Glass tubing drawn out to a capillary.
Running solvent of propan-2-ol, glacial ethanoic acid, and distilled water in the volume proportions 60:20:20.
2 per cent solution of phenylamine (aniline) in propanone.
2 per cent solution of diphenylamine in propanone.
85 per cent aqueous solution of orthophosphoric acid.
Dip-tray **or** chromatographic spray.
Measuring cylinder (25 cm³) to mix locating agent.
Oven maintained at 100°C.
1 per cent aqueous solutions of glucose and fructose.

Experiment 12.10   *Breaking down glucose to ethanol by fermentation*

Each group of pupils will require:

250 cm³ conical flask with fittings shown in Fig. 12.9.
Lime-water.
Glucose.
Yeast (fresh if available).

Ammonium phosphate.
Potassium nitrate.

It is essential that the apparatus is air-tight.

Experiment 12.11 *Making a solution of alcohol in water stronger in alcohol*

If sufficient apparatus for class-work is not available, this must be done as a demonstration.

Each group of pupils or the teacher will require:

Fractionation apparatus shown in Fig. 12.10 or equivalent.
Filtration apparatus.
Fermentation mixture from Experiment 12.10.

The data should suggest that the earlier fractions are richest in ethanol and hence the least dense. If it is required to determine the densities of the fraction, a method depending upon Archimedes' principle will be found suitable.

Experiment 12.12 *Some reactions of ethanol*

The teacher will require:

Supply of sodium stored under naphtha oil and a knife, tile, and pair of forceps to dispense it.

Each group of pupils will require:

Ethanol, dried by standing over calcium and then filtering.
Access to phosphorus(III) chloride stored in fume-cupboard, with teat-pipette for transfer.
Apparatus shown in Fig. 12.11.
Tap-pump.
Ice.
Platinized asbestos.
Magnesium carbonate.
Magnesium ribbon.
Ethanoic acid.
1 M solution of sodium carbonate.
Test-tube with bung and delivery tube as shown in Fig. 12.12.
Cotton wool.
Fragments of porous pot.
Shallow beaker or dish, for collection of gas over water.
Bromine water.
Wooden splints.

The teacher may prefer to carry out part (*c*) as a demonstration. In this reaction, some ethanal (acetaldehyde) is also formed and the characteristic smell of this may be noticed by the class.

Experiment 12.13 *Cracking a saturated hydrocarbon to give unsaturated products*

Each group of pupils will require:

Test-tube fitted with delivery tube as in Fig. 12.14.
Shallow beaker or dish for collection of gas over water.
Iron wool.
Bromine water.
Saturated hydrocarbon such as medicinal paraffin.

Experiment 12.14 *Cracking Polythene*

Each group of pupils will require:

Test-tube fitted with delivery tube as shown in Fig. 12.15.
Shallow beaker or dish for collection of gas over water.
Fragments of Polythene.
Bromine water.

Experiment 12.15 *The breakdown and repolymerization of perspex*

Each group of pupils will require:

Test-tube fitted with delivery tube as shown in Fig. 12.16.
100 cm^3 beaker.
Ice.
Perspex chippings.
Benzoyl peroxide (Lauryl peroxide may be used but it is slower).
Oven at 95°C.
Cotton wool.

NB: The use of fume cupboards should be observed if possible as ill effects of perspex monomer on pupils have been reported. The benzoyl peroxide *must* be stored slightly moist and not used in concentrations above that recommended if the experiment is to be carried out without danger of explosion. Lauryl peroxide is said to be a safer alternative in this respect. It is advisable to use a disposable glass tube for the polymerization. The teacher is advised to have a bottle sample of methyl methacrylate available to supplement that of groups obtaining too small a yield.

Experiment 12.16 *The polymerization of styrene*

Each group of pupils will require:

Styrene.
Benzoyl peroxide (or lauryl peroxide).
Paraffin oil.
Methylated spirit.
250 cm^3 beaker.
Reflux apparatus shown in Fig. 12.17 or equivalent.

Oven at 95°C.

Cotton wool.

The same precautions regarding the use of benzoyl peroxide as specified for Experiment 12.15 should be observed.

Experiment 12.17   *The formation of Nylon 6.6 by interfacial polymerization*

Each group of pupils will require:

5 per cent solution of adipyl chloride in tetrachloromethane.

5 per cent solution of 1,6-diaminohexane in dilute sodium hydroxide solution.

10 cm³ beaker (or small specimen tube as substitute).

Glass rod.

Forceps.

Experiment 12.18   *Converting castor oil into soap, detergent, and margarine*

Each group of pupils will require:

Castor oil.

50 cm³ beaker.

Saturated solution of sodium chloride.

Glass rod.

5 M solution of sodium hydroxide.

Filtration apparatus, preferably Buchner funnel and flask for filtration under reduced pressure.

The teacher will require:

Castor oil.

Three-necked flask fitted with stirrer, inlet and outlet as shown in Fig. 12.19.

0/360°C thermometer.

Oil heating bath.

Cylinder of hydrogen with two-stage control valve.

Source of carbon dioxide (Kipp's apparatus or cylinder).

Finely divided nickel catalyst (obtainable from Unilever Educational Services free of charge. Alternatively the catalyst can be made by the thermal decomposition of nickel formate (nickel methanoate)—the product is pyrophorric and should be handled appropriately).

NB: When carrying out this demonstration, it is essential to displace **all** the air with carbon dioxide before raising the temperature if danger of catalyst ignition is to be avoided.

Use of a heated filter funnel when separating the reaction mixture is recommended.

Experiment 12.19   *How do soaps and detergents work?*

Each group of pupils will require:

> Aluminium disc (about 2 cm diameter × 2 or 3 mm thickness—old French aluminium currency is ideal).
> 250 cm³ beaker.
> Liquid detergent (such as Teepol).
> Square of unused fabric of fine weave.
> Teat-pipette.
> Solution of commercial detergent (such as Tide, but **not** a *biological* detergent, in hot water).
> Strips of bandage (source of untreated fabric).
> Ultra-violet lamp giving little visible light.

Experiment 12.20   *The action of soap on waters of various types*

Each group of pupils will require:

> 25 cm³ pipette.
> Conical flask (250 cm³).
> Soap flakes (such as Lux).
> Temporarily hard water (made by bubbling carbon dioxide through lime-water until no further change takes place then adding an equal volume of distilled water).
> Permanently hard water (made by shaking distilled water with calcium sulphate, filtering, and adding an equal volume of water).

Simple tests will show that calcium carbonate is deposited when temporarily hard water is boiled—to explain this and the origin of calcium hydrogen carbonate in such water see Experiment 12.4(*d*).

Experiment 12.21   *What ions are responsible for hardness in water?*

Each group of pupils will require:

> 25 cm³ pipette.
> 0·2 per cent solutions of sodium chloride, calcium chloride, magnesium chloride, potassium nitrate, sodium sulphate, iron(II) sulphate, magnesium sulphate, and calcium nitrate.
> Conical flask (250 cm³).
> Soap flakes (such as Lux).

The results will show that it is the double-charged metal ions that are responsible for hardness in water. They react with the negative ions in soap thus:

$$M^{2+}(aq) + 2O\!\sim^{-}(aq) \longrightarrow M(O\!\sim)_2(s) \text{ [scum]}.$$

Experiment 12.22 *How may hard water be softened?*

Each group of pupils will require:

25 cm^3 pipette.
Conical flask (250 cm^3).
Washing soda (sodium carbonate decahydrate).
Soap flakes (such as Lux).
Ion-exchange resin Zeo-Karb 215 (British Drug Houses Ltd.)
Ion-exchange column (as illustrated in Fig. 12.21—the outlet tube should rise above the level of the resin in the column to prevent this from drying out. Some glass wool should be packed at the base of the resin.)
'Calgon' (sodium hexametaphosphate).

Experiment 12.23 *The extraction of silicon from sand*

This is safe for class practical work provided the precautions concerning complete dryness are complied with.

Each group of pupils will require:

Thoroughly dried silicon oxide (silica) labelled 'Purified Sand'.
Finely powdered magnesium.
Safety goggles or spectacles.
Filter funnel and papers.
100 cm^3 beaker.
Watch-glass.
Oven at $100°C$.

Experiment 12.24 *Some uses and properties of silicones*

Each group of pupils will require:

Silicone grease.
Hydrocarbon grease (Vaseline).
Elastic band.
$-10/110°C$ thermometer.
250 cm^3 beaker.
1 per cent solution of silicone MS 1107 in propanone.
Cotton wool.
Liquid detergent (such as Teepol).
Oven at $150°C$.
Antifoam RD silicone.
Glass rod.
Microscope slide.
5p piece.
Protractor.

The silicones can be obtained from Messrs. Hopkin and Williams.

The following Nuffield Chemistry film-loops could be shown during the teaching of this chapter:

'Oil Prospecting'
'Petroleum Fractionation'
'Cracking Hydrocarbons'
'Plastics'

Chapter 13   Non-metallic elements and their compounds—II
Group V—nitrogen and phosphorus

Experiment 13.1   *Investigating proteins*

Each group of pupils will require:

Samples of proteinaceous food stuffs (perhaps provided by the pupils).
Soda lime.
Squares of asbestos paper.

Experiment 13.2   *To prepare ammonia and investigate some of its properties*

Each group of pupils will require:

Calcium hydroxide.
Ammonium chloride.
Test-tube fitted with bung and delivery tube as shown in Fig. 13.1.
Wooden splints.
Small flask with fittings as shown in Fig. 13.2.
100 cm^3 beaker.

Experiment 13.3   *Investigating the properties of ammonia solution*

Each group of pupils will require:

Apparatus for testing conductivity as for Experiment 3.1.
Solutions of iron(II) sulphate, iron(III) chloride, magnesium sulphate, copper(II) sulphate, and zinc sulphate.

NB: There is no merit in the old name 'ammonium hydroxide', there being no such un-ionized species in aqueous solution. The properties of ammonia solution are better explained in terms of the Lowry–Brönsted equilibrium, the equation for which is given in the pupils' text.

Experiment 13.4   *Breaking down ammonia*

Each group of pupils will require:

Apparatus illustrated in Fig. 13.4 consisting of an ammonium chloride/calcium hydroxide mixture in the base of a test-tube, above which is packed lumps of calcium oxide. This should be connected to the tube packed with dried wire-form copper(II) oxide which leads to a delivery tube ending in a bunsen valve.

Shallow beaker or dish for collection of gas over water.
Wooden splints.

Experiment 13.5   *The composition of ammonia*

The teacher or each group of pupils will require:

Three gas syringes.
Three three-way taps.
Rubber sleeves.
Two silica tubes (each about 10 × 0·3 cm internal diameter), one containing steel wool which has been de-greased with ether, the other containing dried copper(II) oxide in the wire-form; the contents of these tubes are best kept in place by pieces of glass rod of slightly smaller diameter than the inside of the silica tube, one at each end.
Syringe bench (or set of clamps).
Cylinders of hydrogen and nitrogen with appropriate control gear.
Apparatus shown in Fig. 13.6 for generation of dry ammonia.
Wet cloth.

If this experiment is to succeed, all apparatus must be dried in an oven before use, or the volume of ammonia produced will be too small. It should be noted that syringe experiments such as this need considerable practice if they are to be reliable.

Experiment 13.6   *To make ammonia from nitrogen and hydrogen*

The teacher or each group of pupils will require:

Two gas syringes.
One three-way tap.
Rubber sleeves.
Silica tube containing steel wool treated as in Experiment 13.5.
Syringe bench (or set of clamps).
Cylinders of hydrogen and nitrogen with appropriate control gear.
Wet cloth.

Experiment 13.7   *To prepare a fertilizer—ammonium sulphate*

Each group of pupils will require:

100 cm³ beaker.
25 cm³ measuring cylinder.
Glass rod.
1 M sulphuric acid.
Filter funnel and paper.

Experiment 13.8 *To separate and detect amino-acids by chromatography*

Each group of pupils will require:

Chromatography paper and tank.
0·01 per cent solutions in propan-2-ol of a variety of amino-acids, glycine, alanine, and leucine being particularly suitable.
Running solvent of ethanol, 0·880 ammonia solution and distilled water in the volume proportions 45:2.5:2.5.
0·2 per cent solution of ninhydrin in propanone (or aerosol preparation).
Dip-tray **or** chromatographic spray.
Oven at 110°C.
Glass tubing drawn out to a capillary.

Experiment 13.9 *The amino-acids in orange juice*

Each group of pupils will require:

Samples of commercial orange juices and/or squashes.
Fresh orange (optional—see directions in pupils' text).
Ethanol.
Filter funnel and paper or centrifuge and tubes.
Apparatus for Experiment 13.8.

Experiment 13.10 *The reactions of ammonia with oxygen*

The teacher will require:

Wide-bore glass tube fitted with bung and inlet tubes and packed at base with glass wool, as illustrated in Fig. 13.9.
Cylinder of oxygen with appropriate control gear.
Apparatus for preparation of dry ammonia shown in Fig. 13.5.
Wide-necked conical flask (250 cm^3).
Coil of platinum wire on glass rod or wooden splint.

Experiment 13.11 *Some properties of nitric acid*

The teacher will require (for test (*a*)):

Copper turnings.

Each group of pupils will require:

Apparatus to test electrical conductivity as for Experiment 3.1.
Copper(II) oxide, magnesium oxide, calcium hydroxide, lead(II) carbonate and sodium carbonate.
Magnesium and copper turnings.
Potassium iodide solution and iron(II) sulphate solution.
Test reagent for iron(III) such as ammonium thiocyanate.

The chemistry of these tests appears later in the chapter.

56

Experiment 13.12 *Some properties of nitrates*

Each group of pupils will require:

Selection of nitrates including those of sodium, potassium, calcium, copper(II), lead(II), and ammonium.
Iron(II) sulphate.

In the 'Brown Ring' test, nitrate ions are reduced to nitrogen monoxide by iron(II) ions and this reacts with more iron(II) ions:

$$NO(g) + Fe^{2+}(aq) \longrightarrow [Fe(NO)]^{2+}(aq)$$

which is brown.

The pupils should learn that metals high in the activity series have nitrates that decompose to give the nitrite and oxygen. Less active metals decompose to give the oxide, oxygen, and nitrogen dioxide. The teacher may care to tell them that very unreactive metals (such as mercury) have nitrates that decompose further to give the metal. It is not recommended that the class heat mercury(II) nitrate because of the very toxic nature of mercury vapour.

Experiment 13.13 *The oxides of nitrogen*

Each group of pupils will require:

Test-tube fitted with delivery-tube as shown in Fig. 13.13.
Shallow beaker or dish for collection of gas over water.
Copper turnings.
Iron(II) sulphate solution.

[The teacher may like to show the pupils how the equations on page 264 can be obtained using the method for balancing redox equations shown in chapter 8.]

Test-tube fitted with delivery-tube as illustrated in Fig. 13.14 leading to side-arm test-tube as shown.
250 cm^3 beaker.
Ice.
Lead(II) nitrate.
Length of rubber tube.

Experiment 13.14 *To investigate some of the properties of white and red phosphorus*

The teacher will require:

White and red phosphorus (the former must be stored under water) with knife and dish of water for cutting and forceps for handling.
Carbon disulphide.
Filter paper.
Strip of steel about 30×2 cm.

The pupils should recognize the much greater reactivity of white than red phosphorus which suggests that the latter allotrope is the stable form.

NB: Great care must be taken when handling white phosphorus, because of its potential inflammability. For this reason, it should be cut under water (hence the dish of water mentioned earlier). Handling must always be carried out with forceps as the substance will cause serious burns in contact with the skin. As a precaution against such contact, a dish of aqueous copper(II) sulphate should be nearby on the bench while working. If fingers, etc., are immersed in this solution, having accidentally touched some phosphorus, no damage will be done as harmless copper phosphide is formed.

The following Nuffield Chemistry film-loops could be shown during the teaching of this chapter:

'Ammonia Manufacture'
'Ammonia—Uses'
'Giant Molecules—Proteins'

Chapter 14   Non-metallic elements and their compounds—III
Group IV—oxygen and sulphur

Experiment 14.1   *To prepare some oxides of elements within a period (sodium to chlorine)*

The teacher will require:

Oxygen cylinder, with appropriate control gear.
Test-tube fitted with bung and tubes as shown in Fig. 14.2.
Small samples of sodium, magnesium, aluminium, silicon, phosphorus, and sulphur.

The aluminium remains unoxidized under these conditions. The oxides thus prepared could be used in Experiment 14.2, if convenient. (This would be the case for the oxides of sodium, magnesium, silicon, and phosphorus.)

Experiment 14.2   *Investigating the properties of the oxides of the elements in the sodium period*

The teacher will require:

Fresh samples of sodium and phosphorus(V) oxides.

Each group of pupils will require:

Fresh samples of magnesium, silicon, and aluminium oxides, the latter prepared by the thermal decomposition of aluminium nitrate.
Source of sulphur dioxide (Kipp's apparatus or cylinder).

Experiment 14.3   *To prepare some different varieties of sulphur and examine the effect of heat on the element*

Each group of pupils will require:

Powdered roll-sulphur.
Carbon disulphide.
Xylene.
Filter-paper.
Watch-glass.
100 cm³ beaker.

The effect of heat on sulphur (rhombic) is to melt it at 113°C. At this temperature the fluid is runny because the rings of atoms can slide easily over one another. As the temperature increases, the rings of atoms open and join to form chains of atoms. This causes the liquid to become very viscous. At higher temperatures still, the chains of atoms start to rupture and the liquid becomes runny once more. If the liquid sulphur is now dropped into cold water, long chains are re-formed and an unstable solid, plastic sulphur, consisting of these long chains is produced before ring formation is again achieved.

Experiment 14.4   *To make a model of the S₈ molecule*

Each group of pupils will require:

Eight expanded polystyrene spheres of the same diameter.
Piece of stout cardboard ⎫ or special template (see Experiment 12.3).
Protractor.   ⎭
Scissors.
Lengths of pipe-cleaner (2 to 3 cm).

Experiment 14.5   *To prepare sulphur dioxide and investigate its properties*

Each group of pupils will require:

Test-tube fitted with bung and delivery tube as in Fig. 14.6.
Sodium sulphite.
Solutions of potassium permanganate and potassium dichromate.
Iodine solution.
Wooden splints.
Short length of magnesium ribbon.

NB: The existence of 'sulphurous acid molecules' is doubtful and the teacher is advised to use the name sulphur dioxide solution.

Experiment 14.6   *The oxidation of sulphur dioxide*

The teacher will require:

Conical flask (250 cm³) with wide neck and fitted with bung and tubes as in Fig.
14.8 and containing concentrated sulphuric acid.

Silica or hard-glass tube containing platinized asbestos, with corks and tubing as
illustrated.

Dreschel flask connected to a second (not shown on diagram) containing sodium
hydroxide solution to absorb excess reactant.

Ice bath, e.g. large beaker.

Cylinders of oxygen and sulphur dioxide, fitted with appropriate control gear.

The entire apparatus shown should be kept for several hours in an oven at 100°C
immediately prior to assembly.

Experiment 14.7   *Investigating the properties of sulphuric acid*

Each group of pupils will require:

Apparatus for testing electrical conductivity as in Experiment 3.1.

Watch-glass.

Copper(II) oxide, magnesium oxide, zinc hydroxide, and sodium carbonate.

Magnesium and copper turnings.

Sodium chloride and sodium nitrate.

Copper sulphate pentahydrate.

Concentrated cane sugar solution in water.

Experiment 14.8   *Investigating the properties of sulphates*

Each group of pupils will require:

A selection of sulphates including at least those of calcium, sodium, potassium,
magnesium, and ammonium.

Solutions of lead(II) nitrate and calcium chloride.

Experiment 14.9   *Distinguishing between sulphites and sulphates*

Each group of pupils will require:

Solutions of sodium sulphate and sodium sulphite.

Barium nitrate solution.

Potassium permanganate solution.

Solid sodium sulphate and sodium sulphite.

NB: The use of barium nitrate is preferable to that of barium chloride in the test for
sulphates as the possibility of precipitation of insoluble chlorides is avoided.

The Nuffield Chemistry film-loops 'Liquid Air Fractionation' and 'Sulphur
Crystals' could be shown during the teaching of this chapter.

Chapter 15   Non-metallic elements and their compounds—IV
Group VII—the halogens

Experiment 15.1   *To prepare chlorine from hydrochloric acid*

Each group of pupils will require:

Potassium dichromate, lead(IV) oxide, potassium permanganate, manganese(IV) oxide.

Experiment 15.2   *To prepare the chlorides of the elements within the sodium period*

The teacher will require:

Test-tube fitted with bungs and tubes as shown in Fig. 15.1.
Dreschel bottle containing sodium hydroxide solution (to absorb excess chlorine).
Sodium, magnesium, aluminium, silicon, phosphorus, and sulphur.
Cylinder or generator of dry chlorine.

Experiment 15.3   *The reaction between chlorine and hydrogen*

The teacher will require:

Experiment I

A plastic washing-up liquid bottle, fitted with a stopper and with a section cut out and covered with Sellotape, as shown in Fig. 15.2.
Trough or large beaker.
Cylinders or generators of chlorine and hydrogen with a suitable delivery-tube.

This experiment should be carried out away from sunlight, or a premature reaction may occur!

Experiment II

250 cm^3 ground-glass flask with stopper and fittings as shown in Fig. 15.3.
500 cm^3 beaker.
Cylinders or generators of chlorine and hydrogen (these gases must be dry).

NB: The apparatus should be dried in an oven at 100°C immediately prior to the experiment.

Experiment 15.4   *Investigating the properties of hydrochloric acid*

Each group of pupils will require:

Apparatus to test for electrical conductivity as in Experiment 3.1.
Copper(II) oxide, magnesium oxide, zinc hydroxide, and sodium carbonate.
Magnesium and copper turnings.

Experiment 15.5   *Investigating the properties of chlorides*

Each group of pupils will require:

Selection of chlorides including at least those of sodium, potassium, ammonium, magnesium, calcium.
Solutions of lead(II) nitrate and silver nitrate.

Experiment 15.6   *To distinguish between chlorides, bromides, and iodides*

Each group of pupils will require:

Sodium chloride, bromide, and iodide as solids and solutions.
Manganese(IV) oxide.
Silver nitrate solution.
Chlorine water (made by bubbling the gas through water).

Experiment 15.7   *To investigate the reactions between the halogens and aqueous iron(II) ions*

Each group of pupils will require:

Freshly prepared solution of iron(II) sulphate.
Chlorine water, bromine water, and iodine solution.
Potassium thiocyanate solution.

Experiment 15.8   *A survey of liquid bleaches*

Each group of pupils will require:

Selection of liquid bleaches with purchase price noted.
Access to large measuring cylinder (at least 1 dm^3 capacity).
25 cm^3 pipette.
Burette.
250 cm^3 volumetric flask.
Conical flask (250 cm^3).
5 per cent solution of sodium thiosulphate.
10 per cent solution of potassium iodide.

The following Nuffield Chemistry film-loops could be shown during the teaching of this chapter:

'Fluorine Manufacture'
'Uses of Fluorine Compounds'
'Chlorine Manufacture'
'Chlorine—Uses'
'Bromine Manufacture'
'Bromine—Uses'
'Iodine Manufacture'
'Iodine—Uses'

Answers to end-of-chapter questions

Chapter 1

    1. Half-life = 25 minutes

Chapter 2

    3. 10^6 atoms

Chapter 3

    1. Venn diagram

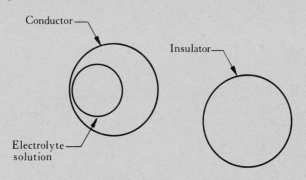

    4. 0·17 g

Chapter 4

    1. A, 28·8 kJ mol^{-1}; B, 40·6 kJ mol^{-1}
       B is more polar than A and has the higher boiling point.

Chapter 5

    1. Pb_3O_4
    3. (a) 5×10^{-2}, (b) 10^{-2}, (c) 2×10^{-3}, (d) 2×10^{-3}, (e) $2·4 \times 10^{-2}$.
    4. $2Ag^+(aq) + CrO_4{}^{2-}(aq) \rightarrow Ag_2CrO_4(s)$
    5. $2Al(s) + 3Cu^{2+}(aq) \rightarrow Al^{3+}(aq) + 3Cu(s)$
    6. (a) 100, (b) $2·5 \times 10^-3$, (c) $2·5 \times 10^{-3}$,
       (d) e.g., $CaCO_3(s) + 2HCl(aq) \rightarrow CaCl_2(aq) + H_2O(l) + CO_2(g)$
    7. (a) 100 cm^3, (b) 40 cm^3, (c) 0·29 g
    8. Molecular mass = 34; formula PH_3
    9. (a) $36·4 \text{ cm}^3$, (b) $5·4 \text{ cm}^3$
   10. (a) $5·6 \text{ dm}^3$, (b) $33·6 \text{ dm}^3$
   11. (a) $59·5 \text{ cm}^3$, (b) 76

Chapter 6

    2. (b) 0·65 g

Chapter 7

    1. (a) 33·6 kJ, (b) 17·8 kJ
    2. $\Delta H = +16·8$ kJ mol^{-1}
    4. $\Delta H = -284$ kJ mol^{-1}
    5. (b) methanol 720 kJ mol^{-1}, ethanol 1360 kJ mol^{-1}, propanol 2004 kJ mol^{-1}
       (c) 2644 kJ mol^{-1}
    6. $\Delta G = -61·8$ kJ mol^{-1}

Chapter 12

    10. Venn diagram

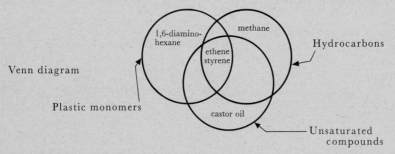

    13. Needle moves to the right; antimony

Chapter 13

    1. 33 g
    2. 1·21 kg
    6. N_2O

Chapter 14

    2. 3·06 kg